Teaching Durkheim

AMERICAN ACADEMY OF RELIGION

TEACHING RELIGIOUS STUDIES SERIES

SERIES EDITOR
Susan Henking, Hobart and William Smith Colleges

A Publication Series of
The American Academy of Religion
and
Oxford University Press

TEACHING LEVI-STRAUSS
Edited by Hans H. Penner

TEACHING ISLAM
Edited by Brannon M. Wheeler

TEACHING FREUD
Edited by Diane Jonte-Pace

TEACHING DURKHEIM
Edited by Terry F. Godlove, Jr.

Teaching Durkheim

EDITED BY TERRY F. GODLOVE, JR.

OXFORD
UNIVERSITY PRESS

2005

OXFORD
UNIVERSITY PRESS

Oxford   New York
Auckland   Bangkok   Buenos Aires   Cape Town   Chennai
Dar es Salaam   Delhi   Hong Kong   Istanbul   Karachi   Kolkata
Kuala Lumpur   Madrid   Melbourne   Mexico City   Mumbai   Nairobi
São Paulo   Shanghai   Taipei   Tokyo   Toronto

Copyright © 2005 by The American Academy of Religion
Published by Oxford University Press, Inc.
198 Madison Avenue, New York, New York 10016

www.oup.com

Library of Congress Cataloging-in-Publication Data
Teaching Durkheim / edited by Terry F. Godlove, Jr.
p.   cm.—(AAR teaching religious studies series)
Includes bibliographical references and index.
ISBN 0-19-516527-6; 0-19-516528-4 (pbk.)
1. Durkheim, Emile, 1858–1917—Study and teaching.   2. Religion and
sociology—Study and teaching.   I. Godlove, Terry F. II. AAR teaching
religious studies.
BL60.T45 2004
200'.92—dc22   2004002171

9 8 7 6 5 4 3 2 1

Printed in the United States of America
on acid-free paper

For H. R. G. and B. R. G.

Preface

In 1966, in "Religion as a Cultural System," Clifford Geertz made the then-startling claim that we must count Emile Durkheim (1858–1917) as belonging in the pantheon of "transcendent figures" in the study of religion.[1] Today this claim strikes us as commonplace. One recent commentator notes that the 1980s and '90s witnessed "an unparalleled flourish in Durkheimian studies in Europe and in North America."[2] Others write of "Durkheim's Religious Revival."[3]

But while these forty years have cemented Durkheim's position within the arena of scholarship and research, his place in the classroom is not as secure. First, there are problems intrinsic to the writings themselves. For example, for all its brilliance, many teachers find *The Elementary Forms of Religious Life* too uneven and difficult for inclusion in introductory courses, and too lengthy and unwieldy to assign in upper division or even graduate semester-length courses in "theory and method." Second, there are extrinsic factors, having to do with the development of the field of religious studies in the academy since the publication of Geertz's essay. Durkheim's basic claim that "religion is something eminently social" has too often been dismissed as "reductionistic," both by those concerned to secure an institutional niche for autonomous religious studies departments and by those who would prefer the new field not stray too far from its theological roots.[4] The result is that even today many students are more likely to read authors who are either extending Durkheim's basic program (for example, Robert Bellah, Peter Berger, Mary Douglas, Geertz, Erving Goffman, Victor Turner), or who are self-consciously inverting or rejecting one of its main tenets (for example, Mircea Eliade, Claude Lévi-Strauss, Colleen McDannell, Rodney Stark and William Bainbridge) than they are Durkheim himself.

This volume aims to be useful to those teachers and students who would like to hear Durkheim's voice more directly. It does not pretend to cover the entire expanse of Durkheim's work on religion. It does, however, attempt to represent a range of points of views and a range of disciplines, including anthropology, gender studies, history and history of religions, sociology, and philosophy. The book is divided into three parts of progressively widening scope. Part I focuses on the activity of introducing—on issues of what pages to assign in what sorts of courses, and on how to present them to students of varying background, preparation, and motivation. Part II turns to context, to assessing the four available English translations of the *Elementary Forms* (two, one whole and one partial, published within the last ten years), and to teaching the historical, critical, and biographical framework of Durkheim's work on religion. Part III takes up questions of how to incorporate Durkheim's work in courses concerned with ethics, gender studies, and social theory.

I would like to thank Susan Henking for encouraging me to pursue this project, and, more than that, for seeing the Teaching Religious Studies series through from conception to fruition. Thanks also to Hannah Rubin Godlove for help with preparation of the manuscript, and for contributing so much to the local effervescence.

NOTES

1. Clifford Geertz, "Religion as a Cultural System," in Michael Banton, ed., *Anthropological Approaches to the Study of Religion* (London: Routledge), 1–42. Max Weber, Sigmund Freud, and Bronislaw Malinowski round out Geertz's pantheon.

2. Edward A. Tiryakian, "Review of On Durkheim's Elementary Forms of Religious Life," *American Journal of Sociology*, 105/1 (Jul. 1999): 258.

3. Philip Smith and Jeffrey C. Alexander, "Durkheim's Religious Revival," *American Journal of Sociology* 102/2 (Sept. 1996): 585–92.

4. William Paden writes that "the Berlin Wall of religious studies amounted to a methodological bulwark against the likes of Durkheim." See Paden, "The Creation of Human Behavior: Reconciling Durkheim and the Study of Religion," in Thomas A. Idenopulo and Brian C. Wilson, eds., *Reappraising Durkheim for the Study and Teaching of Religion Today* (Boston: Brill, 2002), 16. See also Russell McCutcheon, *Manufacturing Religion: The Discourse on Sui Generis Religion and the Politics of Nostalgia* (New York: Oxford University Press, 1997).

Contents

PART THREE: Courses

Contributors

Carlos Bertha
Assistant Professor of Philosophy
United States Air Force Academy
Colorado Springs, CO 80840

Jacques Berlinerblau
Associate Professor of Comparative Literature and Languages
Hofstra University
Hempstead, NY 11549

Karen E. Fields
Independent Scholar
Richmond, VA 23229

Terry F. Godlove, Jr.
Professor of Philosophy and Religion
Hofstra University
Hempstead, NY 11549

Robert Alun Jones
Professor of Religious Studies, History, and Sociology
University of Illinois in Urbana-Champaign
Urbana, Illinois 61801

Jean Elisabeth Pedersen
Associate Professor of History
University of Rochester
Rochester, NY 14627

Warren Schmaus
Professor of Philosophy
Illinois Institute of Technology
Chicago, IL 60616

Jonathan Z. Smith
Robert O. Anderson Distinguished Service Professor of the Humanities in the College and the Committees on the Ancient Mediterranean World and on the History of Culture
University of Chicago
Chicago, IL 60637

Ivan Strenski
Holstein Family and Community Professor of Religious Studies University of California
Riverside, CA 92521

Edward A. Tiryakian
Professor of Sociology
Duke University
Durham, NC 27708

Stephen P. Turner
Professor of Philosophy
University of South Florida
Tampa, Florida 33620

PART I

Introducing

I

Introducing Durkheim

Jonathan Z. Smith

If one thinks about the enterprise of introducing Durkheim's *Elementary Forms* to college students, the emphasis must fall on the activity of introducing rather than on the contents of Durkheim's work. That is to say, within the context of an introductory course, the question becomes what one is seeking to introduce for which Durkheim will serve as an effective exemplum.

One way of thinking about this question is in terms of subject matter. To introduce Durkheim's text as part of a larger course on social theory is a different project from introducing Durkheim as part of a larger course on the study of religion. In the case of social thought, one might want to emphasize Durkheim's sociology of knowledge, or to take advantage of the possibility of comparison with other figures that might be read in the course (most usefully, Marx); in the case of the study of religion, one might want to emphasize Durkheim's explanatory translation of the language of religion (for him, in the *Elementary Forms*, the unknown) into the language of society (for him, the known), or to compare his translation with alternative constructions that use some similar vocabulary, but with profoundly different agendas (for example, selections from Mircea Eliade's book *The Sacred and The Profane*, or, preferably, Roger Caillois's *Man and The Sacred*).[1] Both of these intentions are different from introductory courses devoted to Durkheim's works, or to the Durkheimian tradition, that still presume a focus on *Elementary Forms*. While such courses will differ, again, depending on whether their more general setting is social thought or religious studies, in either case, there is, necessarily, more interest in contextualizing Durkheim (for example, in terms of Auguste Comte and "positive science," or various neo-Kantianisms), and much thought needs to be given, in the first instance, to the choice of other Durkheimian readings, or, in the second, to what constitutes the 'tradition.' With respect to the former question, if social thought is the focus, then selections from Durkheim's book *The Rules of Sociological Method* may prove an appropriate first reading; if religious studies, then perhaps the three lectures on the "Right of Property" from Durkheim's *Physics of Morals and of Rights* would be an effective first reading. Alternatively, *The Division of Labor in Society* works well as a first reading in Durkheim regardless of whether the interest is in social thought or the study of religion.[2] If the course is concerned with the Durkheimian tradition, a pressing pedagogical issue would be how broadly to extend that tradition. Regardless of other readings chosen, I have found it most useful to spend a good bit of time on W. Lloyd Warner, less on his Australian than on his American ethnography, especially, *The Living and the Dead*, as an example of the power of a Durkheimian 'defamiliarization.'[3] If the course's primary interest is in questions of theory, the inclusion of either Claude Lévi-Strauss's *Totemism* or *The Savage Mind* provides important occasions of explicit and implicit comparison. Alternatively, for introductory purposes, it might be better to begin with Lévi-Strauss's more accessible inaugural lecture, "The Scope of Social Anthropology."[4]

I have introduced Durkheim to college students in each of these contexts, sometimes in more than one in a single year. Not only are the readings different, but *Elementary Forms* reads differently, so much so that it is impossible (as well as irresponsible) for the instructor to use the same underlined, annotated copy of the text in these various settings.

As important as clarity on subject matter goals may be, with the implicit assumption that Durkheim is a self-evidently significant figure, it is even more important to be clear as to general educational goals. Here the need to give explicit reasons for the choice of Durkheim becomes acute. In some classes, for example, Durkheim has been chosen because his work is a model of argument. Here, the first class may well be spent on general questions as to what constitutes an argument (the role of data, the importance of anticipating objections, etc.) as well as the building blocks of argument (including, definition, classification, explanation), and initial class discussions and assignments are built around these topics.[5] This is to insist, again, that one cannot think about introducing Durkheim without thinking as much about the enterprise of introducing as one does about Durkheim.[6]

Such a curricular thought carries with it pragmatic consequences for reading Durkheim. In an introductory course, one presumes the reading will be done in English translation, and, more than likely, will not entail reading the work in its entirety. These strictures, in turn, present their own pedagogical issues. We now have available two complete and two significant partial translations of *Elementary Forms* (or, as I prefer, *Elemental Forms*), each in a relatively inexpensive paperback edition. The choice between them depends, in part, on what it is one understands the text to be introducing.[7] The same understanding will also inform decisions as to the pages assigned, as well as to those particular passages to be emphasized in class discussion.[8]

Introductory courses, throughout the human sciences, are, above all, courses in reading, in verbal and written communication, in reasoning, and in gaining critical perspectives. While this presumes a good bit of activity such as frequent short writing assignments, it also entails an instructional ethos that focuses class discussions on understanding processes of thought rather than on reporting summary conclusions. I have written elsewhere against "a false generosity with respect to method and theory, presenting this method or theory in summary one week, that method or theory the next. None of them is allowed to have the kind of monomaniacal imperialist power a good theory or method displays. Lacking this force, theories and methods have been reduced to gossip, to mere opinions, without entailments or consequences."[9] To interrupt this tendency—"seven theories of religion"—the class must become interactive with Durkheim's thought rather than passive underliners of his text, let alone of secondary accounts of his work. For this reason, one of my chief rules of introducing is to *always begin with the question of definition*. Before opening *Elementary Forms*, after discussing the logic and forms of definition, it is useful to take time in class to have the students write out their definitions of terms such as 'religion,' 'sacred/profane,' and 'church' and, later, to have them re-write their definitions in light of Durkheim's, accounting for each revision with specific reference to Durkheim's counterintuitive proposals. This makes the opening pages of *Elementary Forms* crucial. What kinds of definitions does Durkheim employ? Why is the definition of 'religion' deferred? What has been gained, argumentatively, in the interim? Why, in the initial characterization, is religion defined in terms of "society"? Why the dual definition, "simplest" and "most primitive"? Why the stipulation that these characteristics must be determined with reference to groups "that observation can make known to us"? Preliminary answers to such questions will have to be revised in light of subsequent readings. *Elementary Forms* is one of those cunning argumentative works in which time must be taken to reread the introduction and discuss it again after the class has read through to Durkheim's conclusion.

A second rule of introducing insists on the importance of *making arguments explicit*. In the case of *Elementary Forms*, this is best accomplished by having the students outline, in two or three pages, the central spine of Durkheim's argument, at least until page 231 with its claim, "given the idea of the totem, the emblem of the clan, all the rest follows," and label each operation (see note 5). I expect students to identify not only definitions, classifications, analogies, analytic descriptions, explanations, and anticipations of objections, as well as techniques such as concomitant variation, but also to locate crucial turning points in the argument that Durkheim must win. One such point is the linguistic analogy with respect to the "marks" on the *churinga* (pp. 125–126), made in order to demonstrate both the arbitrariness of the signs (that is to say, that they are not natural), and to support his argument that sacredness is "super-added." I find this the only occasion at which some introduction of supplementary Australian ethnographic materials becomes crucial. The students need to see examples of native Australian art that demonstrates the natives' capacity to "imitat[e] the forms of things," as well as decoded churingas to reinforce Durkheim's claim as to the conventional nature of the "geometric designs."[10] Finally, such an outline should note those places where Durkheim appears to violate the stipulations of his own argument. For example, it is worth discussing what warrants Durkheim's use of the Oceanic notion of *mana* as a central element in his theory of religion when it does not occur in his privileged example, Australia.[11]

A third rule of introducing is that *nothing must stand alone*, with the idea that comparison opens up space for criticism. Each item encountered in an introductory course should have a conversation partner, so that each may have, or be made to have, an argument with another in order that students may negotiate difference, evaluate, compare, and make judgments. While historically grounded contrasts are common, whether to works contemporary to Durkheim or within the Durkheimian tradition (as suggested earlier), I find that anachronistic, surprising juxtapositions are often more useful pedagogically.[12] Taking advantage of our students' highly developed visual literacy, one social sciences core sequence at the College of the University of Chicago, in which I have taught selections from *Elementary Forms* for some twenty years, shows and discusses Leni Riefenstahl's classic propaganda film of the Nazi Nuremberg rally, *The Triumph of the Will*, after reading Durkheim's unproblematized account of "collective effervescence" (especially pp. 211–213 in relation to pp. 217–219).[13]

Closely related to comparison is a fourth rule: that students be asked to demonstrate their mastery of Durkheim by exhibiting a *capacity to 'play' with the argument*, applying it to an example quite different from the Australian aboriginal data on which *Elementary Forms* is based. As a simple assignment, I have students take a familiar object of social interest, such as the Vietnam War Memorial in Washington, D.C., and ask them to provide a Durkheimian redescription. In a more complicated exercise, I use Supreme Court cases, preferably ones with closely split decisions. I do this for a variety of general pedagogical reasons. Students often know the results reached by the Court; they rarely have any sense of the intellectual processes by which these decisions are reached. At the level of the Supreme Court, the data are stipulated, and there is general agreement as to the relevant constitutional provisions and legal precedents. In such a situation, difference is not, as students often suppose, a product of one side knowing something the other side doesn't know, or knowing more. In the justices' written opinions, students are able to observe the construction of alternative arguments and plausibility structures, reasoned from a common base, concerning issues of social consequence. Of several cases, the most successful in the classroom has been *Lynch v. Donnelly* (45 U.S. 668, 79 L. Ed. 22nd 604, 104 S. Ct. 1355 [1984]). After completing *Elementary Forms*, I have my students read the text of this crèche case where the arguments depend on the question of whether the crèche, and other displayed symbols, serve a primarily "religious" or a "secular" purpose. I ask the students to imagine that Durkheim presented a brief to the Court. What would he write? For example, would he accept the majority opinion's presupposition that religion requires only the presence of sacrality, or would he have argued that religion requires the dual, oppositional relations of sacred/profane? By the conclusion of the exercise, both Durkheim and the American issue of "separation," with its implicit understandings of religion, have become mutually complicated. The students, because of their reading of Durkheim, 'see' aspects of the case that the Court ignored; likewise, the students, having read a case that describes a familiar rather than an exotic aboriginal religious activity, discover new implications in Durkheim's position. They have come to learn, moreover, that complexity does not result in either paralysis or some form of naive relativism; rather, as with the court, a decision must be made, a decision for which one must bear the consequences.[14]

In this essay on thinking about the enterprise of introducing Durkheim to college students, with its insistence that the emphasis be placed more on the activity of introducing than on Durkheim, I have sought, among other goals, to keep faith with aspects of Durkheim's own pedagogical reflections. What he wrote about 'secondary education' can be applied, *mutatis mutandis*, to what is termed, at the collegiate level, 'general education.' Its object, above all,

> is to arouse and develop a capacity for thinking without trying to tie
> it down to any one particular vocation. . . . The object of cultivating
> the mind can only consist in the acquisition of a certain number of
> intellectual habits and attitudes, which enable the mind to form ade-
> quate conceptions of the most important kinds of things.

What he wrote about the human sciences can be applied, *mutatis mutandis*, to the study of Durkheim within the larger context of social thought and the study of religion, that we should "make the diversity of human nature the basic subject-matter of education"; that "as we should expect, our conception of man is also capable of affecting our conduct"; and that "we must fashion rationalists, that is to say men who are concerned with clarity of thought; but they must be rationalists of a new kind who know that things, whether human or physical, are irreducibly complex and who are yet able to look unfalteringly into the face of this complexity."[15]

NOTES

1. M. Eliade, *The Sacred and The Profane: The Nature of Religion* (New York: Harcourt Brace, 1959); R. Caillois, *Man and the Sacred* (Glencoe, Ill.: Free Press, 1959).

2. E. Durkheim, *The Rules of Sociological Method* (Chicago: University of Chicago Press, 1938; reprint, New York: Free Press, 1950); Durkheim, "The Right of Property," in Durkheim, *Professional Ethics and Civic Morals* (London: Routledge, 1957; reprinted 1992): 133–170; Durkheim, *The Division of Labor in Society* (New York: MacMillan, 1933; reprint, Glencoe: Free Press, 1960).

3. W. Lloyd Warner, *A Black Civilization: A Study of an Australian Tribe* (New York: Harper and Row, 1938; 2nd ed., 1958; reprint, 1964); Warner, *The Living and the Dead: A Study of the Symbolic Life of Americans* (New Haven: Yale University Press, 1959; reprint, Westport, Conn.: Greenwood Press, 1975), Yankee City series 5. A revised, abridged, and supplemented version was prepared by Warner, *The Family of God: A Symbolic Study of Christian Life in America* (New Haven: Yale University Press, 1961).

4. C. Lévi-Strauss, *Totemism* (Boston: Beacon Press, 1963); Lévi-Strauss, *The Savage Mind* (Chicago: University of Chicago Press, 1966); Lévi-Strauss, *The Scope of Social Anthropology* (London: Jonathan Cape, 1967), reprinted in Lévi-Strauss, *Structural Anthropology* (New York: Basic Books, 1963–76), 2:3–32.

5. For example, (1) as a first assignment it is useful to have the class outline the argument of the initial three paragraphs of *Elementary Forms*, labeling each argumentative activity. This exercise often reveals that the students do not spot Durkheim's anticipation of an objection in paragraph 3, a crucial stratagem throughout Durkheim's work. (2) Early on, I sometimes have the students prepare an abstract of Durkheim's first treatment of the sociology of knowledge (Fields translation, pp. 8–12 [see note 7 in this chapter]), reducing it to a single paragraph using no words not found in Durkheim, but allowing them to reorder the material if necessary. The abstracts indicate that students frequently reverse Durkheim's argument, 'if religious then social,' reading it as 'if social, then religious.' This is often because they fail to grant Durkheim's initial appeal to common knowledge (which, therefore, requires no argumentation), "it has long been known . . ." (8). Such exercises go a long way toward making students' reading explicit.

6. I will presume, throughout, the sorts of issues raised with respect to introducing in J. Z. Smith, " 'Narratives into Problems': The College Introductory Course and the Study of Religion," *Journal of the American Academy of Religion* 56 (1988): 727–739. See further Smith, "The Introductory Course: Less is Better," in *Teaching the Introductory Course in Religious Studies: A Sourcebook*, edited by M. Jurgensmayer (Atlanta, Ga.: Scholars Press, 1991): 185–192; Smith, "Teaching the Bible in the Context of General Education," *Teaching Theology and Religion* 1 (1998): 73–78.

7. In recent years, the translation by Karen E. Fields, *The Elementary Forms of Religious Life* (New York: Free Press, 1995), has come to be the most widely used. (For this reason, I have cited Fields's pagination throughout this essay.) It is complete, clear, sensitive to technical vocabulary, and at times helpful in its notes, with a wonderfully useful index. Its translator's introduction, when it speaks of matters of translation (esp. li–lvii), is worth assigning; but its idiosyncratic interpretative sections (esp.

xxv–xxvi, xliii–li) invite misreading and are best passed over. Two unfortunate decisions mar the work: the omission of Durkheim's editorial 'we' (an essential feature of Durkheim's positivist style) and the division of his lengthy paragraphs into smaller units. If one is teaching Durkheim as an example of a type of argumentation in which one is interested in 'seeing Durkheim's mind at work,' these two emendations are fatal. For most other purposes, Fields is, by far, the most useful version.

Joseph Ward Swain's earlier version, *Elementary Forms of the Religious Life* (London: Allen and Unwin, 1915, reprinted 1926, 1954; reprint, New York: Crowell-Collier, 1961; reprint, New York: Free Press, 1965—at times with different paginations), for all its occasional misprints, infelicitous word choices, syntactical errors, and omissions, still reads more like Durkheim than any other English translation. I would hope that the Free Press allows it to remain in print.

Carol Cosman's splendid new translation, abridged by Mark S. Cladis, *The Elementary Forms of Religious Life* (Oxford: Oxford University Press, 2001), in its World's Classics series, is based on the best construction of the underlying French text. It is unusual in that Cladis preserves the majority of the text by largely cutting (chiefly ethnographic) sentences out of individual paragraphs rather than deleting entire sections with a genuine effort to perturb Durkheim's argument as little as possible. Similarly, Durkheim's footnotes and references have been sharply reduced. One would have to judge the costs of this reduction in terms of one's purpose in teaching the book, and in terms of one's own selections of readings in *Elementary Forms*. It is of little help, for example, in classes where I juxtapose Durkheim with Lévi-Strauss. Besides, knowing that the reading is for an introductory course and that, therefore, the student may well have occasion to return to Durkheim's text, and given the small difference in price between the two versions, the Fields translation would seem the better choice. (I hope that Oxford will yet bring out an unabridged translation by Cosman; if so, it would be my preference.)

Jacqueline Redding's fresh translation of selections from *Elementary Forms*, in Emile Durkheim, *Emile Durkheim: Durkheim on Religion*, ed. W.S.F. Pickering (London: Routledge and Kegan Paul, 1975; reprint, Atlanta, Ga.: Scholars Press, 1994): 102–156, American Academy of Religion Texts and Translations series 6, is so abbreviated in its choices as to be useless for anything longer than an introductory course that devotes one or two class sessions to Durkheim. (*Even* in such a situation, the omission of any selection from book 3 makes it problematic.) Its great value lies in the range of other Durkheim materials on religion that it prints, often in their first appearance in English.

Curiously, of the four translations, only the Redding version retains Durkheim's subtitle, *The Totemic System in Australia*.

8. Assuming ten to twelve hours of class time devoted to *Elementary Forms*, I would propose the following selections as a minimum (in Fields's pagination), with the instructor responsible for supplying the argumentative links from the omitted portions: pp. 1–22, 33–44, 84–85, 90–157, 190–241, 265–275, 298–299, 303–329, 348–373, 392–448. It is also important to specify those footnotes that should be read. (For example, given the scientistic interests of many students, it is useful to call attention to notes ranging from p. 17 n. 22, to p. 349 n. 55). In specifying these pages, I resist the tendency to omit book 3. Among other matters, one cannot get the force of Durk-

heim's deployment of the crucial prefix 're' without it. (I usually ask my students to keep a running list of Durkheim's 're words.')

9. Smith, " 'Narratives into Problems,' " 737.

10. As students, in fact, have no idea of what a churinga looks like, a photograph helps. For sentimental reasons, I usually pass around the photographs in one of Durkheim's sources, B. Spencer and F. J. Gillen, *The Native Tribes of Central Australia* (London: MacMillan, 1899; reprint, New York: Dover, 1968): 129, 131, 163, 174, 175. However, the decoded churingas in Spencer and Gillen (for example, 145–150) are not as clear as those in G. Róheim, *The Eternal Ones of the Dream: A Psychoanalytic Interpretation of Australian Myth and Ritual* (New York: International Universities Press, 1945): 240–243. If one is juxtaposing Durkheim to Lévi-Strauss, Lévi-Strauss's argument with Durkheim over the churinga (*Savage Mind*, esp. 237–244) becomes an occasion for revisiting the issue; but see my discussion in J. Z. Smith, *To Take Place: Toward Theory in Ritual* (Chicago: University of Chicago Press, 1987), 174, 175 n. 44. For aboriginal representative art, I use Louis A. Allen, *Australian Aboriginal Art: Arnhem Land* (Chicago: Field Museum of Natural History, 1972), esp. p. 4, figs. 7–10, chiefly because it is a local, accessible collection; but many other illustrated volumes are readily available.

11. Note that, through a misprint, the Fields translation has one instance of *mana* in Australia! On p. 333, the vegetable gum 'manna' (*la manne*) is misrendered 'mana' (*le mana*). See, further, my discussion of Durkheim and *mana* in J. Z. Smith, "Manna, Mana Everywhere and /./././," in *Radical Interpretation in Religion*, edited by N. K. Frankenberry (Cambridge: Cambridge University Press, 2002), 188–212.

12. I have adapted some of these sentences from Smith, " 'Narratives into Problems,' " 735. For the Vietnam War Memorial example, see the Durkheimian redescription in J. Z. Smith, "Topography of the Sacred," in Smith, *Relating Religion: Essays in the Study of Religion* (Chicago: University of Chicago Press, 2004), 101–116.

13. *The Triumph of the Will* is available as a videotape (among several prints, Celluloid Chronicles Home Video is the most complete with the most intelligible subtitles). For the instructor, it may be useful to review the English translation of the original shooting script and D. C. Smith's scene-by-scene shot list, in D. C. Smith, *Triumph of the Will: Document of the 1934 Reich Party Rally* (Richardson, Tex.: Celluloid Chronicles Press, 1990), in the Chronicle Film Script Series.

14. In presenting the rationale for the use of a Court case, I have drawn on Smith, " 'Narratives into Problems,' " 735–736; see 733–734. I have presented a set of ten alternative Durkheimian readings of the 'facts' in *Lynch v. Donnelly* in J. Z. Smith, " 'God Save This Honourable Court': Religion and Civic Discourse," in Smith, *Relating Religion: Essays in the Study of Religion* (Chicago: University of Chicago Press, 2004), 375–390.

15. E. Durkheim, *The Evolution of Educational Thought: Lectures on the Formation and Development of Secondary Education in France* (London: Routledge and Kegan Paul, 1977): 320, 327, 329, 348.

REFERENCES

Allen, Louis A. 1972. *Australian Aboriginal Art: Arnhem Land*. Chicago: Field Museum of Natural History.

Caillois, Roger. 1959. *Man and The Sacred.* Glencoe, Ill.: Free Press.

Durkheim, Emile. 1933. *The Division of Labor in Society.* New York: MacMillan.

———. 2001. *The Elementary Forms of Religious Life.* Translated by Carol Cosman and abridged by Mark S. Cladis. Oxford: Oxford University Press.

———. 1995. *The Elementary Forms of Religious Life.* Translated by Karen E. Fields. New York: Free Press.

———. 1915. *The Elementary Forms of the Religious Life.* Translated by Joseph Ward Swain. London: Allen and Unwin.

———. 1975. *Emile Durkheim: Durkheim on Religion.* Edited by W.S.F. Pickering and translated by J. Redding. London: Routledge and Kegan Paul.

———. 1977. *The Evolution of Educational Thought: Lectures on the Formation and Development of Secondary Education in France.* London: Routledge and Kegan Paul.

———. 1957. *Professional Ethics and Civic Morals.* London: Routledge, 1957.

———. 1938. *The Rules of Sociological Method.* Chicago: University of Chicago Press.

Eliade, Mircea. 1959. *The Sacred and the Profane: The Nature of Religion.* New York: Harcourt Brace.

Lévi-Strauss, Claude. 1966. *The Savage Mind.* Chicago: University of Chicago Press.

———. 1963–76. *Structural Anthropology.* New York: Basic Books.

———. 1963. *Totemism.* Boston: Beacon Press.

Róheim, G. 1945. *The Eternal Ones of the Dream: A Psychoanalytic Interpretation of Australian Myth and Ritual.* New York: International Universities Press.

Smith, D. C. 1990. *Triumph of the Will: Document of the 1934 Reich Party Rally.* Richardson, Tex.: Celluloid Chronicles Press.

Smith, J. Z. 2004. " 'God Save This Honourable Court': Religion and Civic Discourse." In Smith, *Relating Religion: Essays in the Study of Religion.* Chicago: University of Chicago Press, 2004.

———. 1991. "The Introductory Course: Less Is Better." In *Teaching the Introductory course in Religious Studies: A Sourcebook,* edited by M. Jurgensmayer. Atlanta, Ga.: Scholars Press.

———. 2002. "Manna, Mana Everywhere and /./././." In *Radical Interpretation in Religion,* edited by N. K. Frankenberry. Cambridge: Cambridge University Press.

———. 1988. " 'Narratives into Problems': The College Introductory Course and the Study of Religion." *Journal of the American Academy of Religion* 56: 727–739.

———. 1998. "Teaching the Bible in the Context of General Education." *Teaching Theology and Religion* 1: 73–78.

———. 2004. "Topography of the Sacred." In Smith, *Relating Religion: Essays in the Study of Religion.* Chicago: University of Chicago Press, 2004.

———. 1987. *To Take Place: Toward Theory in Ritual.* Chicago: University of Chicago Press.

Spencer, B., and F. J. Gillen. 1899. *The Native Tribes of Central Australia.* London: MacMillan. Reprint, New York: Dover, 1968.

Warner, W. Lloyd. 1938. *A Black Civilization: A Study of an Australian Tribe.* New York: Harper and Row.

———. 1959. *The Living and the Dead: A Study of the Symbolic Life of Americans.* New Haven: Yale University Press.

2

Durkheim Sings

Teaching the "New" Durkheim on Religion

Ivan Strenski

The New Durkheim

As an undergraduate majoring in philosophy and sociology at the University of Toronto, with special interests in religion, I had been dunned with the standard orthodox drill about Durkheim. He was a dull and confused combination of old fashioned 'scientist'—the number-crunching Positivist of *Suicide* or *The Division of Labor in Society*—and head-in-the-clouds theorist of the hopelessly metaphysical *Elementary Forms of the Religious Life*. His overgeneralized and reified concept of Society put him into a theoretical never-never land and out of touch with the particularities of the diversity of societies and certainly their detailed histories. Yet, as a classic 'great man,' he single-handedly created sociology and pioneered sociology of religion. In terms of religion, however, not much was there to be learned, since he crudely reduced 'God' to 'society' and flew in the face of everything believers said about their own experience of religion. In terms of his underlying vision of human life, morality, and the like, he 'misplaced' the 'concreteness' of the individual and imagined that Society writ large was itself some kind of 'thing.' As a stiff and naive moralist, he had his mind fixed only on the problem of social order, which, above all things, he sought to maintain in classic conservative, if not statist, ways.

With the publication in 1974 of Steven Lukes's *Emile Durkheim: His Life and Work*, however, a new Durkheim came into focus. A new generation as well of historical reappraisal and study was initiated into the life and works of Durkheim, the benefits of which we are only now, a quarter century later, beginning to reap. Here, Durkheim is located within the context of his real life and times and not tailored to fit the needs of theorizing in the social sciences, such as quantitative sociology, or the dogmas of mainstream ideologies, such as bourgeois individualism.

This historical reevaluation of Durkheim has resulted in a view of the great thinker that departs substantially from the received view dominant in the human sciences since the mid-1950s. It became clear in the wake of Lukes's great work that, far from working alone in the splendid isolation typical of history's 'great men,' Durkheim presents us with a paradigm of collaborative multifaceted scholarship. In the France of the late nineteenth and early twentieth centuries, Durkheim had assembled a 'team' of research around the periodical he had founded in 1897, the famous *Anneé Sociologique*. At the center of this active 'team' of collaborators in the crosscultural and comparative study of societies, he directed research across a wide range of subjects that was unequaled in the history of the human sciences for the real collective work it embodied. He emerges as a thinker still alive to the problems of philosophy and respecting the status of the historical sciences, even as he sought to transform both older disciplines. While seeing sacredness resident in the interaction of human beings in collective enterprises, Durkheim was alert to the sacrality and importance of the individual in society—as witnessed by his singular defense of Dreyfus in the face of the conservative political forces of his day. Far from being a simplistic sociological reductionist, Durkheim was always the eclectic: he was as active in thinking about the social nature and function of religion in society as he was in exploring the moral or religious nature of society. All the while, Durkheim was a passionate and thoughtful progressive thinker who was as skeptical of communism or socialism, patriotic jingoism or mob rule as he was of the myths of an abstract and selfish individualism embodied so thoroughly in classic utilitarian economic ideology and in many of the social arrangements connected with the market mentality. How then could and should this 'new' Durkheim be taught in religious studies?

"The Problem of Religion" and the Causes of Religious Experience

I speak from the experience most recently of having taught Durkheim for the past six years in a one-quarter undergraduate course called "The Problem of Religion" at the University of California, Riverside, and for some years previously at the University of California, both Santa Barbara and Los Angeles.[1] Parenthetically, I might add that this course has been taught for the past six years as an interactive video conference course tying in the Davis and Los Angeles campuses of the University of California system. In terms of content and authors read, this course ranges from the theorists and advocates of what has been variously called 'natural religion,' Jean Bodin and Lord Herbert of Cherbury, through the classic 'naturalist' thinkers of religious studies, such as David Hume, Friedrich Max Müller, E. B. Tylor, J. G. Frazer, Sigmund Freud, Max Weber, Robertson Smith, Gerardus van der Leeuw, Ninian Smart, Eliade, and Durkheim. Of each figure introduced, I ask how they have 'problematized' religion—how have they made a problem for religion?

Although this array of thinkers might signal the stock 'methods and theories' course, "The Problem of Religion" is far from it. It is my view that these so-called methods and theories courses are in reality 'wannabe' analytic philosophy of religion courses. One takes the theoretical views of the founders and considers them solely as collections of *arguments* and for the sake of their arguments. The propositions in these arguments are then analyzed critically to determine their viability. Little or no attention is given the historical contexts in which these arguments are situated, nor is there any sense that such attention would really advance our understanding of the founders and their thought.

The two most frequent results of the 'wannabe' philosophical approach are what I call 'the tool box' or 'Prince Charming.'[2] As Tool Box, one regards most or all of the contributions of the classic thinkers as having some utility, like the variously useful items collected in a good box of tools. These Tool Box 'methods and theories' courses in principle never come to a single conclusion as to the best theory or method sufficient to guide students in their work. Pragmatic in its outlook, the Tool Box approach finds bits of each theory or method of potential use. So, when one needs theoretical help, one just dips into one's Tool Box of theories to pick out the one, or the parts of one, most useful to the particular task to hand. All the theories are *right* in their own ways and for their own purposes. On the other hand, in Prince Charming, we meet the 'methods and theories course' as ideology. Here the instructor is wedded to a certain single theoretical approach and seeks in this way and that to vindicate it at the expense of those dead white men who made so many stupid mistakes about the study of religion. Prince Charming method and theory courses then become elaborate contrivances aimed at showing how a *true* theory thankfully arrives amid all the other benighted wrong ones littering the history of past theorizing. Thus, when treated as philosophy, these 'methods and theories' courses become either forays into the Tool Box or preparations for the coronation of Prince Charming.

As its title indicates, "The Problem of Religion" seeks to show how religion has been 'problematized' in the course of the study of religion. If anything, the course is much more a *history* of the study of religion, built around the notion of religion *becoming a problem* for Western thought than an attempt critically—acontextually or abstractly—to decide or pronounce on the truth or falsity of various approaches to the study of religion. What *historical* conditions have led thinkers to see religion as a *'problem'*? Thus, the main question guiding the course is not whether a given conception of religion or its study is *true*—although these questions can and should be *entertained*—but why the thinkers in question *thought they were right* in speaking and thinking of religion as they did. Why did this array of classic thinkers bother to *interrogate or theorize* religion, instead of, for example, just *being* religious? And why did they think their questions were the right ones to ask? What sorts of happenings in the context of our culture have forced people to think about the nature and function of religion as they have? An example that comes to mind is the impact of critical history and philology of the Bible on our entire conception of the status of sacred texts. Much the same scholarly skills were to be applied as well to the scriptures of India, as was pioneered by, among others, Friedrich Max Müller. And, in addition to the application of methods honed in the higher criticism of the Bible, the nineteenth-century discovery of 'alternate bibles,' such as the Vedas, produced *problems* of religion of their own.

Durkheim's Problems with Religious Experience

Taken together with the emergence of the 'new' Durkheim, this orientation to religion as a source of problems suggests a certain way to teach Durkheim in religious studies. While I shall only describe my own efforts in "The Problem of Religion," I would submit that the new scholarship on Durkheim makes him, his thought, and that of those he influenced available across a much wider spectrum of courses in religious studies than has ever been imagined. The writings of Durkheim and his 'team' might inform many a course in our curricula—Durkheim himself on morality, ritual, and nationalism, Henri Hubert, Marcel Mauss, and Georges Bataille on gift and sacrifice, Maurice Halbwachs on memory, Michel Leiris on the sacred in everyday life, and Robert Hertz on pilgrimage, shrines, and saints, to mention a few examples. Let me discuss how I teach Durkheim in "The Problem of Religion."

The classes on Durkheim come toward the end of the second part of the 10-week run of the course, just before Eliade and just after Freud. In the second part of the course, I argue that the focus of theoretical problems in the study of religion, at a certain point in the nineteenth century, doubtless the result of Schleiermacher's influence, became religious *experience*. This focus contrasts, on the whole, with the way problems of religion arose from issues having to do, for example, with predominantly historical quests for the identity of the first or most fundamental religion—the discourse of 'natural religion'—typical of sixteenth-century thinkers such as Jean Bodin, seventeenth-century thinkers such as Lord Herbert of Cherbury, and the eighteenth-century Deists. Likewise, the relatively modern obsession shared by Durkheim with making sense of religion by making sense of religious *experience* contrasts as well with the nineteenth-century critical philological and historical focus on the way the study of sacred *texts*—the Bible as well as the Vedas and other religious *docu-*

ments—problematized religion in the West by putting into question the status of religious *texts*. Here one not only thinks of D. F. Strauss and the 'higher criticism' of the Bible but also of Friedrich Max Müller's historical and philological criticism of the scriptures of India, which Max Müller and his ilk thought were an alternative—'Aryan'—bible.

These contrasts make the case that the work of Durkheim on religion is better seen as akin to other investigations of religion focused on the *experiential* dimension of human religious life. In his day, even while the quest for natural religion persisted, as, for example, with Max Müller, it took a distinctly *psychological* turn, as in the work of Cornelis P. Tiele and the liberal Protestant neo-Deists who dominated the study of religion in France in Durkheim's time—Albert Réville and his son, Jean Réville. To wit, in the same league, although 'playing' for different 'teams' than Durkheim, would be Rudolf Otto, Bronislaw Malinowski, Weber, Freud, Carl Jung, and Eliade, among others. Thus, like Freud or Otto, for example, Durkheim sought to explain the *psychological state* or *individual experience* of dependence on the sacred that seemed characteristic of religion. But, unlike Freud or Otto, for example, Durkheim argued that this feeling of dependence was not some residue of early childhood experiences or instead a 'being experienced' by the "Wholly Other," respectively, but ultimately a function of participation in social groups—effervescent or otherwise.

A Plausible Durkheim: The Case of 'Strong' and 'Weak' Durkheimianisms

If we accept that Durkheim's approach to religion is fundamentally a critique of religious *experience*, the first challenge in pedagogy would be to make Durkheim's view plausible to students typically hostile to its societist character. Here I do not primarily have in mind that part of the Durkheimian view that urges us to study religious *institutions and social organizations*. This aspect of the 'sociological apperception' that Durkheim contributes to the study of religion is fairly easily accepted, even if it is still not as 'natural' a part of present-day religious studies as the study of beliefs, doctrines, morality, and such have been. Historically speaking, positions in anthropology or sociology of religion in *religious studies* departments are far outnumbered by those in the historical, philosophical, or theological study of religion. This appropriation of Durkheim would indeed take religious studies beyond these more prevalent approaches to the study of religion in terms of religious beliefs, myths, morals, and the like. To me, it is altogether a salutary development in our field. But, for all its virtues, this appropriation of Durkheim would be what one might call a 'weak' Durkheimianism.

What I would call a 'strong' Durkheimianism, however, generally meets fierce resistance among students of religion. 'Strong' Durkheimianism asserts that religious experience is *caused* by social forces, by the action of groups on the psychology of their members. It is not then surprising that, given our native Western individualism, often coupled to an individualist religious piety, students instinctively object to Durkheim's social view of the *origins and causes* of religious experience. They protest that religious experience is essentially transcendent and personal. It cannot in principle have social *causes*, such as Durkheim describes, for example, in his discussion of the relation of totemic *beliefs* to the *collective activities or rituals*—essentially *social* features—of totemic religion itself. Since God dwells within and since the individual human person is thought to be an absolutely autonomous being, the occurrence of religious experience is therefore felt to be independent of extrapersonal or worldly location. Put in another form, the objection raised is how the Durkheimian account of the causes of religious experience explains the frequent occurrence of religious experience in solitude. Therefore, in order to get students to make Durkheim plausible, one needs to confront 'strong' Durkheimianism and the issue of why Durkheim would have thought he was right in advancing his 'strong' societist view of the *causes* of religious experience.

Since 'strong' Durkheimianism goes well beyond the fairly acceptable propositions of 'weak' Durkheimianism, namely, that we should attend to religious institutions as well as religious beliefs, myths, morals, and the like, a little more argumentation is required. This takes us into some fairly sophisticated intellectual territory. To begin, we need to attend to *epistemology* and then to what I would call *social ontology*.

Epistemology, Public Knowledge, and 'Strong' Durkheimianism

In terms of epistemology, early in "The Problem of Religion," I argue that the *study* of religion differs from *being* religious, and that this has certain consequences for the way we proceed in talking about religion in the public domain. In our discussion of the problems for religion thrown up by the critical study of the Bible and religious texts in general, I argue that one needs, for example, to distinguish between what Christians *believe* Jesus to be and what, *as a matter of history*, it is possible to say about Jesus' life and works. We can thus distinguish between the claims made about Jesus by a particular Christian community from those it is possible to affirm in the broader public domain. This is not to say that one is true and the other not—that, say, the Jesus of faith or of a particular Christian group is a 'myth' and thus not true, while the Jesus of 'history' or of the public domain necessarily tells the truth about Jesus. It is, however, to say that 'history' and the demands of the public realm in diverse and pluralist societies differ in certain key respects from 'myth' and the demands of a believing community. To wit, we can ask what it is possible to say about Jesus from the viewpoint of the epistemological standards of 'history' as a *public academic discipline* and to compare that with what it is permissible to say about Jesus from the standpoint of a particular Christian *community and faith*. In the classroom of a public university such as the University of California, we are situated in the public domain, and in that sense we are governed by a different set of rules about what constitutes 'knowledge' from that in a particular Christian church. Interestingly enough, Durkheim was aware of this distinction and was, moreover, dedicated to addressing this broader *public* domain. Although, for example, there are elements of liberal Judaism in the thought of Durkheim and his collaborator, Marcel Mauss, as well as aspects of liberal modernist Roman Catholicism in Henri Hubert, another close coworker in the Durkheimian group, none of these Durkheimians participated in articulating or in any way developing the respective confessional discourses of religious liberalism proper to either the Judaism or Roman Catholicism of their day. Their focus was *public* and *extra*-ecclesial, so to speak.

In studying Durkheim, we are therefore considering someone *studying* religion, someone seeking, moreover, expressly to advance *knowledge* about religion in the public domain. This aim, in turn, calls forth an epistemology governing Durkheim's claims about the nature of religion, the causes of religious experience, and such. To wit, Durkheim must play by the same rules governing what counts as public 'knowledge' as any other player in the arena of knowledge about the world. One of the requirements of such claims made about the world would be that they must be in some sense be empirical and publicly falsifiable, as in the case of the historical 'sciences.' With his efforts shaped by these rules, Durkheim could not, *in principle*, advance a claim about religion that made appeal to religious faith or transcendent causes—even had he wanted to do so. The reason of course lies in Durkheim's seeking to advance public knowledge. While one may not *like* his claim that association with a social group causes religious experience, such a claim is legitimate within the world as it is bounded by the epistemology of public knowledge about the world.

Social Ontology, Religious Reality, and 'Strong' Durkheimianism

Once, however, students get over the issue that inquiry is *public*, and that *public* knowledge is sought, we can begin taking the measure of the more fruitful appreciations of Durkheim's 'strong' approach to religion. This brings me to the issue of the *social ontology* of religion. This issue arises immediately concerning Durkheim's views about the underlying reality of religion—the *ontology* of religion—best summed up in his religion-society/society-religion identity, the identity of society and the object of religion (the sacred).

As an identity relation, "Religion, God, the Sacred = Society" (I call this D1) is interestingly ambiguous. (One will note as well that Durkheim and his peers called his sociology of religion by the equally ambiguous title *sociologie religieuse.*) Our identity is ambiguous because it can just as fairly be read: "Society = Religion, God, the Sacred" (I call this D2). That is to say that the identity expressed is to be read in *both* directions at the same time—either with 'society' being the object of predication (D1) or with 'religion' playing the same grammatical role (D2). Yet, when scholars speak of the religion-society/society-religion identity, they are often tempted to read this identity in the typical reductionist way characteristic of the old scholarship as Durkheim (D2). Thus, by this reading, "Religion, God, the Sacred = Society" implies that Durkheim argues simply that the underlying reality of religious experience, and thus of the nature of God or the sacred and so on, is *society.* Religious experience is thus caused by the very social forces that can be detected and investigated in the public way I have just discussed.

Logically speaking, however, this reductionist reading is not logically privileged. Strictly speaking, no member of a pair in an identity is prior. No member of the pair identified is privileged with position in the expression of identity: the religion-society identity is just as much a society-religion identity; neither D1 nor D2 are prior. This means we can read this identity (D2) as saying "Society = Religion, God, the Sacred" with equal logical justification as D1. Read in this way as D2, from the point of view of what is predicated of society, it follows that Durkheim is asserting that society, social life, and so on have a *religious* nature. Society is for Durkheim no mere sociobiological massing of individual organisms but a collectivity informed with what one might call *spirituality* or, in older parlance, values, ideals, and such. Durkheim is predicating religious traits necessary to the existence and maintenance of society, not only the other way around. Durkheim 'sings.'

Society And—Not Or—the Sacred

The main point in drawing these deductions is to shift the typical religious studies student's perspective on Durkheim, sufficient for giving Durkheimian scholarship on religion a plausibility it may not have hitherto had. Beyond, then, the benefit of 'weak' Durkheimianism, of taking a social approach to religion, there is thus more. Beyond the benefit of focusing on religious institutions and social forms—for example, asceticism and monasteries come into focus as *social* institutions and forms of *social* organization, rather than just the beliefs, morals, or myths of monks—there is the core of at least part of 'strong' Durkheimianism that can be appreciated. To wit, the 'strong' Durkheim, properly understood as affirming the religion-society/society-religion identity, is asserting that all social reality can be said to participate in *religious* reality. This would be no more nor no less than one saying that society participates equally well in political or esthetic dimensions of human life. Since there is no society without values, without what Durkheim himself called a non-materialist or natural 'spiritual' dimension, there is no society without a *religious* dimension.

How then does appreciating Durkheim's positing of religious traits onto society play itself out in a course in religious studies? Here the choice of texts is crucial. Instead of the better known classics like *The Elementary Forms of the Religious Life*, I have used Durkheim's passionate and brilliant polemic essay of 1898, on behalf of the innocence of Dreyfus, "Individualism and the Intellectuals."[3] This piece is most effective in showing how Durkheim links certain social arrangements and values to the sacred or religiousness in a way that hardly seems to make his societism an obstacle to thinking seriously about the propositions made about the nature of religion.

Durkheim here is arguing against the attacks made on the defenders of Dreyfus led by the Roman Catholic writer and polemicist Ferdinand Brunetière. At the time Durkheim wrote, it was becoming increasingly clear that Dreyfus was quite plausibly innocent and thus both unjustly condemned and punished. To stem the tide of a popular movement to exonerate Dreyfus, Brunetière argued, in effect, that the honor of the army and state required that protests should cease and Dreyfus's conviction should not be challenged. In a time of national danger, said Brunetière, matters of mere individual innocence must be subordinated to 'saving the face' of the national government. Better, like Jesus, that one man—even though innocent—suffer for the sake of the people of France than that the nation's key institutions be humiliated and perhaps delegitimated by admitting their errors. The trouble in the France of his day, argued Brunetière, was those noisy protesting 'intellectuals,' who were the chief advocates of Dreyfus's innocence. In the name of transcendent values of justice and the integrity of the individual, they argued that Dreyfus should be rehabilitated, no matter what embarrassment this would cause to the nation as a whole.

Going by expectations normally associated with Durkheimian societism, the case Durkheim made for Dreyfus is remarkable, and shows how crude the old view of Durkheim was. Against Brunetière, Durkheim argued nothing less than the case for the *sacredness* of the human individual. As sacred, an individual like Dreyfus was due justice absolutely. His rights as a sacred being were transcendent and could not be compromised to the national interest, as Brunetière wished. Indeed, for us, Durkheim says, the human individual is a *sacred* being.

This move then establishes at least one feature about the place of religion in Durkheim's thought—namely that he approved of at least *certain kinds* of religion—here a version of the 'religion of humanity,' that neoreligion affirming the transcendent sacredness of the human individual. If Durkheim be a reductionist and in this sense insincere about his claim that the individual is sacred, then we would no longer have a "new" Durkheim but just the old one.

But recent scholarship—at least since Lukes but also anticipated by Robert Bellah and his notion of 'civil religion'—shows that we do indeed have a "new" nonreductionist Durkheim. We have a Durkheim who saw religion as something valuable in itself and a pervasive element in modern societies—especially the ideal of the sacredness of the human person.

Readers may ask, however, what has become of Durkheim the reductionist sociologist? I answer that Durkheim is still present at the heart of this argument, although not in a way I think ought to be called 'reductionist.' Durkheim here resists reductionism because he integrates his societism and his individualism, rather than making one an epiphenomenon of the other. By arguing, first, that the individual is a *value* for 'us,' at least for France, and, second, that it is so because to be a value is be valued by the *community*—whether the historical or present-day community does not matter—Durkheim links individual and society internally. Thus, in defending Dreyfus, Durkheim is defending the rights of the *individual* as an instance of the more general French national and *social* values inscribed in such foundational documents as, for example, the Declaration of the Rights of Man and Citizen. Although there is a social causality, in that our values—like all human values—are necessarily the products of groups, there is no reductionism, because the sacredness of the individual is real, and as real as anything emanating from the human realm could be.

Making Durkheim Plausible: Beyond History and Phenomenology of Religion

Another source of antipathy to Durkheim among students of religion stems from the assumption that he does not belong to the lineages of religious studies. He is, for example, neither a historian nor a phenomenologist of religion. As either a secularizing pedagogue or sociologist, Durkheim's institutional affiliations are not those of anyone in the main institutions of the study of religion in France—the "Science Religieuse" (Fifth) Section of the École Pratique des Hautes Études in Paris. Nor does he even seem much aware of his contemporaries, Albert Réville, the doyen of the École Pratique, Fifth Section, Jean Réville, his son and successor, or Maurice Vernes, founder of the august *Revue de l'histoire des religions*. Likewise, Durkheim does not seem to be in conversation with the founders of the classic origins of religious studies in the late nineteenth and early twentieth centuries like a Sir James Frazer, Friedrich Max Müller, Edward Burnett Tylor, Cornelis P. Tiele, or Pierre Daniel Chantepie de la Saussaye. From this perspective, Durkheim is not 'one of us' but rather a foreign intruder into our field of religious studies, and worst of all, someone seeking to 'reduce' it to sociology.

For those who have read Durkheim closely, it is clear that most, if not all, of these assumptions are groundless. Since Lukes and the basic efforts at pub-lication made by Victor Karady and Philippe Besnard of the Maison de Sciences de l'Homme in Paris, among others, we now can begin to see how Durkheim and his group worked in tight collaboration with one another in intense intel-lectual labors (Besnard 1983, Besnard and Fournier 1998, Karady 1968, Mauss 1968). In this sense, the references in Durkheim's *Elementary Forms* to familiar names in the study of religion such as Max Müller, Sir James Frazer, E. B. Tylor, Abel Bergaigne, William Robertson Smith, or Albert Réville carry a spe-cial significance for our understanding of the Durkheimian conception of their intellectual program: to wit, they saw themselves as fully belonging to the academic study of religion—even as they played the role of revolutionaries aiming to overthrow its theological tendencies. Indeed, one of the first con-certed acts of the Durkheimians with respect to the major institution of the study of religion in France—the École Pratique des Hautes Études, Fifth Sec-tion—was to seek to have Hubert and Mauss appointed there to major profes-sorial chairs.

These connections are additionally significant because both Hubert and Mauss trained as 'historians of religion' at the École Pratique, Fifth Section, in the very French 'science religieuse' that dominated the study of religion in France in their day. The Roman Catholic–born Henri Hubert had trained in the study of Judaism and Near Eastern religions under the leading scholar of rabbinic Judaism of France, Israel Lévi, while the Jewish-born Marcel Mauss worked on the religions of India under Sylvain Lévi. And even beyond their concern with particular religions, Hubert and Mauss also had theoretical and phenomenological interests. For example, they had also been attracted to Tiele's morphology of religion—a precursor to van der Leeuw's phenomenol-ogy. Durkheim had gone so far as to have sent Mauss on a mission to study with Tiele in Leyden as part of a year's tour of leading foreign university efforts in studying religion—a study tour including residence under Tylor at Oxford and Frazer at Cambridge. The common desire of the Durkheimians (especially Mauss) and Tiele was to produce a history of religion that was "philosophical" rather than merely documentary.[4] Both Durkheimians and the early phenom-enologists sought to go beyond the 'facts' by seeking the structures underlying them.

In the end, however, the Durkheimians and Tiele parted company over Tiele's theological ambitions and theistic conclusions. Initially, for example, Mauss lavished praise on Tiele's efforts at "morphology"[5]—his creative clas-sification and grouping of religion into different forms. For Mauss, category formation, such as he and Hubert undertook in their *Sacrifice: Its Nature and Functions*, was the part of Tiele's work closest to the ambitions of the *Année*. Tiele's morphology, like the similar Durkheimian efforts, were, Mauss tells us, essential rudimentary scientific work, even if Tiele preferred in the end to make a theology of religion rather than the real science of religion Mauss wanted.[6]

In a similar spirit, Henri Hubert's French edition and translation of Pierre Daniel Chantepie de la Saussaye's lengthy 1887–89 "phenomenological" handbook of the world's religions, *Lehrbuch der Religionsgeschichte*, showed how much Durkheimians wanted to revolutionize the study of religion.[7] Interested as they were in new ways of studying religion beyond what the historians and theologians of their milieu had put forward, in 1904, Henri Hubert and Isidore Lévy gathered a team of translators to produce a French edition of this massive work, under the title *Manuel d'histoire des religions*.[8] This translation and French edition was, however, not done in the spirit of 'pure' scholarship. It was shot through with a thoroughly disingenuous political purpose, which is embodied in Hubert's most peculiar introduction to the book. In it, Henri Hubert severely attacks most of Chantepie de la Saussaye's main theses! While saluting Chantepie de la Saussaye's conceptual sorting of classes of religious phenomena, Hubert charged it with sectarian partisanship. Saussaye excluded both Judaism and Christianity from the *Manuel*. For Chantepie de la Saussaye, they were not 'religions' like the rest but 'true' revelations of divine will.[9] As such, they could never be the object of scientific study in the way the other 'religions' were. For Hubert, such theological biases made the *Manuel* "useless" in its present form and made it useless "to remake it."[10] Instead, Hubert tried to turn Saussaye's effort to Durkheimian purposes and methods in the study of religion.

Thus, lacking knowledge of the activity of the Durkheimians with respect to the more widely recognized founders of religious studies, it has been all too easy to overlook the way the Durkheimians fit into the study of religion. Until recently, we have known next to nothing about the historical location of the Durkheimians with respect to the study of religion in Europe. One of the major contributions of the scholarship behind the 'new' Durkheim is precisely, however, to bring such connections to light.

In this connection, several texts illustrate how the Durkheimians worked within the discourse of the study of religion. Their books on magic and sacrifice, for example, are at one level nothing other than elaborate works of religious *phenomenology*, in that what they seek to do is spell out what we should understand by these classic commonplaces of the study of religion. Of course, they are much more than phenomenologies or works of religious morphology, like those of Tiele or Chantepie de la Saussaye (Hubert and Mauss 1972; Hubert and Mauss 1964). But they are at least that. Much the same can be said, as well, for Durkheim's article "Concerning the Definition of Religious Phenomena," but here about the category of 'religion.' It is here as well that Durkheim first argues that Buddhism ought to be classified as a religious *phenomenon* despite its lack of a central idea of God.[11]

But perhaps there is no handier text available for showing students how much a part of the classic discourse of religious studies were the Durkheimians than Durkheim's address to a joint meeting of the Free Thinkers and Free Believers, "Religious Sentiment at the Present Time." There, decades before van der Leeuw, for example, Durkheim argued for the importance of empathy in the study of religion. To his freethinker fellows, Durkheim says these remarkable words:

> what I ask the free thinker is that he should confront religion in the same mental state as the believer. It is only by doing this that he can hope to understand it. Let him feel it as the believer feels it; what it is to the believer is what it really is. Consequently, he who does not bring to the study of religion a sort of religious sentiment cannot speak about it! He is like a blind man trying to talk about colour.[12]

The beauty of using this particular text in "The Problem of Religion" is that it concerns the matter of religious experience, and thus brings us back to the central organizing concept of the course—namely, that in the modern period, the main reference of the critical study of religion, in the West, at least, has been religious *experience*. Thus, Durkheim's instructions to the freethinkers are precisely to begin their inquiries—as he does—there with the insider's data of what religious experience is.

NOTES

1. For further information, consult the course website: http://religiousstudies.ucr.edu/Web/Strenski1oooutline.htm.

2. I thank Wendy Doniger for the usage 'tool box.'

3. Durkheim, "Individuals and the Intellectuals 1898," in *Durkheim on Religion*, ed. W. S. F. Pickering (London: Routledge, 1975).

4. Cornelis P. Tiele, *Elements of the Science of Religion*, part I, *Morphological* (Edinburgh: Blackwood, 1898), 17–18.

5. Mauss, 1899 review of Cornelis P. Tiele, *Enleidung: Part I*, in *Marcel Mauss, Oeuvres*, vol. 1, *Les Fonctions sociales du sacré*, ed. Victor Karady (Paris: Éditions de Minuit, 1968): 540, 544.

6. Mauss, review, 544.

7. Pierre Daniel Chantepie de la Saussaye, *Lehrbuch der Religionsgeschichte*, 2 vols. (1887–92), 2nd ed. (Freiburg: n.p., 1897).

8. Henri Hubert, introduction to the French translation, in Pierre Daniel Chantepie de la Saussaye, *Manuel de l'histoire des religions* (1897), 2nd ed., trans. Henri Hubert and Isidore Lévy (Paris: Colin, 1904).

9. Saussaye responded to such criticism by promising to deal with Christianity separately and then later integrate this into a general phenomenology. This was reported in Hubert, introduction, vi. This excuse did not please Saussaye's arguably sharpest critic, the Catholic modernist Alfred Loisy, either. In reviewing both the French translation of the second edition and the subsequent third German language edition, Loisy says:

> Christianity has the completely negative privilege of not being represented. This form of respect may have its inconveniences. Without doubt, a time

will come when the history of religions—in its own interests—will see that it cannot do without Christianity; and a time will come when Christian theology will recognize that it ought—for the same reason as well—make a place for the history of religions.

Albert Loisy, review of Hubert, introduction, *Revue d'histoire et de littérature religieuses* 9 (1904): 479. See also Loisy, review of Chantepie de la Saussaye, *Lehrbuch der Religionsgeschichte*, 3rd ed., *Revue d'histoire et de littérature religieuses* 10 (1905): 505–506. In his review of the third edition of Saussaye's *Manuel*, Loisy observed that Christianity is still left out. But this time Loisy spares the charm: "Christianity might figure there [in comparison with other religions] with damage to the faith of its adherents; [but] for the good of science, it should already have been introduced."

Jean Réville also found Saussaye's omission of Christianity "inexcusable"—but only because in excluding Christianity from comparison with other religions, Saussaye had missed a great chance to demonstrate its superiority!

All histories of religion which systematically leave aside Christianity—insofar as the focus of such history is religious—are deprived of the crown of the religious evolution of humanity; in its different forms and in its progressive evolution, Christianity has been for the last five hundred years the religion of those peoples who have marched at the head of civilization.

Jean Réville, review of Chantepie de la Saussaye, *Lehrbuch der Religionsgeschichte*, 2nd ed. (1897), *Revue de l'histoire des religions* 38 (1898): 69.

10. Hubert, introduction, v.

11. Durkheim, "Concerning the Definition of Religious Phenomena," in *Durkheim on Religion*, 74–99.

12. Durkheim, "Religious Sentiment at the Present Time," in *Durkheim on Religion*, 184.

REFERENCES

Besnard, Philippe. 1983. *The Sociological Domain.* Cambridge: Cambridge University Press.

Besnard, Philippe, and Marcel Fournier. 1998. *Emile Durkheim: Lettres à Marcel Mauss.* Paris: Presses Universitaire de France.

Durkheim, Emile. 1975. "Concerning the Definition of Religious Phenomena." In *Durkheim on Religion*, edited by W. S. F. Pickering. London: Routledge.

———. 1975. Contribution to Discussion 'Religious Sentiment at the Present Time.' " In *Durkheim on Religion*, edited by W. S. F. Pickering. London: Routledge.

———. 1975. "Individuals and the Intellectuals 1898." In *Durkheim on Religion*, edited by W. S. F. Pickering. London: Routledge.

Hubert, Henri. 1904. Introduction to the French translation. In Pierre Daniel Chantepie de la Saussaye, *Manuel de l'histoire des religions* (1897), 2nd ed., translated by Henri Hubert and Isidore Lévy. Paris: Colin.

Hubert, Henri, and Marcel Mauss. 1972. *A General Theory of Magic.* Translated by R. Brain. London: Routledge.

———. 1964. *Sacrifice: Its Nature and Function.* Vol. 13. Translated by W. D. Halls. Chicago: University of Chicago Press.

Loisy, Albert. 1904. Review of Henri Hubert, introduction to the French translation, in Pierre Daniel Chantepie de la Saussaye, *Manuel de l'histoire des religions* (1897), 2nd ed., translated by Henri Hubert and Isidore Lévy, *Revue d'histoire et de littérature religieuses* 9 (1904): 479.

Mauss, Marcel. 1968. *Oeuvres.* Vol. 1. *Les Fonctions sociales du sacré.* Edited by Victor Karady. Paris: Éditions de Minuit.

———. 1899. Review of Cornelis P. Tiele, *Enleidung: Part I* in Loisy, review of Chantepie de la Saussaye, *Lehrbuch der Religionsgeschichte,* 3rd ed. *Revue d'histoire et de littérature religieuses* 10 (1905): 505–506.

Réville, Jean. 1898. Review of Chantepie de la Saussaye, *Lehrbuch der Religionsgeschichte,* 2nd ed. (1897). *Revue de l'histoire des religions* 38: 64.

Tiele, Cornelis P. 1898. *Elements of the Science of Religion. Part I. Morphological.* Edinburgh: Blackwood.

3

Three Levels of Teaching Durkheim

Edward A. Tiryakian

In his recent imaginative exegesis, Donald Nielsen proposes that there is an emergent "sociological monism" in Durkheim's oeuvre, an attempt at finding unity or totality in the civilizational currents and encounters of modernity. Foremost, in Durkheim's days (but also in ours), are the major encounters of traditional religion, philosophy, and science, encounters that generate ontological, epistemological, and ethical disputes, inside and outside academic walls. While Durkheim—like Marx and Weber—did not live to complete his magnum opus (in his case, it was to be his Ethics), Nielsen makes the case that Durkheim's overarching final philosophy is a vision of the unity of Nature, society, and religion, the three faces of God.[1]

In a complementary secular trinitarian mode, I will in this essay present a pedagogical approach to Durkheim, essentially what might be thought of as three faces, or three levels, of Durkheim to present primarily to undergraduate and graduate students. The first is for students getting their initial exposure to Durkheim, typically in introductory courses of sociology; the second is at a level of more advanced undergraduate courses, notably a level where students take the sociology of religion and some overview of sociological theory (depending on the academic institution, these courses may be open to both undergraduates and graduates). The third level is for those who are in a doctoral program or the equivalent. I will draw on my experiences and observations in the course of a lengthy academic career in which my commitment to sociology has been coextensive with my unabashed acceptance of Durkheimian sociology as being of central significance for our discipline, not only historically but also presently. I think it safe to say that other contributors to this book feel the same way, though perhaps for different reasons, intellectual and otherwise.

My starting point is that teaching Durkheim to American students is a challenging, if not difficult, assignment, particularly if the audience consists of undergraduate novices, rather than professionals or those training to become professional social scientists or scholars of religion. There are several factors that are likely to make Durkheim and his central concerns seem very distant to college students. Since cognoscenti may easily neglect these, let me indicate the most serious obstacles.

First, Durkheim *may appear so distant in time and space to our students.* The social world of the French Third Republic and its intellectual milieu are far removed from those of the contemporary American academic setting. It is hard enough to get students to have empathy with the American setting of, say, the 1950s—the era of Eisenhower, McCarthyism, structural-functionalism, and cultural sobriety. How much harder is it to get them to view with interest the world of Paris (and Bordeaux) one hundred years ago: not the *belle époque* and the glitzy world of the Moulin Rouge depicted in films but the social and academic world, with its bitter political chasms climaxing in the Dreyfus affair, alongside the great (radical) republican struggle to wrest education away from the traditional tutelage of the Catholic Church that culminated with the complete disenfranchisement of religion under the prime ministry (1902–1905) of Emile Combes. Also part of the ferment now dimmed by the passage of time were the new intellectual and social currents, such as socialism, militant conservatism, radical syndicalism, and the American import, pragmatism, that provided leaven for a new generation of the French intelligentsia. All this, in perspective, may seem to be nothing more than a ballpark of "dead white males."

Second, Durkheim *operates with a different set of presuppositions from that of the great majority of American students.* Years ago I made the argument that of the three great sociological approaches to modernity, it is that of Weber that comes closest to making sense of the American reality (Tiryakian 1975), partly because of his profound knowledge of the Puritan matrix of American culture, which he saw in action in the course of his 1904 visit to the United States.[2] Without reopening the issue, let me advance the argument that Durkheim's social realism, however different from that of Marx, nevertheless gives ontological priority to the societal group over the individual. The bundle of presuppositions (or, in other terminology, "domain assumptions" or "assumptive framework") that we are first and foremost a part of a collectivity to which we owe obligations, that society (and the group) are an emergent reality greater than the sum of its individual parts, that group identity is fundamental to our personal identity, and that group well-being is essential to our personal well-being—all this cluster runs against the basic and tacitly held presuppositions of (most) students in the United States.

The "mainstream" presuppositions of the American institutional structure, however these may be weakening today, accentuate (liberal) individualism, the rational individual as the ultimate determinant and arbiter of her or his actions.[3] The whole tenor of public education, including higher education, is to encourage self-development, and popular culture and its mass media reinforce this individualism with the emphasis on freedom of choice (today as much for women as previously for men). Although undergraduates may not know what "eudemonism" means, they live, partake, and enjoy this major orientation of contemporary modernity, which has become deeply imbedded in consumerism—the antipode of the this-worldly asceticism that Weber noted gave so much leverage to modern capitalism, especially American style. While it would be erroneous to think that students bring no moral baggage to the table—they certainly do, according to the surveys analyzed in the recent study of Alan Wolfe (2001)—unlike the "unisex" haircut, there is no uniform moral code transcending individual preferences and experiences, no moral code taken as binding on the nation or binding the individual to a larger collectivity than himself or herself. "Moral freedom," as uncovered by Wolfe in this decade, updates the "Sheilaism"—religious individualism—that Robert Bellah and his associates came across in the 1980s;[4] unlike the latter in *Habits of the Heart* and Bellah's earlier attempt to recover an American communitarian tradition lost from sight (Bellah 1975), Wolfe's present assessment seems to have as its message: "moral pluralism is the new American way of life."

I have alluded to the sense of obligation, of a moral duty that is part of Durkheim's presupposition. Put in so many terms, it is a sort of *Kantian republicanism*. While this ethical and moral framework undergirded the institutions of Durkheim's Third Republic and, for that matter, was congruent with the basic institutional framework of the United States for most of the twentieth century, it may well be out of sync in today's setting. But since one is not likely to discuss presuppositions with undergraduates in introductory sociology courses (or even at higher levels), it is altogether possible for those teaching Durkheim to overlook that students do not connect with him at the level of presuppositions. In contrast, though Marx's presuppositions of collectivism and class conflict as the motor of history are equally alien to the basic American experience, along with the more abstruse notion of dialectical materialism, the idealistic and quasi-romantic inclinations of college students can find in Marxist and contemporary neo-Marxist themes of "exploitation," oppression, and "alienation" elements of a vast historical morality play that are lacking in Durkheim.

From this preliminary caveat about an initial invisible barrier separating Durkheim from American college students, how do we proceed to bridge the chasm and involve students with him, starting with their initial encounter in the introductory course?

Level 1: Introductory Durkheim

The introductory sociology course, at least in the United States, does not have a standardized curriculum, not even (at a medium-sized or large university) in the same department. This means that the nature and extent of exposure to Durkheim in general, much less to his sociology of religion, is subject to the vagaries of who happens to be the instructor in the course. As a first approximation of the treatment of Durkheim at this level, I shall briefly consider how he fares in four currently available introductory textbooks, which I randomly selected from an array made available by a colleague currently in charge of the introductory course. The texts are, alphabetically, Giddens and Duneier (2000), Landis (2000), Macionis (2001), and Nolan and Lenski (1999)—all successful, judging by the fact that one is in its third edition, two are their eighth, and the fourth is in its eleventh edition.

Giddens and Duneder, very global in overall scope, devote an entire chapter to religion, with a strong focus on comparative and contemporary religions. Durkheim is mentioned briefly as "a good example of the *functionalist* school of thought in sociology" (Giddens and Duneder 2000, 410), and then, in the chapter summary that lumps the "classical" thinkers, Marx, Durkheim, and Weber, one reads: "all believed that religion is fundamentally an illusion."[5] In the text's introductory chapter, Durkheim receives a more extensive treatment as an influential figure, but with a very brief mention of *The Elementary Forms of Religious Life* as signaling "the importance of religion in maintaining moral order in society."[6] Landis gives ample place to Durkheim in various chapters, from mentioning him among evolutionary theories to a discussion of anomie as related to social disorganization, and to his contribution to the sociology of deviance. One of the four chapters covering social institutions is devoted to religion: without explicit mention to the *Forms*, Durkheim's functionalist perspective on the integrative and regulative functions of religion is discussed (Landis: 266), and later in the chapter, his stimulus for research in pointing to the association of religion and suicide.[7]

Of the introductory textbooks examined, Macionis offers the broadest coverage of global aspects of religion and religiosity. Durkheim's concepts of the *profane* and the *sacred* and of *totemism*, the basic thesis of religious life as people engaging "to celebrate the awesome power of their society,"[8] and the structural-functional analysis of religion are abstracted with reference to the *Forms*. The author goes on to discuss (to a lesser extent) theoretical alternative perspectives, such as symbolic interactionism and social conflict *theory*, with further brief mention of Weber. (An earlier chapter on theories of society and social change gives greater scope to Weber's analysis of rationalization as a master process of social change, noting in particular major points of the *Protestant Ethic* thesis.)

Polar to Macionis is the nugatory discussion of religion presented in the Nolan and Lenski textbook: religion is briefly mentioned as a declining ideology in modern industrial societies after having played a role, via the Protestant Reformation, in the early spread of democratic beliefs and values. Given the authors' broad evolutionary and materialistic orientation as a frame of organization, it is revealing that Durkheim merits just a single entry—in a brief footnote reference to the *Forms* there is a cursory mention of "belief in a god in technologically less advanced societies."[9]

In checking with four departmental colleagues who in the past six years have each been in charge of the introductory course, I found the same variability in their presentation of Durkheim to beginning students. At one end were two colleagues who make little, if any, mention of him. By contrast is a colleague who reported making extensive use of Durkheim, including linking Durkheim's discussion of totemism to network analysis (she informed me that students readily took to this linkage), along with discussing Durkheim's analysis of suicide in evaluating social versus personal causes, and the bearing of *The Division of Labor* on studies of social stratification. Intermediary was the fourth, who structured the introductory course in terms of three broad perspectives: conflict theories, cultural studies, and functionalist theories; she reported that students found reading Durkheim on "What is a social fact?" stimulating as a springboard to their own location of social facts.

My own inclination in exposing students to Durkheim at the introductory level is to take C. Wright Mills's book *The Sociological Imagination* (1959) as a springboard to present Durkheim as an exemplar of *the sociological imagination*. In one lecture—which may be all that an instructor has to present a figure from the past in this kind of course—one can organize Durkheim's overarching task for sociology being, first, in order to establish its academic identity, to identify, analyze, and measure *social solidarity* in different societal forms. Second, as a critical task for the broader legitimation of sociology, to innovate, restore, and renovate solidarity, without which society, like a sandcastle or a house of cards, can topple overnight, witness, for example, the explosion of ethnic violence in Northern Ireland, Bosnia-Herzegovina, or Rwanda-Burundi. After this preface, I can in the remainder of the hour highlight how Durkheim boldly demonstrated the social reality of social solidarity in three different kinds of substantive studies.

One can begin with Durkheim's *Division of Labor in Society* (1964). Students can be told that Durkheim laid out in this work a broad overview of the transformation of human society from small-scale to large, complex, modern, urban society and that he proposed that accompanying the structural changes are changes in the relative proportion of two forms of social solidarity, *mechanical* and *organic*. But how to demonstrate changes in solidarity, which is not tangible or "objective"? That was his initial challenge. Perhaps it would be well to pause and ask students if they have any idea as to what a *social indicator* of solidarity might be. (If that seems daunting or too abstract, one can ask students if they would suggest a social indicator of, say, *community ties* at their college or university.) After seeing what suggestions are made, the instructor can then put forward Durkheim' s show of the sociological imagination by his latching onto *law* as an external index of what is an internal, social-psychological condition of social existence (Durkheim 1964, 64). One can indicate Durkheim's differentiation of the legal code into the criminal and the civil code, and his argument that in the evolution of society, the criminal code diminishes as the civil code becomes of greater significance in the regulation of conduct between individuals.

I will not repeat Durkheim's argument, but in the context of this book, it may be of interest to point out to students Durkheim's knowledge of various religious traditions of antique civilizations, and certainly of the Hebrew Bible, in the framing of the penal code.[10]

To offer students a challenge here, one may invite some students (in particular, any who think of themselves as prelaw) to do a term paper testing out the relevance of Durkheim by looking at a setting that underwent regime transformation, from a tight authoritarian or totalitarian regime to a modern democratic one. If Durkheim's thesis has validity, one would expect that in a few decades, the corpus of law would shift from a "repressive" and penal emphasis, defining a multitude of actions as offensive to the moral sentiments of the collectivity, to a greater emphasis on "restitutive" and civil emphasis on rights of individuals. As a test case, one can examine the *Book of General Laws* of the Massachusetts Bay Colony in its heyday as a Puritan stronghold and, say, the Massachusetts legal code in the latter part of the nineteenth century: in looking over *Division*, I did not see any reference to "modern America," but it might appeal to American students to see whether his general evolutionary scheme (which provided much fodder for the modernization and secularization perspectives of a generation ago) applies to the United States.

The second instance of Durkheim's sociological imagination is *Suicide*, a hallmark contribution to enduring sociological classics, as may be noted by at least three important centennial volumes appraising its significance (Borlandi and Cherkaoui 2000; Lester 1994; Pickering and Walford 2000). What is most daring about the study, students in the introductory course might be told, is that Durkheim took what is seemingly an irrational, individual act par excellence, and showed his spellbound audience that there are demonstrable structural factors that underlie differentiated group rates of suicide. To challenge students, they need be told that Durkheim took suicide rates as an indicator of the health of a society or a nation and changes in the rates as indicators of the changing health. Where does the United States stand today, relative to the students' parents' generation, and relative to other countries? This is always a question that can generate good discussion.

But again, in terms of teaching Durkheim on religion, perhaps equally challenging is to delineate the typology of suicide that Durkheim drew up, giving attention to the type he associated with excessive integration of the individual to group attachment and, more specifically, *obligatory altruistic suicide* (Durkheim 1951, 221). Although Durkheim drew on antiquity, on Asian societies (India, Japan), on early Christianity for instances of this kind of suicide, the remnant in modern society that he found rich in altruistic suicide was the military. One could ask students whether they thought our present volunteer army would have higher or lower rates of suicide than, say, fifty years ago when the draft prevailed, and whether there might be differentials between officers and nonofficers, or between different branches of the service. But in terms of actuality, there is in the news an instance of altruistic suicide not covered by Durkheim: *the suicide bomber.* Though occurring elsewhere sporadically, it is in the Palestinian-Israeli escalation of violence that the suicide bomber, combining killing the self and killing "the other," has made dramatic headlines. To the individual who commits the single act of violence, the words of Durkheim apply: "[it] springs from hope; for it depends on the belief in beautiful perspectives beyond this life. It even implies enthusiasm and the spur of a faith eagerly seeking satisfaction" (225). It is hard for Westerners to understand a certain religious mentality that would promote killing of self and killing of others, except perhaps in wartime, but apparently the Palestinian suicide bombers have the motivation of religious martyrdom in the context of Islam and ultimate sacrifice for Palestinian nationhood. On the other hand, from an Israeli perspective, there is nothing glorious in this act but only execrable terrorism by an agent of a despicable organization. The ontological ambiguity of suicide in relation to its social context—an act of valor or an act of cowardice—is fully dramatized on the contemporary scene in the Middle East, and should provoke interest in Durkheim's analysis.[11]

The third instance of Durkheim's demonstration of the sociological imagination is the *Forms.* At the introductory level, beginning students may be informed that in his last major work, written ninety years ago at a time when the influence of religion in the public sphere in Europe was rapidly waning,[12] Durkheim combined anthropological materials with materials of religion of the French Revolution—neither being components of what is today termed "Judeo-Christian"—to propose that the hub of social organization and large-scale social change is a complex religious one. To arouse students' interest one more notch, one can conclude the lecture by pointing out that Durkheim's analysis gives weight to the significance of *symbols of the totem,* and one paramount symbol is the emblem or the flag. What, the instructor could conjecture, would be the reaction on the campus if we burned either the American flag or the flag of the university? Are these "mere" bits of cloth or do they have a more profound significance as symbols of collective identity?

The introductory level, then, is the occasion for students to become aware of Durkheim as a trailblazer of modern sociology, and as a challenge, this hopefully by inviting students to develop their own sociological imagination while retaining how and in what fields Durkheim demonstrated his.

Level 2: Intermediate Durkheim

The intermediate level is one of a substantive course or a sociological theory course that students take either as a requirement for the major or as an elective for nonmajors. I will restrict myself to the two courses at this level that I have repeatedly taught, the sociology of religion and what I call "The History of Social Thought."[13]

The Sociology of Religion

I begin at the first meeting of this course by asking students to fill out a short anonymous questionnaire that asks them a few simple questions, including "What do you understand by 'sacred'?" and "What, if anything, is sacred for you?" In the initial class discussion, I draw students into reflecting on the difference between "sacred" and "religion," and I emphasize that the course will explore the multidimensional ties between "sacred" and "religion" on the one hand and between "religion" and "society" on the other. To engage students at the onset, I pose the question that is at the crux of American exceptionalism: what factors are involved in the United States being the most advanced, modern capitalist society in the world *and* the one with the greatest level of across-the-board religious participation of its population . . . and this with a very distinctive separation of church and state? Drawing on the students' name recognition from their introductory sociology exposure, I will mention that none of the major figures of classical sociology—Marx, Durkheim, Weber (one can add Simmel)—was "religiously active." Further, in terms of their paramount perspective on modernity, none of them would give a sociological explanation of the American phenomenon. The course does not pretend to provide an answer to the American enigma, but it is heuristic at the start to pose an intriguing problem.

For many years teaching this course, I would begin by having students read, in their entirety, *Forms* and Weber's book *The Protestant Ethic and the Spirit of Capitalism* as basic frames for the field. Neither is a "light" reading, but I still think that undergraduates should be exposed to enduring works. However, more recently I sequence these two "classics" differently: I begin with two descriptive books that, like the two classics, have different settings from the customary ones that are familiar to students (churches and synagogues, mainly): Orsi's *Gods of the City* (1999) and Forbes and Mahan's *Religion and Popular Culture in America* (2000). Students can engage with the materials at the very start, and both works point to American religious vitality in adjusting to environments of modernity—the environment of the American metropolis and the entertainment environment.[14] Moreover, they prepare students for *Forms* in providing empirical materials regarding religious associations and their social organization, beliefs, and rituals, which most middle-class students are unlikely to have experienced, even if living in the same metropolitan region. The interpenetration of religion and society, even at the level of religion and popular culture, is a major component of Durkheim's analysis of the symbolic nature of organized society; this is better appreciated by students after they have considered that (immigrant) urban dwellers from different traditions can experience antinomies of modernity: secularization *and* sacralization.[15]

In addition to readings and lectures, my course in the sociology of religion has as a major component rather extensive field research. Students are asked to attend during the semester at least eight different religious "events," which may be institutionalized worship services but may also include some unscheduled religious activity: a revival meeting, a funeral, a procession or religious parade, or even some "secular" event that brings the community together in an outburst of collective enthusiasm. Students are told they have discretion as to what they attend, *as long as it is not a religious service that is part of their own family tradition.* And to enhance the learning experience, I ask white students to attend two African American services and conversely, African-American students to attend white services (one of a mainstream church, the other a Pentecostal or charismatic community). They are instructed to observe the *interaction rituals* of the service, the interaction between the religious virtuoso heading the service, the acolytes, and the general public of the congregation; they are to note what doctrinal *beliefs* are professed collectively or by the head of the congregation; they are to note what seems to them the *sacred symbols* of the service. Students are given written guidelines that outline how to write up their observations, and they turn in their field report at the end of the semester. I have found that students find this one of the best experiences they have, and it is a way for them not only to see in practice the reality of Durkheim's analysis but also to discover the extensive religious resources and diversity of the environment in which their university or college is located.[16]

In my lectures on *Forms*, I also indicate that for Durkheim, there was a quest for a new Holy Grail of modernity, that is, a new source of collective inspiration of ideals. Modern society is full of rituals, of feasts (holidays) and symbols, but in Durkheim's evaluation, they belong to an earlier era, while the present is "a period of transition and moral mediocrity" (1995, 429). And, drawing on the French Revolution as a setting that generated collective enthusiasm and ideals, Durkheim was hopeful for a similar rebirth that might launch a new era, a new society. He would have been dismayed at the revolutions of the twentieth century—the Bolshevik and the Nazi revolutions in particular—which for a generation in Russia (expanded to the Soviet Union) and Germany, respectively, generated collective enthusiasm and a feeling of empowerment.

Is it then futile to search for a religion and moral ideals that can integrate modern society, especially one as heterogeneous as American society? I pose that question to students and then draw in materials regarding civil religion, which Robert Bellah reintroduced as a focus in the sociology of religion, drawing on his readings in Durkheim, among other sources (Bellah 1970, 1973). The next time I give the course, I will have some new perspectives and new materials on American "civil religion," as discussed in the epilogue to this chapter. But in any case, I think the field research provides students with the basis for seeing firsthand some structural similarities in how the "sacred" is socially organized, while at the same time enhancing the authenticity and specificity of the religious experience of each religious community.

The History of Social Thought

This course is taken as a requirement for the sociology major and as an elective for nonmajors. It is for the most part taken by juniors and seniors. I tend to cover a lot of ground, extending the scope to social theory from Plato and Aristotle to Foucault and Habermas; consequently, the exposure to Durkheim is rather concentrated. In my lectures, besides other material, I like to point out that Durkheim is a link in an interesting sociological tradition that goes back to Henri de Saint-Simon and Auguste Comte (whose basic models have been covered in previous lectures), characterized by the theorist turning his attention to the strategic significance of religion for societal integration. Saint-Simon, after his early seminal works on the new industrial order, saw the need for something else to bind social actors besides their place in the emergent industrial society—hence his "New Christianity" to renovate the Golden Rule. Comte realized that the system of positivism, for all its systematic rationality embodied in "sociocracy," did not guarantee social cohesion—hence his final elaboration of a "Religion of Humanity." And Durkheim completes the French connection by his later preoccupation with religion as not a vestige of the past but as intimately connected to modernity. I will also on occasion bring out that Max Weber's sociological odyssey bears comparison, since Weber begins his research in economic history and economic sociology, but then later turns to the religious sector as both a source of motivation in worldly conduct and as a cultural anchor for civilizations.

For reading selections in this course, I like to have a mixture of solid overviews (Tiryakian 1978b; Poggi 2000), with at least one selection from *Su-*

icide, since the latter is uniformly praised as a sociological exemplar that combines empirical data analysis and theorizing. I tend to change which particular chapter(s) I select for required reading, as long as their actuality may be pointed out, in lectures or in discussion sessions. So, for example, book 2, chapter 2 ("Egoistic Suicide") would be relevant in the context of this discussion, since this is where Durkheim lays out differential suicide rates by religious affiliation. Students from Protestant, Catholic, and Jewish religious backgrounds find the materials in this brief chapter intriguing, and it is part of the assignment to predict whether similar patterns of differentiation prevail today in the United States, given the changes in the social situation of Protestants, Catholics, and Jews from that of turn-of-century Europe. Alternatively, chapter 2 of book 3 is rich in actuality, since after a quick historical overview of the relation of suicide to morality, Durkheim considers various religious aspects of suicide, including its relation to homicide (I discuss this further in the epilogue).

For a second reading by Durkheim, I alternate between "Individualism and the Intellectuals" (1973b) and "The Dualism of Human Nature" (1973a). The first is a concise presentation of major versions of individualism, undoubtedly a central notion of Western civilization. Durkheim's disposal of Spencer and utilitarianism may puzzle our students and strike them as fighting a windmill, but they can be informed as to the persistence of this mode of individualism in contemporary economics, in rational choice theory, and in various writings of a certain conservative icon, Ayn Rand. Durkheim then moves on to the political individualism expressed in the Declaration of the Rights of Man and in our own Bill of Rights. Students will find in this passage a conception of the individual with which they should have some familiarity, touching on aspects of the dignity of every individual and the egalitarian premise of modern society (equality before the law, equality of opportunity). This part of the essay relates to themes of individualism that students may have been given to read earlier in the course in taking up Tocqueville and John Stuart Mill.

The latter and longer part of the essay is more thought-provoking, because it is here that Durkheim shifts his perspective on the individual, seeing in man a transcendental dimension worthy of a veritable cult, the "religion of humanity."[17] While students might appreciate Durkheim's historical note of the originality of Christianity in "the remarkable development of the individualistic spirit" (1973b, 52), some may find it difficult to accept that the modern cult of the individual and the scientific spirit of our times supersedes the traditional religious aura. But class discussions around this essay can bring in how today the still evolving doctrine of human rights, framed in the thirty-article United Nations Universal Declaration of Human Rights of 1948 does in fact approximate what Durkheim saw as modernity's religion of the individual. At the same time, the debates regarding stem cell research and the use of fetal tissues in this research also suggest that the traditional view of the sacredness of the individual still commands numerous adherents who are not willing to have a purely scientific, rational, instrumental approach prevail, even in research that promises to benefit ultimately humankind.

As to "The Dualism of Human Nature," it is also a good discussion piece in raising for students the question of what are the images of human nature held by sociology (and, by extension, in other social sciences). As one of his last sociological writings published in his lifetime, the essay is an extension of *Forms*, of course, but students need not to have read the latter to appreciate (and react to) Durkheim's sociological attempt to deal with a basic feature of human existence: the dual aspects of selfhood. One part of us is the body that individualizes us in the here-and-now relative to other beings. The other part of us transcends the body and the immediate; it is what the religious traditions of our civilization have taken to be "the soul," which belongs to a realm other than the biological. And in his discussion of human beings as *homo duplex* (quite in contrast to economic man, *homo economicus*), Durkheim notes the innate tension we feel between these two poles of our being: tension between self-interest and impersonal, moral demands. An attempted resolution of what Durkheim terms "this chronic and universal state of malaise" is to view this duality as an illusion (1973a, 154–158). Durkheim rejects this and provides a sociological justification for religious notions of a sacred aspect of the self— essentially, the internalization of the ideals of group life (1973a, 160).

What can add leaven to this assignment is to have students read at the same time the closing chapter of Freud's *Civilization and Its Discontents* (1961).[18] There is also an image of *homo duplex* in this late "sociological" essay of Freud. It is a pessimistic view of modernity, written after World War I, when Freud became increasingly aware of the destructive side of humankind, of *thanatos* as opposite to *libido*. And Freud, while categorically rejecting a transcendental basis for belief in the soul, accepts the psychological reality of civilization as the *superego* that, rather in a despotic way, curbs the aggressive impulses of the individual by turning these impulses inward by the mechanism of guilt. It is interesting that Freud in the guise of therapy negates the function of the superego (that which has traditionally been called conscience), particularly in its command of "loving one's neighbor as oneself," for allegedly contributing to neurosis, so that, he inquires, "may we not be justified in reaching the diagnosis that, under the influence of cultural urges ... some civilizations have become 'neurotic?' " (1962, 91).

Freud has difficulty in accepting the reality of morality (he is in this respect in the mold of Nietzsche), and that involves rejecting the professed ideals of humankind as being an illusion. Yet, after the carnage of World War I and the disturbing mass movements of the 1920s that preceded the dictatorships of the 1930s, Freud was also all too aware of the need for humankind to succeed "in mastering the disturbance of their communal life by the human instinct of aggression and self-destruction" (1962, 92). For Durkheim, the ideals of civilization—first the Christian ideals and then the principles of 1789 (and those of human rights)—are not "illusions" but what elevate humankind above the biological self, even if they can only be partially realized.

Level 3: Advanced Durkheim

The third level typically has as clientele graduate students in two kinds of course structure: either a "basic" history of sociological theory with a focus on the "classics" or an independent study course (designated, say, as "Readings in the Sociology of Religion"). The latter may be requested either by a student who wishes to make a specialty area of the sociology of religion or by a graduate student in religious studies who wants to focus on major theoretical approaches in sociology that might assist her or him in dissertation research. Because of space considerations, I shall treat both of these as if they were the same module of Durkheim's sociology of religion. (I have not had the occasion or privilege of teaching an entire semester solely on Durkheim's sociology of religion.)

Graduate students should certainly read *Forms* in its entirety, noting that Durkheim is addressing extremely important epistemological issues (the Kantian legacy of the a priori categories of knowledge)[19] and ontological ones (the symbolic nature of ultimate reality in the human being's experience of the world). They should note that methodologically, *Forms* is an early sociological classic in secondary analysis of the "theoretically informed" Australian ethnographies of Baldwin Spencer and F. J. Gillen (Morphy 1998). In addition, it is a pioneer in sociological phenomenology, in its placing the analysis in terms of the lived experience of subjects (the Australians, but also modern subjects experiencing moments of enthusiasm, for example, in 1789 (Durkheim 1995, 215–216). And students might be apprised of an interesting paradox regarding Durkheim's complex attitude in dealing with religion: he saw traditional religious institutions, such as the Catholic Church in France, as outmoded, an anachronism of modern times; yet not only was the religious life *la vie sérieuse* but also, as Prades points out (1990, 113), Durkheim even cautioned in 1914 that "no one can speak about the study of religion who does not bring a sort of religious sentiment: he would be like the blind seeking to speak about colors."

In reading and discussing Durkheim's *Forms*, graduate students will become aware of a functionalist perspective with which Durkheim treats religion—the social organization of the sacred—as a social institution related synchronically and diachronically to other institutions. Religion is for Durkheim a sort of *primus inter pares*, or even a tissue of stem cells, so to speak. But lest students take this as only a conservative ploy, they should also be encouraged to pay close attention to the very dramatic sections in chapter 7 of book 2—a chapter with the innocuous title "Origins of These [Totemic] Beliefs (Conclusion)." It is here that Durkheim presents the "dynamogenic" aspect of religion in terms of the religious life being able to generate collective enthusiasm ("effervescence") that puts in play the sacred; consequently, this can lead to collective action that disrupts but can also renovate and reorganize the frames of the quotidian with new symbols of collective representation.[20] This should serve graduate students to see in this section the germs of a general theory of social change that is as applicable to modern societies as to colonized and Third World societies: the cultural sector as not just the one for the *reproduction* of the institutional framework but on extraordinary occasions as one for its new *production*, in giving actors an empowerment they lack in the everyday setting.

Besides reading the original text, students should also be familiar with some of the major (modern) secondary literature on *Forms* and Durkheim's sociology of religion. Certainly, as I have suggested (2000), Talcott Parsons became increasingly keen on the significance of Durkheim's later phase of study of symbolism and the nexus of religion and society (for example, Parsons 1973). Students can also add to their repertoire of the sociology of knowledge by readings in different accounts of the *context* of *Forms*, for example, in the intellectual context that Jones has addressed in various pieces (1977, 1986) or the republican context I have proposed (Tiryakian 1988a). They should also have on their list secondary readings and interpretations, such as the relevant works of Jeffrey Alexander (1982, 1988), whose reading of Durkheim led him to promote in American sociology a new emphasis on cultural sociology.

What graduate students need to know is the existence of two sets of Durkheimians, Durkheimians *then* and Durkheimians *now*. By *then* I mean the extremely talented group of young scholars, starting with Durkheim's first graduate student, his own nephew, Marcel Mauss (on their recently published correspondence, see Durkheim 1998). I will not dwell on their various and significant contributions to various fields of sociology. (For a discussion of the Durkheimians, see Besnard 1983; for a useful, but now incomplete, bibliography of their writings grouped in terms of their relative importance, see Nandan 1977.) In the context of this discussion, what is important for students to retain is that the original Durkheimians were generally social democrats (non-Marxist socialists), intellectuals "of the left," imbued, with very few exceptions, with the rational, skeptical, scientific spirit of the Enlightenment that was so integral to higher education in republican France.

Yet, like Durkheim, some of their best works and research dealt with the religious life of societies and civilizations. So for example, Mauss prepared (but did not complete) a dissertation on prayer and wrote extensively on various of its aspects and other themes of "the sacred" (1968). He collaborated with a long-term companion Henri Hubert (a specialist on Celtic civilization) on a series of brilliant essays in religious sociology (Hubert and Mauss 1929), including the landmark analysis of a basic ritual, that of sacrifice (Hubert and

Mauss 1964). Robert Hertz, a founder of the *Cahiers du Socialiste*, wrote in his short lifetime seminal essays on "death," on "the left hand," and on the Alpine cult of a saint and had begun a momentous study of sin and expiation before being killed early in World War I (Hertz 1928, 1994). Halbwachs, who gave a seminar on demography at Chicago—he was one of the few Durkheimians to visit the United States—added to his early studies of social classes and economic sociology several studies in religious sociology, including a pathbreaking study of collective memory in the construction of the Holy Land (1971). And the list can be extended to lesser known figures: among others, Maurice Cahen, a sociologist of Scandinavian civilization, who worked on the notion of the sacred in Germanic religions and the "name of God" in Germanic languages, and Edmond Doutté, a sociologist of the Maghreb, whose major work was *Magic and Religion in North Africa* (Mauss 1927).

What, one may ask of students, accounts for the Durkheimians exploring religious or quasi-religious topics, given their seemingly secular background? I will not seek to answer this extremely complex question, which has not been rigorously addressed, though an interesting debate regarding the relation between liberal Protestants and Durkheimians has recently surfaced (Mucchielli 1998; Strenski 2000).[21]

There is also a *current* group of Durkheimian scholars on both sides of the Atlantic doing dedicated archival and historical research. The French-speaking world has ongoing research undertaken on the original Durkheimians by Philippe Besnard in Paris and Marcel Fournier in Montreal, among others, and Raymond Boudon is renovating the famed *Année Sociologique*, which our students should know served as a sort of "laboratory" of research for Durkheim and his associates. On the American side, A. Tristan Riley and Jennifer Mergy recently completed in France doctoral dissertation research on the Durkheimians, in the footsteps of the research done a generation ago on the institutionalization of the social sciences by Terry Clark (1973).

Still, it may be argued that the main hub of Durkheimian studies currently is in England, which in Durkheim's days was devoid of academic sociology.[22] Besides a host of individual names, students should be aware of the actual British Centre for Durkheimian Studies, founded by W. S. F. Pickering, which has found a home in the Institute of Social and Cultural Anthropology at Oxford University. Pickering and other notable Durkheim scholars like Ken Thompson, William Watts-Miller, and Mike Gane organize periodic conferences on themes related to Durkheim and publish occasional papers and a yearly *Durkheimian Studies/Etudes Durkheimiennes*, often containing some newly discovered documents, correspondence, and even original texts previously unpublished or translated. (Further information can be obtained via e-mail to william.pickering@anthropology.oxford.ac.uk and w.watts-miller@ Bristol.ac.uk.)

I would end the module for graduate students by pointing out the import of the "Durkheimian tradition" in various fields and areas that relate to or derive from the sociology (and anthropology) of religion, as capably sketched out by Collins (1994). Finally, to add spice, students should note the radical feminist critiques entertained by Jennifer Lehmann (1993, 1994), who sees Durkheim as a promising socialist, waylaid by the bourgeois and masculine prejudices of his days (illustrated, for example, in his treatment of marriage and divorce).

The three levels of teaching Durkheim—more or less, at the underclass, upperclass, and graduate level—should provide a fairly comprehensive approach to Durkheim's sociology of religion. They do not exhaust the research possibilities regarding Durkheim, the Durkheimians, and religious currents and countercurrents in early twentieth-century France (including Freemasonry), but what might be viewed as a "fourth level" lies beyond the scope of this discussion.

Epilogue

The preparation of this essay was interrupted by the catastrophe of the multi-pronged attack on New York and Washington on September 11, 2001, and its aftermath. What the total impact will be, short-term and long-term, of this unprecedented national trauma, including the reactions of an aroused nation internally and externally, is impossible to assess at this writing. Nonetheless, I would like to offer as a concluding reflection that the disaster and at least the immediate postdisaster situation render the actuality of Durkheim—particularly Durkheim's sociology of religion—even more salient.

First of all, the notion of anomie as a generalized normlessness gained momentary salience on that Tuesday, with the realization that the United States had been unexpectedly hit in its twin heartland of New York's financial center and Washington's military defense hub. What other destruction might be forthcoming anywhere and everywhere made for a highly ambiguous and anxious moment. It is very seldom that a country faces the *néant*, an abyss of nothingness, but September 11, 2001, was such a rupture in the social order, as horrendous if not more than the anomie of November 22, 1963.

Second, the mode of destruction—manned American aircraft that had been hijacked—gave new significance and amplification to Durkheim's concept of *altruistic suicide*. Ken Morrison has recently drawn attention to its overlooked significance because "it stands alone as a social type of suicide independent of individual considerations and points to a form of self-sacrifice imposed by social ends" (Morrison 2001, 107). While the destruction of the World Trade Center and the wing of the Pentagon was an act of terrorism, presumably it was also, on the part of the hijackers, an act of suicide for a transcendental cause. Suicide bombers have been a recent phenomenon in numerous other settings, and of course entail not only a voluntary death to the self for greater social ends but also the death of others, that is, homicide: the sacrifice of self entails at the same time the destruction of "the other." But there was another instance of altruistic suicide on September 11. It appears from wireless communication that the passengers on United Airlines flight 93, realizing that their plane might become a weapon of immense destruction, arose and, at the cost of their lives, averted a greater disaster by crashing their plane and the hijackers into a field in Shanksville, Pennsylvania. Hence terrorism and heroism are intrinsically mixed in the events of September 11.

Third, the postdisaster setting in the United States is de facto a Durkheimian laboratory for the study of rituals. Drawing from Durkheim, Etzioni recently has drawn attention to the significance of public rituals, placing his focus on holidays (2000).[23] I would propose that the national scene in the United States, especially in New York, the zone of the greatest disaster impact, has witnessed since the attack on the United States an interrelated set of rituals of integration that embrace the entire societal community, namely, what Durkheim termed *piacular rites*. These are rites of mourning, which provide meaning in an anomie setting. They differ from the televised national mourning of President Kennedy in 1963 or the funeral train of Lincoln in April 1865 because of a prominent display of a symbol of American unity and resolve, the flag. Durkheim (1995, 228) had mentioned the flag as an important symbol, but his discussion bears more on the flag of the military and not as a generalized affective symbol of the entire nation. But American civil religion gives a privileged place to "Old Glory," and in the wake of the attack the ritual of integration—bringing together civil religion and traditional mainstream religion of all faiths—has made the American flag a matter of intense devotion, complete with the singing of "God Bless America" at baseball games and the renewal of the Pledge of Allegiance, which had fallen into desuetude. A myriad of other new or resuscitated rituals have sprung forth that would require a much fuller analysis.

I close this epilogue with a last reference to Durkheim's actuality. In his discussion of piacular rites, Durkheim notes that sadness is not the only feeling expressed during rituals of mourning. "A kind of anger is usually mingled with it. The relatives apparently need something to avenge the death suffered. . . . A pain that reaches such great intensity does not go without anger" (1995, 397). In America, as in the Holy Land, piacular rites today are vivid and tragic aspects of the social landscape. We see and will continue to see the suffering of family members grieving over the loss of victims of terrorism, whether the victims are those of New York, Tel Aviv, or Gaza. But the mourning is also utilized to mobilize the population against "evildoers," and demonization—which Durkheim did not analyze—can be used to justify dire retribution, not in rituals, but in actions seeking to destroy those who are seen as the agents of death.

NOTES

1. See Nielsen 1999, 243–244.

2. Some might wish to make the sociological trinity into a quaternity by adding the figure of Simmel. He did, of course, influence a good deal of American sociology via the Chicago school, Lewis Coser, Donald Levine, and others. While his essays on the structures of everyday life can still be read with enjoyment by students at all levels, his basic overarching societal framework is recondite, especially regarding key factors of social change.

3. At least this would apply *after* secondary school. Prior to that, there is in the United States strong pressure to conform to the demands and tastes of the peer group and the youth culture of the day.

4. See Bellah, Madsen, Sullivan, Swidler, and Tipton 1985, 221, 235.

5. See Giddens and Duneier 2000, 427.

6. See Giddens and Duneier 2000, 12.

7. See Landis 2000, 266–268, 272.

8. See Macionis 2001, 490.

9. See Nolan and Lenski 1999, 80. Sociologists of religion may recall with some dismay that the technological emphasis of Lenski is in marked contrast with his earlier pioneering survey research study of the relevance of religion as an independent variable in modern life (*The Religious Factor: A Sociological Study of Religion's Impact on Politics, Economics, and Family Life*, Garden City, N.Y.: Doubleday, 1963).

10. For example, Emile Durkheim, *The Division of Labor in Society*, trans. George Simpson (New York: Free Press, 1964 [1893]), 138–143.

11. This passage was prepared shortly before the calamitous events of September 11, 2001. The set of suicide homicides they engendered may well make a rational discussion of this impossible for years to come, but I venture a few remarks in the epilogue to this discussion.

12. The continuing waning of traditional religious commitment in Europe today, even allowing for interesting national variations, is captured by Grace Davie (2000) in her discussion of the contemporary scene characterized as "belonging without believing."

13. Of course, devotees of Durkheim may find it easy to insert some of his writings in other substantive courses, for example, his "Two Laws of Penal Evolution" can make for an interesting selection in a course on criminology, especially if one couples it with Foucault's book *Discipline and Punish* (1999).

14. As Orsi points out in his introduction, the materials he presents "provide a series of soundings into the cultural creativity and religious improvisations of city people over the last fifty years" (Orsi 1999, 61).

15. As an optional reading, I have on occasions in giving this course lectured on or assigned the essay "Sacrifice" (Hubert and Mauss 1964). Readings and videos of some contemporary transplanted cults, like Santeria, provide graphic images of this primary ritual, which Hubert and Mauss gleaned information about from ancient texts.

16. I provide students with copies of the listings under "Churches" in the Yellow Pages.

17. W. S. F. Pickering has an excellent discussion of Durkheim's cult of the individual (1993); see also the comments of Thompson (1993).

18. As Strachey notes in his introduction (1962, 5), Freud completed the work in 1929 and gave it the title *Das Unglück in der Kultur* ("Unhappiness in Civilization"), later changed to "Das Unbehagen in der Kultur," which has no exact English equivalent. But *Unbehagen* can be rendered in French as *malaise*, which adds to the overlap between Freud and Durkheim's view that the progress of civilization does not lead to the greater happiness of individuals.

19. Although most graduate sociology students may lack the philosophical background, they should be aware of Kant's tremendous influence on modern thought, including the field of ethics and moral education and, very broadly speaking, on what has come to be termed, following Parsons, "action theory." Durkheim sought in *Forms* to give a sociological grounding to the categories of understanding, and by extension, Münch has cogently argued, "Parsons's sociology cannot be understood apart from a consideration of Kant's critical project" (Münch 1981, 713).

20. I have discussed the bearing of Durkheim's analysis of "collective effervescence" to the settings of modern revolutionary settings wherein authoritarian regimes were overthrown in popular uprisings (Tiryakian 1988b). A seminal piece for social anthropology is to be found in Wallace (1956).

21. Nielsen (1999, 227–244) has argued that one influence on Durkheim's "sociological monism" was a Jewish inspirational tradition that includes Philo, Maimonides, and especially Spinoza. For a broader discussion of religion and French Jewry in Durkheim's France, see Strenski (1997).

22. The renewal of sociological interest in Durkheim in Great Britain, after the great postwar anthropological contributions of Evans-Pritchard and Rodney Needham and their many students at Oxford (especially regarding rituals, religion, and symbolic beliefs), was facilitated by the publication thirty years ago of a comprehensive study of Durkheim by Steven Lukes (1972).

23. He distances himself from the functionalist premise of Durkheim regarding the integrative aspect of rituals, which Etzioni sees as limited to either homogeneous premodern societies or to groups in the larger, modern society.

REFERENCES

Alexander, Jeffrey C. 1982. *The Antinomies of Classical Thought: Marx and Durkheim.* Berkeley: University of California Press.
———, ed. 1988. *Durkheimian Sociology: Cultural Studies.* Cambridge: Cambridge University Press.
Allen, N. J., W. S. F. Pickering, and W. Watts-Miller, eds. 1998. *On Durkheim's Elementary Forms of Religious Life.* London: Routledge.
Bellah, Robert N. 1970. *Beyond Belief: Essays on Religion in a Post- Traditional World.* New York: Harper and Row.
———, ed. 1973. Introduction to *Emile Durkheim on Morality and Society.* Chicago: University of Chicago Press.
———. 1975. *The Broken Covenant: American Civil Religion in Time of Trial.* New York: Seabury Press.

Bellah, Robert N., R. Madsen, W. M. Sullivan, A. Swidler, and S. M. Tipton. 1985. *Habits of the Heart: Individualism and Commitment in American Life*. Berkeley: University of California Press.

Besnard, Philippe, ed. 1983. *The Sociological Domain: The Durkheimians and the Founding of French Sociology*. Cambridge: Cambridge University Press.

The Book of General Laws of the Inhabitants of the Jurisdiction of New-Plymouth. 1685. Boston: Samuel Green.

Borlandi, Massimo, and Mohammed Cherkaoui, eds. 2000. *Le Suicide un siècle après Durkheim*. Paris: PUF.

Cladis, Mark, ed. 1999. *Durkheim and Foucault: Perspectives on Education and Punishment*. Oxford: Durkheim Press.

Clark, Terry N. 1973. *Prophets and Patrons: The French University and the Emergence of the Social Sciences*. Cambridge, Mass.: Harvard University Press.

Collins, Randall. 1994. *Four Sociological Traditions*. New York: Oxford University Press.

Davie, Grace. 2000. *Religion in Modern Europe: A Memory Mutates*. Oxford: Oxford University Press.

Durkheim, Emile. 1951 [1897]. *Suicide*. New York: Free Press.

———. 1964 [1893]. *The Division of Labor in Society*. Translated by George Simpson. New York: Free Press.

———. 1973a [1914]. "The Dualism of Human Nature." In *Emile Durkheim on Morality*, edited by Robert Bellah. Chicago: University of Chicago Press.

———. 1973b [1898]. "Individualism and the Intellectuals." In *Emile Durkheim on Morality*, edited by Robert Bellah. Chicago: University of Chicago Press.

———. 1995 [1912]. *The Elementary Forms of Religious Life*. Translated with an introduction by Karen Fields. New York: Free Press.

———. 1998. *Lettres à Marcel Mauss*. Edited by Philippe Besnard and Marcel Fournier. Paris: Presses Universitaires de France.

Etzioni, Amitai. 2000. "Towards a Theory of Public Ritual." *Sociological Theory* 18 (March): 44–59.

Forbes, Bruce David, and Jeffrey H. Mahan, eds. 2000. *Religion and Popular Culture in America*. Berkeley: University of California Press.

Freud, Sigmund. 1961 [1929]. *Civilization and Its Discontents*. New York: Norton.

Giddens, Anthony, and Mitchell Duneier. 2000. *Introduction to Sociology*, 3rd ed. New York: Norton.

Halbwachs, Maurice. 1971 [1941]. *La topographie légendaire des évangiles en terre sainte; Etude de mémoire collective*. With a preface by Fernand Dumont. Paris: Presses Universitaires de France.

Hertz, Robert. 1928. *Mélanges de sociologie religieuse et folklore*. With a preface by Alice Hertz. Paris: Alcan.

———. 1994. *Sin and Expiation in Primitive Societies*. Translated and edited by Robert Parkin with a preface by W. S. F. Pickering. Occasional paper 2. Oxford: British Centre for Durkheimian Studies.

Hubert, Henri, and Marcel Mauss. 1929. *Mélanges d'histoire des religions*. Paris: Alcan.

———. 1964. *Sacrifice: Its Nature and Function*. Chicago: University of Chicago Press.

Jones, Arthur Alun. 1977. "On Understanding a Sociological Classic." *American Journal of Sociology* 83 (September): 279–319.

———. 1986. "Durkheim, Frazer, and Smith: The Role of Analogies and Exemplars in the Development of Durkheim's Sociology of Religion." *American Journal of Sociology* 92 (November): 596–627.

Landis, Judson R. 2000. *Sociology: Concepts and Characteristics.* 11th ed. Stamford, Conn.: Thomson Learning.

Lehmann, Jennifer. 1993. *Deconstructing Durkheim.* London: Routledge.

———. 1994. *Durkheim and Women.* Lincoln: University of Nebraska Press.

Lester, David, ed. 1994. *Emile Durkheim: "Le Suicide" One Hundred Years Later.* Philadelphia: Charles Press.

Lukes, Steven. 1972. *Emile Durkheim, His Life and Work, a Historical and Critical Study.* New York: Harper and Row.

Macionis, John J. 2001. *Sociology.* 8th ed. Upper Saddle River, N.J.: Prentice-Hall.

Mauss, Marcel. 1927. "Notices Biographiques." *Année Sociologique,* n.s. 2: 3–9.

———. 1968. *Oeuvres. Vol. 1. Les fonctions sociales du sacré.* With an introduction by Victor Karady. Paris: Editions de Minuit.

Mills, C. Wright. 1959. *The Sociological Imagination.* New York: Oxford University Press.

Morphy, Howard. 1998. "Spencer and Gillen in Durkheim: The Theoretical Construction of Ethnography." In Allen, Pickering, and Watts-Miller 1998.

Morrison, Ken. 2001. "The Disavowal of the Social in the American Reception of Durkheim." *Journal of Classical Sociology* 1, 1: 95–125.

Mucchielli, Laurent. 1998. "Les Durkheimiens et *la Revue de l'histoire des religions* (1896–1916): Une zone d'influence méconnue." *Durkheimian Studies/Etudes Durkheimiennes,* n.s. 4: 51–72.

Münch, Richard. 1981. "Talcott Parsons and the Theory of Action. I. The Structure of the Kantian Core." *American Journal of Sociology* 86 (January): 709–739.

Nandan, Yash. 1977. *The Durkheimian School: A Systematic and Comprehensive Bibliography.* Westport, Conn.: Greenwood Press.

Nielsen, Donald A. 1999. *Three Faces of God: Society, Religion and the Categories of Totality in the Philosophy of Emile Durkheim.* Albany: State University of New York Press.

Nolan, Patrick, and Gerhard Lenski. 1999. *Human Societies: An Introduction to Macrosociology.* 8th ed. New York: McGraw-Hill.

Orsi, Robert A., ed. 1999. *Gods of the City.* Bloomington: Indiana University Press.

Parsons, Talcott. "Durkheim on Religion Revisited: Another Look at *The Elementary Forms of Religious Life.*" In *Beyond the Classics? Essays in the Scientific Study of Religion.* New York: Harper & Row, 1973.

Pickering, W. S. F. 1993. "Human Rights and the Cult of the Individual: An Unholy Alliance Created by Durkheim?" In *Individualism and Human Rights in the Durkheimian Tradition,* edited by W. S. F. Pickering and W. Watts Miller. Occasional papers 1. Oxford: British Centre for Durkheimian Studies.

Pickering, W. S. F., and Geoffrey Walford, eds. 2000. *Durkheim's "Suicide": A Century of Research and Debate.* London: Routledge.

Poggi, Gianfranco. 2000. *Emile Durkheim.* Oxford: Oxford University Press.

Prades, José A. 1990. *Durkheim*. Paris: Presses Universitaires de France.

Strenski, Iva. 1997. *Durkheim and the Jews of France*. Chicago: University of Chicago Press.

———. 2000. "Durkheimians and Protestants in the Ecole Pratique, Fifth Section: The Dark Side." *Durkheimian Studies/Etudes Durkheimiennes*, n.s. 6: 105–114.

Thompson, Kenneth. 1993. "Wedded to the Sacred." In *Individualism and Human Rights in the Durkheimian Tradition*, edited by W. S. F. Pickering and W. Watts Miller. Occasional papers 1. Oxford: British Centre for Durkheimian Studies.

Tiryakian, Edward A. 1975. "Neither Marx nor Durkheim . . . Perhaps Weber." *American Journal of Sociology* 81 (July): 1–33.

———. 1978a. "Durkheim and Husserl: A Comparison of the Spirit of Positivism and the Spirit of Phenomenology." In *Phenomenology and the Social Sciences: A Dialogue*, edited by Joseph Bien. The Hague: Martinus Nijhoff.

———. 1978b. "Emile Durkheim." In *A History of Sociological Analysis*, edited by Tom Bottomore and Robert Nisbet. New York: Basic Books.

———. 1988a. "Durkheim, Mathiez and the French Revolution: The Political Context of a Sociological Classic." *European Journal of Sociology* 29: 373–396.

———. 1988b. "From Durkheim to Managua: Revolutions as Religious Revivals." In Alexander 1988.

———. 1995. "Collective Effervescence, Social Change, and Charisma: Durkheim, Weber and 1989." *International Sociology* 10 (September): 269–281.

———. 2000. "Parsons's Emergent Durkheims." *Sociological Theory* 18 (March): 60–83.

Wallace, Anthony F. C. 1956. "Revitalization Movements: Some Theoretical Considerations for Their Comparative Study." *American Anthropologist* 58 (April): 264–281.

Wolfe, Alan. 2001. *Moral Freedom: The Impossible Idea That Defines the Way We Live Now*. New York: Norton.

PART II

Context

4

Translating Durkheim on Religion

What Teachers and Students Should Know

Karen E. Fields

"What sort of science is it whose principal discovery is that the subject of which it treats does not exist?"[1] So ends book 1, chapter 2, section 5 of *The Elementary Forms of the Religious Life*. The English is the work of Joseph Ward Swain, in his 1915 translation of Emile Durkheim's 1912 masterpiece, *Les Formes élémentaires de la vie religieuse*. Short and sharply worded, outrageously rhetorical, that question virtually jumps off the page: "Qu'est qu'une science dont la principale découverte consisterait à faire évanouir l'objet même dont elle traite?"[2] Here is Durkheim the scientist, delivering his *coup de grâce* to a theory whose refutation begins even before the book does, right from the table of contents entry for 1.2.5:[3] "Conclusion. Animism reduces religion to nothing more than a system of hallucinations." And here is Swain the translator, giving Durkheim forceful English that still radiates heat from long-dead debates to which Durkheim was contributing. In sum, he faithfully renders sense, nuance, atmosphere, and even attitude. Notice the hissing *s*'s that launch the English sentence.

And yet, Swain is inexact. There is a gap between what Durkheim says and what his translator makes him say,[4] for the phrase "does not exist" (*n'existe pas*) figures nowhere in the French. Durkheim writes: *faire évanouir*. If literally translated, he is indicting a science that "makes [its own subject] disappear" or "vanish into thin air" like a ghost or a phantom.[5] That shadow's worth of distance between the two sentences displays general features of translation, as process and as product, that I propose to explore, using three editions of *Forms* that have sought to improve on Swain's work: excerpts by W. S. F. Pickering and Jacqueline Redding (1975);[6] my own complete retranslation (1995),[7] and an Oxford World's Classics Abridgement by Mark S. Cladis and Carol Cosman (2001).[8]

I first explore those features. Next comes a comparison of the four English renderings of *Forms*. That comparison is both accompanied and followed by a discussion of some hard-to-translate terms and concepts that can open wide windows to incomprehension: some that, by convention, often appear in italics (like *représentation* and *conscience collective*); others that do not but perhaps should (*moral, idéal,* and *spirituel; élémentaire, simple,* and *primitif*); and still others that cannot, as a practical matter (French for "the" and "it"). Along the way, I reexamine certain of my own and others' solutions to various difficulties. These difficulties challenge not only the translator from French to English but also the teacher, whose task, in a sense, is to translate from English to English.

The Translator Chooses

Begin with an elementary question and an elementary answer: What is a translation? It is a product and a process. As a product, it cannot help but appear to be what it cannot possibly be: the text itself, though in a different language. But a text cannot move; it has to be rebuilt with materials and on terrain that are foreign to it. Not only do vocabulary, grammar, and sentence structure differ between languages but so do the rhetorical and stylistic conventions that authors deploy (and their translators, later on). Every translation is thus a reconstruction, and every translator works like an artisan, not a medium. As a process, translation is an affair of making choices, many or most of which could be made differently. Moreover, the choices can be very consequential. As the Kant translator W. H. Werkmeister writes, "any translation is *ipso facto* an interpretation." To succeed, therefore, a translator must bring to bear not only sufficient philological understanding to render a text accurately ("finer nuances and overtones" included) but also sufficient understanding of the author's point of view to know "what the author has to say in defending his point of view."[9] In short, translation means navigating not only individual trees but large forests. The Swain passage just cited meets those standards, showing how a nonliteral translation can depart from the original yet keep faith with it. Contrarily, literal translation can betray the original by navigating trees alone and without concern for their distinctiveness. If an author's text is literate and luminous, can dim prose faithfully render it?

Since some of my examples will be trees and others forest, note the two edges of Werkmeister's tidy phrase "has to say": on one side, a point of view with a certain content, and on the other, *given* a point of view, what an author is *led* to say. Before proceeding, then, let me disclose what I take to be the expositional arrow of the book as a whole. It takes flight in the table of contents entry just quoted, it passes through Durkheim's rhetorical shout that science can and must treat religion as being about something real, and then it flies on toward the ethnographic ground on which his (intentionally hard-case) proof will be made, from 1.4 onward: that such a science of religion can be built *even* on the study of totemic rites. Since totemic rites presuppose kinship between people and plants or animals, the arrow cannot stop short of socially constructed knowledge and, with it, socially constructed reality. Both are called for by the author's initial insistence on keeping the object of such a science real. Durkheim brings all these elements together in 2.7.

Keeping that arrow of argument in mind, I turn now to a celebrated passage at 2.7.3. In it, using evidence gathered by the British ethnographers Sir Baldwin Spencer and Francis James Gillen, Durkheim recounts an *effervescence collective*, in which the Uluuru phratry of the Warramunga people of Australia affirm their common kinship and common descent from a snake. The centrality of this passage can be gauged from its location, the climactic midpoint of a chapter that knots together separate threads of several arguments that have been deployed over the preceding 342 pages. The theorists Jeffrey Alexander and Philip Smith singled it out in a review essay about *Forms*. They quote the French and two English renderings:

> Tandis que les feux, allumés de tous les côtés, faisaient ressortir violemment la blancheur des gommiers sur le fond des ténèbres environnantes, les Uluuru s'agenouillèrent les uns derrière les autres à côté du tumulus, puis ils en firent le tour en se soulevant de terre, d'un mouvement d'ensemble, les deux mains appuyées sur les cuisses, pour s'agenouiller à nouveau un peu plus loin, et ainsi de suite. En même temps, ils penchaient leurs corps tantôt à droite, tantôt à gauche poussant tous à la fois, à chacun de ces mouvements, un cri retentissant, véritable hurlement, *Yrrsh! Yrrsh! Yrrsh!*[10]

Here is Swain's quite literal rendering:

> While fires were lighted on all sides, making the whiteness of the gum trees stand out sharply against the surrounding darkness, the Uluuru knelt down one behind the other beside the mound, then rising from the ground they went around it, with a movement in unison, their hands resting on their thighs, then a little further on they knelt down again, and so on. At the same time, they swayed their bodies, now to the right and now to the left, while uttering at each movement a piercing cry, a veritable yell, *Yrrsh! Yrrsh! Yrrsh!*
> (248–249)

Here is mine:

> With fires flickering on all sides, bringing out starkly the whiteness
> of the gum trees against the surrounding night, the Uluuru knelt in
> single file beside the mound, rising in unison with both hands on
> their thighs, kneeling again a little farther along, and so on. At the
> same time, they moved their bodies left and then right, at each
> movement letting out an echoing scream—actually a howl—at the
> top of their voices, *Yrssh! Yrssh! Yrssh!* (219)

Smith and Alexander correctly observe that neither of these English reconstructions "quite captures the urgent yet supple rhythm of Durkheim's own
writing."[11] Something is always lost in translation. But if translation is *"ipso
facto* interpretation," something is also gained. That gain percolates, willy-nilly,
up from the translator's understanding of what the author had to say and into
the translation. To add in this sense, moreover, is sometimes to subtract. Both
of the partial retranslations choose to omit this passage. And both designate
"ethnographic material" as a rubric for what may safely be omitted—cut out
entirely in the case of Pickering and Redding, aggressively pruned in that of
Cladis and Cosman. Those decisions suggest a shared judgment that ethnography is tangential to what Durkheim had to say. At the same time, however,
interpretation is distinct from reconstruction, so if pressed to render this passage, the two teams would most likely produce two more variants.

Having chosen to dismiss ethnography at will, however, they often miss
the distinctive contributions of Durkheim the expert student of ethnography.
If we now recall that Spencer and Gillen were *British* ethnographers, we realize
that we have just met not only Durkheim the writer of "supple yet urgent"
prose but also Durkheim their translator. Analyzing Durkheim's French style
in *Forms*, Jean de Lannoy has shown how carefully Durkheim attended to the
writing itself, not least in his renderings from *Northern Tribes of Central Australia*.[12] "Nowhere else," writes de Lannoy, referring to the passage just cited,
"is Durkheim's care in the construction of his text more apparent."[13] In it, he
translated "almost literally" but selectively; and in reworking the English original, he used various literary techniques to intensify the effects. Thus, for example, the ethnographers' phrase "stand out in strong contrast" contracts into
ressortir violemment, and "the white trunks of gum trees" into *la blancheur des
gommiers.* Meanwhile, "the darkness beyond" expands and elegantly deepens
into *le fond des ténèbres environnants.*[14] To omit this passage is to sacrifice literary
aspects of a book that is known—and to some, notorious—for the way it is
argued and written.

The same kind of omission can be made differently. In an introductory
note, Pickering and Redding alert us that they choose to handle French passages that began in English simply by inserting the original.[15] To see where
that method can lead, consider the result when Swain (with no alert) applies

it to a passage in which Durkheim is quoting the Sanskritist Max Müller. Müller is the scholar who originated an argument Durkheim admired and used in 1.1—that the "supernatural" could not emerge as a distinct idea until positive science had delimited the idea of the "natural." Here is Müller's English as Swain reproduced it:

> In fact, [Müller] says, "at first sight, nothing seemed less natural than nature. Nature was the greatest surprise, a terror, a marvel, a standing miracle, and it was only on account of their permanence, constancy, and regular recurrence that certain features of that standing miracle were called natural, in the sense of foreseen, common, intelligible. . . . It was that vast domain of surprise, of terror, of marvel, of miracle, the unknown, as distinguished from the known, or, as I like to express it, the infinite as distinct from the finite, which supplied from the earliest times the impulse to religious thought and language." (92)

Readers conversant with Müller's writings (many were in Swain's day) would have recognized the passage from Müller's *Physical Religion* (London: Longman's, 1891), 119–120. Without consulting *Forms* in French, however, they would have had no way of knowing that Durkheim's version does not say quite the same thing. One difference, obvious when one consults the French, is that Durkheim chose to delete Müller's parenthetical statement "or, as I like to express it, the infinite as distinct from the finite." Swain put it back.

What most distinguishes the French passage from Müller's original, however, is the subtle yet urgent intervention of Durkheim the storyteller. He does not settle for Müller's phrase "at first sight," but works to engage the reader in this imaginary dawn of human intellect. Adding a subject and a verb, he sets the scene and populates it. He adds the phrase "only later on" [*seulement plus tard*], and the depiction of humanity's march from mere sight to active insight gains the narrative structure of passing time. And while Müller's passage implies the act of discovery, Durkheim's makes it explicit: he adds a verb, *on découvrit*. Meanwhile, he ratchets up Müller's "surprise" and "terror" to the superlative degree—the connotation of *la grande terror* is approximately "the mother of all terrors." Instead of trying to exhaust the subject, I offer Durkheim's passage for further study:

> En effet, dit-il, "au premier regard que les hommes jetèrent sur le monde, rien ne leur parut moins naturel que la nature. La nature était pour eux la grande surprise, la grande terreur; c' était une merveille et un miracle permanent. Ce fut seulement plus tard, quand on découvrit leur constance, leur invariabilité, leur retour régulier, que certains aspects de ce miracle furent appelés naturels, en ce sens qu'ils étaient prévus, ordinaires, intelligibles. . . . Or c'est ce

vaste domaine ouvert aux sentiments de surprise et de crainte, c'est
cette merveille, ce miracle, cet immense inconnu opposé à ce qui est
connu . . . qui donna la première impulsion à la pensée religieuse et
au langage religieux." (104)

In 1995, I tried to construct an equivalent of the translation that Durkheim
carefully wrought for *Forms*, with this result:

> In fact, he says, "at the first glance men cast on the world, nothing
> appeared less natural to them than nature. Nature was for them the
> great surprise and the great fear; it was a permanent marvel and a
> permanent miracle. It was only later, when men discovered their
> constancy, their invariance, and their regular recurrence, that certain
> aspects of that miracle were called natural, in the sense that they
> were foreseen, ordinary, and intelligible. . . . It is this vast domain
> open to feelings of surprise and fear, this marvel, this miracle, this
> immense unknown opposed to what is known . . . that provided the
> first impulse to religious thought and religious language." (71)

Readers who know French will recognize the inexactness of certain renderings
I made: "great fear" for *la grande terreur*; "permanent" made to modify both
"marvel" and "miracle"; and "invariance" for *invariabilité* even though "invar-
iability" works perfectly well. Today, I would approach these and other choices
differently. The 2001 *Forms* tackles the problems of the passage, with this result:

> "At the first glance men cast on the world," he says, "nothing
> seemed less natural to them than nature. Nature was for them the
> great surprise and the great fear; it was a permanent marvel and a
> permanent miracle. It was only later, when men discovered their
> constancy, their invariance, and their regular recurrence, that certain
> aspects of that miracle were called natural, in the sense that they
> were foreseen, ordinary, and intelligible. . . . It is this vast domain
> open to feelings of surprise and fear, this marvel, this miracle, this
> immense unknown opposed to what is known . . . that provided the
> first impulse to religious thought and religious language." (6)

Incorporating my second thoughts about old choices—among them, treating
permanent as if it was identical to the English "permanent," and downgrading
terreur to "fear"—I offer a new version of the passage:

> In fact, he says, "When men first looked at the world, nothing
> seemed to them less natural than nature. To them, nature was the
> ultimate surprise, the ultimate terror; it was a marvel and a perpet-
> ual miracle. Only later on, when men discovered their constancy, in-
> variability, and regular recurrence, were certain aspects of that mira-

cle called natural, in the sense of expected ordinary, and intelligible.
. . . It is this vast domain open to feelings of surprise and fear, this
marvel, this miracle, this immense unknown as opposed to the
known . . . that provided the first impetus to religious thought and
religious language."

Thus far, I have presented general features of translation in several manifestations of translators' choice: nonliteral yet faithful rendering; different yet
literal and faithful renderings of the same passage; literal rendering with literary rearrangement; and deletion. Now I shall examine a literal rendering that
betrays the author's meaning. I give the French first, to exemplify those long
sentences that French grammar accommodates more easily than English,
whose grammar less easily signals what goes with what.

Pour bien comprendre un délire et pour pouvoir lui appliquer le
traitement le plus approprié, le médecin a besoin de savoir quel en a
été le point de départ. Or cet événement est d'autant plus facile à
discerner qu'on peut observer ce délire à une période plus proche de
ses débuts. Au contraire, plus on laisse à la maladie le temps de se
développer, plus il se dérobe à l'observation; c'est que, chemin fais-
ant, toute sorte d'interprétations sont intervenues qui tendent à re-
fouler dans l'inconscient l'état originel et à le remplacer par d'autres
à travers lesquels il est parfois malaisé de retrouver le premier. (10)

The key is the little word "it," whose inability to pinpoint its antecedent as
the French does, through gender, becomes dramatic in a long sentence such
as this one. Here Swain loses the thread of what is advancing and what is being
hidden:

In order to understand a hallucination perfectly, and give it its most
appropriate treatment, a physician must know its original point of
departure. Now this event is proportionately easier to find if he can
observe it near its beginnings. The longer the disease is allowed to
develop, the more it [what?] evades observation; that is because all
sorts of interpretations have intervened as it [what?] advanced, which
tend to force the original state into the background, and across
which it is sometimes difficult to find the initial one. (19)[16]

Here is the same passage as translated by Redding:

In order to understand a delirium properly and to be able to carry
out the best course of treatment, a doctor needs to know how it
started. But this is much more easily ascertained if one can observe
the delirium soon after it began. On the other hand, the longer the
illness is allowed to develop, the more it [what?] eludes observation.
The reason is that, as it [what?] develops, all sorts of interpretations

intervene which tend to drive the original state into the unconscious, and to replace it with others which sometimes conceal the
way leading to the first.[17]

The English of the Pickering-Redding version is more fluid, and, although I
chose "delusion," I agree with their choice of "delirium" (for *délire*), but the
ambiguity of "it" persists, throwing into relief difficulties that arise from the
different structures of French and English.

I end this exploration with a more delicate predicament. What should the
translator do when a holy/profane (*saint/profane*), as opposed to sacred/profane
(*sacré/profane*), dichotomy suddenly pops up? In 1.1, Durkheim establishes the
sacred/profane dichotomy as the fundamental characteristic of religious phenomena, but reverts to holy/profane repeatedly in 2.2 and again in 3.2.[18] Faced
with this seeming lapse, Swain made repairs by sometimes (though not always)
translating *saint* as "sacred" rather than "holy." Perhaps he took that liberty
because Durkheim fixed *sacré* very clearly in a specific definition. Sacred things
are things "set apart and forbidden," he wrote. We generally call things "holy"
if extraordinary properties are held to be inherent in them. True, the two words
are often (though not always) interchangeable in French, as in English. Swain
may have imagined Durkheim thinking of them that way.[19] Still, they diverge
as well, just as "holy" and "sacred" diverge. Compare "sacred cow" and "holy
cow." Who says "the Sacred Bible"? And Durkheim slid sacred excrement into
footnotes.[20] My hunch is that chapters 2.2 and 3.2 may have existed before
Durkheim hit on the sacred/profane dichotomy as fundamental to the definition of religion.[21]

This shifting synonymy has more than antiquarian interest. Many of us
operate with a vague but deeply rooted notion that certain objects are holy
inherently, rather than made sacred by ritual doing. Not so in *Forms*. With
teacherly repetition and wit, Durkheim undercuts that notion of sacredness as
an inherent quality, for it can only exist as a *representation collective*. By the end
of 3.2, the reader (of a complete edition)[22] has encountered three kinds of lice
serving as sacred objects. In terms of meaning, then, it seems that Swain was
right to correct the text.

Or was he? If there is a principle of keeping faith with the author, then it
surely covers fault-lines and inconsistencies too. From that point of view, allowing the holy/profane dichotomy to flash on and off alongside its better
known relative would have been a better choice. But then, what about keeping
faith with the reader? He or she cannot be sure, unless told, who or what is
indicated by the shift in terminology. Translators have no definite rules in the
matter, and so our texts solve this problem differently. The choice did not arise
in the excerpts of Redding and Pickering. I chose to move between the two
terms, following the French text, but to mark the inconsistency with a note and
to supply *saint* in italics wherever it occurs. The Oxford edition opted to move

silently between the two terms. Swain's choice, to make silent changes inter-mittently, betrayed both Durkheim and the reader.

Four Texts

The Elementary Forms of the Religious Life, 1915

Forms was the first of Durkheim's books to be translated into English.[23] There he had a ready audience, as can be seen from the fact that T. S. Eliot com-mented on it in a 1916 review.[24] To my knowledge, Swain left no account of his procedures; and we have no manuscript of Forms. Presumably, however, Durkheim oversaw the work, and either proposed or agreed with dropping the original French subtitle Le Système totémique d'Australie (replacing it with "A Study in Religious Sociology"—subsequently dropped). We know for certain that Swain had very tight deadlines. His English Forms appeared three years after the book's 1912 appearance in French. Moreover, as his bibliography at-tests, one year after he finished with Forms, he defended his doctoral disser-tation in political science at Columbia University, "Hellenistic Influences on Christian Asceticism." An early reviewer recognized the many merits of Swain's translation, judging it "good but of less literary finish than the origi-nal."[25]

Notwithstanding its merits, Swain's Forms harbors many faults of inatten-tion. Teachers who use it should realize that he overlooked bits of French text. Here is one rather important omission: "Now they [religious representations] cannot weaken without the sacred beings' losing their reality, because the sa-cred beings exist only in and through their representations."[26] I will return to it. Other errors born of haste are simple misreadings. For example, Durkheim says this (at 2.7.2) about the social effervescence of the French Revolution: "On vit plus et autrement qu'au temps normal" (301), correctly translated by Red-ding as: "men's lives are more intense and different than they are normally" (129). Swain (241) confused voir with vivre and got it wrong: "men look for each other and assemble together more than ever." Changing the order of Durkheim's elements, Cosman and I arrived at identical solutions: "People live differently and more intensely than in normal times" (Fields, 213, Cladis-Cosman, 159). Other simple mistakes are Swain's use of "imminent" for "im-manent" throughout and regular mishaps with "false friends": inconvénient taken to mean "inconvenience" instead of "disadvantage" or "drawback"; de-mander, or "ask," cranked up to "demand"; végétaux (applied to totems) ren-dered not as "plants" but as "vegetables"; assistants becoming "helpers" rather than "those present" or "the congregation"; failing to recognize that inférieure can mean "lower." I note these not because they compromise understanding but because they can serve to bring out problems of translation in classes where few students know French.

In a much more serious instance, however, Swain buried a pivotal sentence in a key passage, through utterly wrong translation. At 2.7.4, Durkheim wrote:

> Rien ne vient de rien. Les impressions qu'éveille en nous le monde physique ne sauraient, par définition, rien contenir qui dépasse ce monde. Avec du sensible, on ne peut faire que du sensible; avec de l'étendu, on ne peut faire de l'inétendu. (321–22)

Coming on that monster (and, I imagine, with deadlines looming), Swain was stumped. He wrote:

> Nothing is worth nothing. The impressions produced in us by the physical world can, by definition, contain nothing that surpasses this world. Out of the visible, only the visible can be made; out of that which is heard, we cannot make something not heard. (256)

To deal with the pair *étendu* and *inétendu*, he invented. In the made-up solution, *étendu* became *entendu* ("heard"), *sensible* ("able to be felt or sensed") became "visible," and, based on *rien* ("nothing"), *vient* ("comes") became *vaut* ("is worth"). Later I will show how Redding tackled the problem.

Still, when Swain was good, he was very, very good, even if those moments shine like stars in a dark sky of unidiomatic English. I lifted his "thoroughgoing idiocy" for *illogique foncière*, because I think it a brilliant rendering, like the question with which I began. On the whole, however, there is not much for the retranslator to lift from him. Working literally, as a rule, he also preserved Durkheim's long sentences and, to a remarkable degree, even his French syntax. The result is often teetering, heavily accented Franglais. I found this example simply by letting the book drop open: "we shall not forbid ourselves the use of certain facts borrowed from the Indian societies of North America" (117). Nonetheless, as in this instance, the literal accuracy of many passages cannot be improved on. Swain got most things mostly right, and so his English *Forms* went on to inspire almost three generations of ethnographic field work and theoretical reflection. My retranslating was made incomparably easier by his monumental pioneering. Therefore, I differ with him often, but never without respect. In academic life, to do one's own work is, irremediably, to draw on the work of others, living or dead—and acknowledge that fact.

In any event, it would be an exaggeration to claim that Swain's text is inaccessible to students. I first read it while an undergraduate, and I never had the opportunity to teach from any other. Indeed, for some uses—as in classes that hope to follow an author's thought process through the structural features of his writing—Swain's version will always provide a serviceable second-best to reading *Forms* in French. Most of all, though, I have often seen undergraduates make Swain's *Forms* their own, finding in it everything from boot camp and Greek society hazing to the *effervescences* of their own religious milieux, the impersonal rules and ritual hypocrisies of mourning, the attractions of body piercing, and, quite unexpectedly, the peculiar asceticism to which athletes subject themselves. A young man who swam competitively but in general said nothing in class, suddenly spoke up about the exaltation that Swain's Durkheim so poetically evokes:

> Suffering is the sign that certain of the bonds attaching him to his profane environment are broken. . . . So he who is thus delivered is not the victim of an illusion when he believes himself invested with a sort of mastery over things. . . . He is stronger than nature, because he makes it subside. (355)

Teachers who like to excerpt need not always take bits from disparate sections of the book. In its own way, a single chapter, like the one on ascetic rites that so moved my student athlete, is representative of Durkheim's thought in *Forms,* and it can lead to fertile discussions. One year I had students read James Baldwin's novel *Go Tell It On the Mountain* for still more "reality" reading, so to speak, about asceticism closer to home than Durkheim's descriptions, and a young woman promptly enriched the class by suggesting Chaim Potok's novel *The Chosen* as well. One can never anticipate how Durkheim's thick description of flesh-and-blood human doing will affect college students in their often moving efforts to understand what life-in-society is—and sometimes, what "religious life" might mean.

There are moments when those efforts suddenly bring a diverse class to the deepest intellectual and moral layers of *Forms.* I remember how a quick reference to news reports about violence against Sikhs in India brought back our discussion of the Warramungas' *painting* different collective belonging onto their bodies. In the current event, the difference was marked by the wearing of short hair uncovered as opposed to long hair under a turban, but the comparison was plain. A young man gave voice to what many were thinking— *All it took to be safe was to change those outward signs*—but then he trailed off. The dead silence that followed felt like a silence for the dead. Personal truths fluttered within each of us, but we saw elemental truth together.

At other times, students' entirely personal efforts to understand what religious life might mean are instructive too. I remember a religiously committed undergraduate who was working his way through college as an "illusionist" (he emphatically rejected "magician"). As we came to understand, he was reading *Forms* for every detail and nuance of Durkheim's distinction between religion and magic. So he was reading differently from most of us when Swain's Durkheim says: "magic lives on [*vit de*] profanations" (339)—my own and Cosman's word choice is "thrives on." (305 and 223, respectively)—and perhaps even more differently when Durkheim says, in the same long paragraph, "[t]here is no sin in magic." That student's personal questions helped focus our attention on the pluses and minuses of Durkheim's approach to distinguishing religion from magic. At the end of the course, we held an *effervescence collective.* Our illusionist, one of various after-dinner performers, came equipped with cape and cane, scarves, cards, and whatnot. To conclude his act, he placed someone's copy of Swain's *Forms* in his illusionist's box and—what else?—*he made it disappear.*

The Elementary Forms of the Religious Life, *1975*

W. S. F. Pickering edited and collaborated with Jacqueline Redding, translator, to render parts of *Forms* into English for a reader titled *Durkheim on Religion.*[27] As a mixture of editing and translating, their reader offers a new angle on translation as product and as process. In a joint introduction, they disclose their operating principles. Following "common practice," they have "retained the French" for words that "defy translation"—"for example, *conscience, représentation,* together with their associated adjectives."[28] The rendering is "fairly literal," though with the proviso of "acceptable English" and helpfulness to readers.[29] In scientific translation, accuracy must take precedence over style, they tell us. And they "risk only small changes, as in punctuation," but as far as possible leave intact the original structures. To create accurate renderings in acceptable English yet preserve the original structures is hard to do. How did they follow through, and how did the overall result improve on Swain's often unacceptable English?

We can approach that question panoramically by drawing examples from the first few pages of *Forms*, which all four texts have in common. Here, rendered in one long sentence, is Swain's Durkheim explaining the scientific purport of the French term *simple.* Now, it is important for the translator get this not only right but also readable (hence read), because Durkheim's use of the qualifier "simple" can be a magnet for misunderstanding.

> Every time that we undertake [*entreprendre*] to explain something human, taken at a given moment in history—be it a religious belief, a moral precept, a legal principle, an aesthetic style or an economic system—it is necessary to commence by going back to its most primitive and simple form [*sa forme la plus primitive et la plus simple*], to try to account for the characteristics [*chercher à render compte des caractères*] by which it developed and became complicated little by little, and how it became that which it is at the moment in question. (15)

Redding breaks this long sentence but keeps Durkheim's word order and does not divide the huge paragraph to which it belongs.

> Every time we proceed to explain some human fact, related to a specific moment in time . . . it is necessary to go back to its most primitive and simplest form. We must seek to account for the characteris-

tics which help to define it at that period of its existence and then try to see how it has gradually developed and grown more complex, and how it has become what it is now. (105)

Like Redding, I broke the sentence into two but, unlike her, I also reversed the words "primitive" and "simple," for euphony, and I stopped the paragraph after the new second sentence. It seemed to me best to slow the pace a little— Descartes is not at the fingertips of today's English speakers (at least, not at mine), as he was for Durkheim's first audience.

> Thus, whenever we set out to explain something human at a specific moment in time . . . we must begin by going back to its simplest and most primitive form. We must seek to account for the features that define it at that period of its existence and then show how it has gradually developed, gained in complexity, and become what it is at the moment under consideration. (3)

Cosman has the two sentences this way, and chooses to stop Durkheim's paragraph at that place:

> Whenever we try to explain something human . . . we must begin by returning to its simplest and most primitive form. We must try to discover the qualities that define it at this period of its existence, and then show how it gradually developed, grew more complex, and became what it is at the moment under scrutiny. (5)

In support of his designated procedure and its accompanying logic of explanation, Durkheim invoked Descartes: "C'était un principe cartésien," he begins. Swain's (16) Durkheim says: "It was one of Descartes's principles," while Redding's says: "It *is* a Cartesian principle" (105). Feeling that Durkheim intended a nuance of distance between himself and Cartesian principles, I changed the verb: "A cartesian principle had it" (3). Cosman wrote, "A Cartesian principle has it" (5). I thought a nuance of distance was called for, because Durkheim's relationship to Descartes is selective and rather oblique. Later in the same paragraph, we find him attaching the great philosopher's name to a method of defining religion for scientific purposes that he rejects. Redding's rigorously accurate translation has Durkheim say: "To be sure, there can be no question of having an idea formulated in the Cartesian manner as the foundation of the science of religions, that is to say a logical concept, a pure construct, erected by the unaided power of thought" (105).

> Certes, il ne saurait être question de placer à la base de la science des religions une notion élaborée à la manière cartésienne, c'est-à-dire un concept logique, un pur possible, construit par les seules forces de l'esprit. (5)

My own version, less accurate than Redding's, has him insist: "To be sure, it is out of the question to base the science of religions on a notion elaborated in the Cartesian manner—that is, a logical concept, pure possibility constructed solely by force of intellect" (3). Cosman's Durkheim says: "Of course, the science of religion can hardly be based on a notion elaborated in the Cartesian manner—a logical concept, a pure possibility constructed only by the powers of mind" (5).

As a proponent of *science positive*, Durkheim (6) took a dim view of would-be social scientists who defined their object of study not by examining real-world facts but merely by thinking about and identifying (and then engaging in dialectic over) those elements "qui realisent le mieux leur ideal": "which best realize their ideal" (Swain, 16); "which come closest to their ideal" (Pickering and Redding, 106); "that best suit their model" (Fields, 4); or "that best embody their model" (Cosman, 6). Having declared that approach unfruitful, he goes on: "The problem remains intact, and the great service of philosophy is to have prevented its being suppressed[30] by the disdain of scholars" (Swain, 17)—"[L]e problème reste tout entier et le grand service qu'a rendu la philosophie est d'empêcher qu'il n'ait été proscrit par le dédain des érudits."

Quite properly rejecting Swain's solution, Redding (106) tackled again the somewhat cryptic French. By working nonliterally this time, she got this result: "[T]he problem itself has not been forgotten, thanks to the philosophers who grappled with it when other scholars ignored it." I admire the clear English she drew from Durkheim's contrast between *philosophes* and *erudits*, though it remains obscure to me. I wondered if he was gesturing at something or someone outside the text. Anyhow, working the problem differently from Redding, I got this somewhat obscure result: "[T]he problem of definition remains; and philosophy's great service has been to prevent it from being settled once and for all by the disdain of savants" (4). Cosman solved the problem this way: "[T]he problem of defining religion remains; and philosophy's great service has been to prevent it from being settled by the disdain of specialists" (6). Durkheim's huge paragraph begins with: "In the first place, we cannot arrive at an understanding of the most recent religions except by following the manner in which they have been progressively composed in history," and ends with "that is what we propose to do" (Swain, 15). Swain and Redding preserve this long paragraph undivided. Cosman and I divided it in the same way (5 and 3, respectively).

This excursion through details on only two pages has shown what the principle of disturbing the French structures as little as possible can and cannot mean. The underlying good idea, of course, is that an author's thought process is contained therein, and some scholars would even say that to do otherwise is to harm the original, perhaps fatally. To be said as well, however, is that the structural features of a text do indeed embody an individual author's thought process, but not that alone: they also embody prevailing conventions in a given sort of writing and at a given time. In this sense (to use Durkheimian phrasing), the individual writer's own thought process manifests a collective one. Long sentences and paragraphs as long as some I divided (3–4, 225–26, 231–32, and 304–305, for example) were, and still are, accepted form in French academic writing. It therefore does not seem to me that long paragraphs, kept together, convey more than they do separately, millimeters apart. Carol Cosman, a veteran literary translator and retranslator, may perhaps be thought to confirm my view when she divides all of the paragraphs just mentioned exactly as I did. So the proof of that pudding is in the eating. Obviously, those very long paragraphs cannot be quoted here, but I invite readers to judge what difference division makes.[31]

In any case, long sentences and paragraphs are not peculiarly French. We find them among Durkheim's English-speaking contemporaries—for example, his academic peer in America, the sociologist W. E. B. Du Bois, whose writing no doubt reflects the classical education that he, like Durkheim, received.[32] Ultimately, though, even if we hoped actually to retrieve an author's thought process from such structures (not just pickle it), and even if we held that changing those structures harmed a text fatally, we would still have to face the immediate task of retrieving it through word choices—the great majority of which cannot be left unchanged. Finally, as Swain's work shows us, French structures carrying English words are like corn husks in which barley grows. In practice, Redding did not reproduce Swain's Franco-American hybrid.

What is more, she made headway on the problem at 2.7.4 that had stumped Swain sixty years previously:

> Nothing arises out of nothing. The impression made on us by the
> physical world cannot, by definition, embody anything which tran-
> scends this world. The tangible can only be made into the tangible;
> the vast cannot be made into the minute. (134)

Still, notice that Durkheim wrote "impressions," not "impression." I think he had in mind something concrete and objective, a stream of sensory input (a bombardment, perhaps) from the world around us that activates a counterpart within us.[33] To my ear, our everyday use of the word "impression," singular, conveys little of that. Instead, it brings out abstract and subjective connotations of the word, like those that inhabit the old advertisement "You never get a second chance to make a first impression." By keeping "impressions" in the plural (as Swain did), Redding could have allowed concrete and abstract connotations to keep roiling about together in a complicated passage. That aside, all else goes very well until the very end. *Inétendu* and *étendu* do not mean "vast" and "minute."

Now to Pickering's editorial decisions. The retranslated excerpts run to 65 pages (as compared to the 647 pages of the French first edition and the 507 of Swain's translation). Not much more than that would have been feasible in light of the project: a reader composed of newly translated short pieces by or about Durkheim on the subject of religion. The stage is set, then, for interpretation to express itself through selection. Pickering says this about his dilemma as Durkheim's posthumous editor: "A piecemeal reading of this great book cannot but be unsatisfactory; it is a work that has to be read in its entirety."[34] On the other hand, excluding *Forms* from such a reader would mean "travesty and failure."

There are both costs and benefits. One clear benefit is that the reader provides a sense of evolution in Durkheim's ideas and of their place in early twentieth-century history of ideas. The critical reviews[35] show us how *Forms* seemed to its contemporaries. Nowadays, undergraduates in English (say) can trendily toss off the phrase "social construction of reality" with no inkling of its origins in Durkheimian sociology or of the way that notion must have grated in 1912. The material about a defector from Durkheim's circle, Gaston Richard, reveals some contemporaries' offense at his comparing "primitive" religion with their own—as well as individualist objections to Durkheim's ideas about the social, similar to those voiced by T. S. Eliot in the review mentioned earlier. Teachers of *Forms* must still teach against them. To his credit, Pickering is careful to summarize what he has omitted; and he does not minimize the corresponding costs of excerpting *Forms* by giving his readers a less-than-conscientious account of his method.

Pickering takes care to tell us that selections from "the early, middle and late chapters" serve as "points of entry," to "portray Durkheim's methods and findings which have application to religion as a whole."[36] The meaning of "religion as a whole," for purposes of the collection, is spelled out in the additional statement that he has excluded Durkheim's "detailed analysis of the social and religious life of the Arunta." Accordingly, his selections from 2.7 skip 2.7.3, Durkheim's portrayal of that firelit nighttime *effervescence* of painted men, but retain his allusion, in 2.7.2, to comparable scenes in France. So my expositional arrow of awhile ago has been stopped by an interpretation different from mine. My own view is that ethnographic evidence is to Durkheim's *Forms* as, say, biological evidence is to Darwin's *Origin of Species*. (To see what I mean, read through the sometimes-shocking rites for the dead, recounted in 3.5, that let him work out the social machinery by which individual feelings and thought processes disappear into convention and obligation.) Here, by contrast, ethnographic evidence stands as an inert supply of deletables. Thus, all of book 3 (on rites) is "excluded because of the close intertwining of ethnographic material and the generalizations that Durkheim deduces." Excluded, finally, is Durkheim's sociology of knowledge, which for Pickering diverts the focus from the topic of the reader: religion. But Durkheim deployed his sociology of knowledge throughout *Forms*, a book concerned throughout with "religious life"; and as early as 1899, he expressly refused to say simply "religion," full stop.[37] In that way, Pickering's excerpting leads him to an unsettling consequence:

"where well-defined sections on the sociology of knowledge appear in the chapters which have been selected, such sections have been omitted." What Durkheim joined together must be carefully put asunder.

The Elementary Forms of Religious Life, 1995

My translation was a teacher's project, embarked on after many years' use of Swain's *Forms* in classical sociological theory, sociology of religion, and religious studies courses—with the different preparation and preoccupations those imply. To use Swain's *Forms* was to constantly correct it. And to correct it in lectures was to compete with the authority of the printed page. Try standing before thirty copies of Swain, saying, "The book's title is misleading. . . . Along the same lines, you'll also find a misleading extra *the* in the title of book 2, chapter 8," and so on. As every wide-awake lecturer realizes, talk of wrong renderings quickly dead-ends in dullness for all but the translating few. Besides, I had begun to feel that, far more than mistakes, Swain's Victorian diction—native to him but alien to us—was hindering students' access to Durkheim's ideas, if only by slowing their pace. My twofold project, then, was to translate accurately and to give Durkheim less alien English. Inevitably, that led me to study and annotate his references (which are self-contained in each chapter to accommodate various kinds of excerpting by teachers). A rather detailed disclosure[38] of my working principles is given in an extended introduction. I offer here only a few themes.

The book's title did indeed change. I removed the second "the," replacing *The Elementary Forms of* the *Religious Life* with *The Elementary Forms of Religious Life*. At one level, the trouble seems to be only a foreigner's mangled expression—like saying "that's the life" instead of "that's life"—another instance of Swain's Franglais. As a term in normal English, however, "the religious life" poses a different problem. In the first place, it brings to mind the world of nuns and monks. More fundamentally, it has two connotations alien to *Forms*: that of an inward and individual experience, which is certainly valid for some purposes but not for understanding the transformation we witnessed in the Warramunga set-piece; and that of beliefs and practices sealed off within a separate sphere of personal life all their own and compelling for individuals only on a take-it-or-leave-it basis. That is the modern Western definition of "religion," but it is not the subject of *Forms*.

If my change to the book's title proved uncontroversial, another change fared differently. I substituted "I" for Durkheim's conventional use of "we" (but retained the "we" that means "you and I"). Before and after publication, my sometimes heated correspondence with colleagues on that point brought out these main objections to so doing: "we," as the necessary counterpart of Durkheim's positivism; "I," as betraying the collegial norms of his tightly knit scientific community; "we," as in some sense acknowledging multiple authorship of *Forms*. In reply, let me here mention the occasion in *Forms* (only one) when Durkheim the positivist let drop the mask of convention and said, "I mean society"—*j'entends la société* (Swain, 29, Durkheim, 23). In the end, I judged that, like the royal "we" of Louis XIV, Durkheim's positivistic "we" called distracting attention to itself.[39] All the other translators of *Forms* have retained Durkheim's editorial (or collegial) "we." I had no way of knowing that Cosman and Cladis had even opened this issue until I came on two footnotes, one after the other. There was Durkheim saying: "On this question, see *my* report. . . ." and "On the subject of Australian classes in general, see *my* article. . . ." (Cladis-Cosman, 91 and Fields, 107).

I also changed certain words that have English homonyms. Swain's "sentiment" is expunged almost everywhere, because *sentiment* is direct feeling—in French, one can have the *sentiment* that it will rain. The Warramunga at 2.7.3 are gripped by something stronger than "sentiment" (or at least stronger than what that term means in American English today). Similarly, I dropped Swain's word "attitude" from the title of book 3, replacing it with "conduct." Today's usage generally connects "attitude" with invisible inward states, but those chapters deal with outward and visible doing. For that reason, reproducing Swain's word-for-word English for *Les Principales attitudes rituelles* would not do. I chose "The Principal Modes of Ritual Conduct" (compare Cosman's "Principal Ritual Conduct," 219), because activities are classified according to five general types of purpose or posture: ascetic, sacrificial, mimetic (imitative), commemorative (or representative), and piacular (mourning) rites. In 3.2, "Representative or Commemorative Rites," Durkheim examines a dramatic performance (a *représentation*). There, as it turns out, we learn more about the *effervescence collective* of 2.7.3.

The title I gave book 2, chapter 8, "The Idea of Soul" takes us back, by a roundabout route, to the translation Swain botched at 2.7.4. Durkheim wrote *La Notion d'âme*, but because he could have chosen to write *la notion de l'âme*,[40] I took him literally and followed where that led. Even if only another example of Frenglish, (where "ze soul" existed as a type of music), the superfluous "the" would heavily shroud, if not bury, the difference between the two. The further complication in English is that the noun "soul" almost always travels behind an individualizing "a" or "the." Swain's title for 2.8, "The Idea of *the* Soul," has a natural ring. To appreciate the alienness of "soul" without an article, therefore, create a sentence that begins "Soul is . . ." Now, when Durkheim meant *the* soul, something thought of as an inward and individual possession, he said so; and that contrasted with "soul" without the "the," a generic substance or essence thought of as partly independent of individuals. The translation needed both, if it was to convey what Durkheim had to say in advancing his point of view: that the science of religion must be about something real. Here, his case in point about something real, to be studied scientifically, is that writhing horde of philosophical alligators, the idea of soul. He derives the idea of soul by analyzing ethnographic evidence about indigenous theories of descent, and by showing what is real about the Warramungas' collective memory and collective representation of their ancestor the snake.

So as not to ruin the suspense built into that elegantly argued chapter, I stop here, and note only Durkheim's intriguing table-of-contents reference to "impersonal elements of personality." It points to the place, near the end of 2.8, where Durkheim suddenly refers to (what was then) modern psychology: "we know today that the unity of the person is also made up of parts."[41] What could he mean? I wondered if he could have had in mind Freud's id, ego, and superego. I then consulted a textbook on the history of psychology. Quite unexpectedly, it turned out to hold the key to Swain's mistranslation of *l'étendu* and *l'inétendu*. In a passage about Descartes, the words "body" and "soul" seemed to jump off the page, followed instantly by "extended substance" and "unextended substance"—the latter being something that takes up no space. Eureka! Here was raw material out of which might come the Warramungas' shared resemblance to the snake (and to one another). That resemblance depended neither on the biology of procreation nor on that of appearance. Furthermore, it could be felt inwardly and visibly made, all at the same time, painted on and acted out during rites like those dances amid flickering fires and white gum trees. Here, then, is my rendering of the abused passage at 2.7.4:

> Nothing comes out of nothing. The sensations the world evokes in us cannot, by definition, contain anything that goes beyond that world. From something tangible, one can only make something tangible; from extended substance one cannot make unextended substance. (226)

In short, we have something imagined, yet real, that is added to physical things (or to people). The words *moral, idéal, spirituel,* and *social* stand together on this Durkheimian terrain, and their meanings take on shapes unlike those of their English counterparts. In *Forms,* "moral" does not necessarily refer to good and bad, nor does "ideal" refer to the best. Meanwhile, what is "spiritual" is not merely inside individuals but, of necessity, inside and outside them at the same time. Finally, the meaning of "social" unfolds alongside the others, over the full length of *Forms.* All stand together in Durkheim's thought as nonmaterial reality, that is, as mind or soul (not body)—in a word, as *inétendu.* While *sacré* stands with them, *individuel* stands with body opposite them, as *étendu.* Inside this peculiar family of abstractions, then, seemingly exact English equivalents become foreign terms.[42]

I still struggle with that foreignness, because it assigns specialized meanings to words that, having busy lives of their own in everyday English, can easily interfere. I now think I used the wrong strategy with *moral* in Durkheim's phrase *puissances morales et en même temps efficaces* (298). Letting *moral* appear to be the English word "moral," I could not make it convey Durkheim's contrast between physical and nonphysical constraint.[43] Swain's contrast "moral and at the same time efficacious" (239) is right but obscure. Redding's "moral, as well as effective" (127) is right too, but no clearer. My own "moral yet mighty," is both obscure and wrong because it distorts Durkheim's contrast, and so, for the same reason, is Cosman's "moral and forceful" (211 and 156, respectively). How about "at once intangible and potent" or perhaps "in the mind yet muscular?"

Before leaving this account of research and discovery, let me correct another mistake to prevent its further propagation. Because "extended substance" and "unextended substance" are no translation at all for many readers, I supplied a note: "Literally, 'something extended' and 'something unextended,' which correspond to Descartes' opposition between *res extensa* and *res inextensa*, classically the opposition between mind (or soul) and body (226)." The Oxford edition repeats my mistake in a note that reads this way: "The opposition of the French *étendu* (something extended) and *inétendu* (something unextended) is parallel to René Descartes's mind-body opposition, *res extensa* and *res inextensa*" (170, 348). Alas, I now know the term *res inextensa* came from my own effervescence, not from Descartes. His terms was *res cogitans*, and his actual contrast was between "extended thing" and "thinking thing." That makes my phrase "correspond to" imprecise and rather cavalier, for Descartes might well not know what to make of this extension of his idea.[44] "Soul," as manifested in the Warramungas' collectively shared snake-ness (and as distinguished from *the* or *a* soul) could not possibly be a *res cogitans*, a "thinking thing." Perhaps it can be regarded as a "thought thing," a Durkheimian representation.

The Elementary Forms of Religious Life, 2001

The principles of translation applied in this edition cannot be examined, because Carol Cosman gives no general indication of how she approached the usual problems and provides no specific translator's notes. In her review, Jacqueline Redding summarizes all that a reader can infer on the subject: "The translation is based on the easily available 1991 Livre de Poche edition and incorporates Dominique Merlié's corrections to it, as well as editorial improvements made by Fields in her translation."[45]

As a combined exercise of editing and translating, this edition incorporates the same sets of choices Pickering had to make: how best to translate a passage and what passages to translate or delete. But there are consequential differences. Pickering selects material for inclusion in a larger work, so of necessity he excludes most of the book, retaining only sixty-five pages. And, intending a contribution to Durkheim scholarship, he retains all of the pertinent footnotes.[46] Cladis's task, by contrast, is to select material for exclusion, "roughly 25 percent" of the original's 647 pages. This slimmed-down, simplified *Forms* has about 150 fewer pages and 1,050 fewer of Durkheim's notes. It offers no translator's notes, with the sole exception of one, reproduced from the 1995 *Forms*, that speculates about the nineteenth-century French source of a quotation from a fourth-century writer, Procopius of Gaza.[47] "My goal," writes Cladis, "was to produce a readable edition that conveys Durkheim's principal ideas and arguments, not a definitive reference for Durkheimians who are interested in tracking the more antiquarian aspects of his thought."[48]

An abridgement is a form of rewriting and, for that reason, always invites questions of the sort one addresses to authors: "Why say this and not that?" As I will show, Cladis provides a detailed rationale, but let me at least table the prior question: Why an abridgement at all? Why should an ancient university press make a business of cutting classics? Would not something like the 1991 Livre de Poche *Forms* be preferable, a robust edition in a handy pocket size, accompanied by an introduction? As Cladis points out, explaining why he based his work on the Poche edition (not the 1912), it is "readily available and affordable for those who wish to consult the French."[49] There is an irony here. The 1991 Poche gives French-speaking readers, many of them students, access to *all* of Durkheim's ideas and arguments in *Forms* but is called on to give English-speaking readers access to selections from them, by one interpreter. Like original authorship, this sort of rewriting cannot help but reflect particularities of discipline, outlook, teaching experience, and even personal taste. An ethnographer is unlikely to cut *Forms* with the same priorities as a Sanskritist, a researcher in comparative religion, and so on.

Like Pickering, Cladis interprets the connections between "ethnographic material" and "Durkheim's principal ideas and arguments" as relatively loose. But whereas Pickering plainly regrets what he rejects, Cladis's rationale comes close to suggesting that the abridgement corrects flaws in the original: "Digressions, redundant examples, and endnotes referring to dated controversies and ethnographic material supplied most of the deletions." As for the 1,050 deleted notes: "All significant references have been retained"—"significance" being defined as "pivotal influences on Durkheim, or references to his or his colleagues' earlier work." Kept in, as well, are "all passages pertaining to topical issues, for example the role of women in religion." Out go many passages pertaining to Native American religions and to the religions of India. Whether or not one agrees with Cladis's criteria, however, their logic coheres—with one exception: calling for "dated controversies" to be dropped explodes the whole premise of producing a readable new translation of a classic. If datedness defined what should be deleted from a great old book, 25 percent would be a ludicrously small deletion quota for a variety of books in Oxford World's Classics editions—for instance, *The Wealth of Nations*, *Capital*, and the King James

Bible. When as teachers we assign classics and call them "timeless," we mean in fact that they are dated but that well-wrought old books can inspire new readers with new understanding of the world around, and inside, them.

I turn now to what this edition counts as digressions and redundant examples, or discounts as ethnographic material. Comparing the World's Classics edition with the Livre de Poche, looking no further than the table of contents, we find that Durkheim's chapter summaries, the roadmap he created for readers, has gone. The abridged entry for 2.8 says only: "The Notion of Soul." Gone from it is the phrase "impersonal elements of personality" (an early clue to me that Swain had erred in titling the chapter "The Notion of *the* Soul"). The entry for 1.2 keeps the subheading "animism" but deletes "reduces religion to nothing more than a system of hallucinations." Gone from the chapter itself is its provocative concluding question "What sort of science is it . . . ?" And at 2.7.3, dots in square brackets replace the Warramungas' howling, firelit affirmation of their common descent.[50] Indeed, gone, too, is their very name, so they are not easily recognized as the same people who are found again, dramatizing their common history, in the representative rites described at 3.4. More: Durkheim is cut off in midparagraph at the end of 2.7. He is allowed to say that there is no logical gulf between religious and scientific thought, a claim with a secure place in venerable disputes, but he is prevented from drawing his conclusion that scientific thought, in elementary form, inhabits even the world of 2.7.3. Gone, therefore, is another provocative chapter-ending remark: "Elle [la pensée religieuse] emploie, par suite, les mécanismes logiques avec une sorte de gaucherie, mais elle n'en ignore aucun" (342). That remark points toward scholarship like E. E. Evans-Pritchard's 1937 classic *Witchcraft, Magic and Oracles among the Azande* (1937), a study in the sociology of knowledge that asked how seemingly irrational beliefs could be rationally held.[51] To accept this adulterated paragraph as representing a "principal idea or argument of Durkheim's" we would have to invoke the magic principle that the power of a sanctified mummy is fully present in a tooth, a hank of hair, or a thighbone.

The other three translations do not chisel away this provocative parting comment but grapple with its translation. Here is Swain (272): "[I]t [religious thought] consequently employs logical mechanisms with a certain awkwardness, but it ignores none of them." Here am I (241): "As a result, it employs logical mechanisms with a certain gauchness, but none of them are unknown to it." And here is Redding (144), who I think best solved the problem of the verb *ignorer*—which neatly joins "not to know" and "to pay no attention": "as a result, it uses logical mechanisms in a clumsy way, but it does not overlook any of them." Some deletions are as short as a single sentence or two razored from the midst of paragraphs or hacked from paragraph endings; others extend to a page or more. This one lops off the nine lines that are Durkheim's final touch to the intense and celebrated argument of 2.7. The reader of this *Forms* will never know how far Durkheim was willing to go in defending the logical capacities of "primitive" humanity.[52]

Finally, the declared principles of this editorial surgery are often violated. Some references that are "significant," by the editor's own definition, are in fact dropped. These include references to Marcel Mauss; they even include Durkheim's own directive notes to help readers keep track of his argument.[53] Elements about the role of women in religion vanish as well: exclusion from blood rituals,[54] fertility-related mutilation, self-inflicted torture the better to fulfill gender-specific roles,[55] and sexual license at big *effervescences collectives*.[56] Various references on Vedic religion are dropped—whether as insignificant, untopical, dated, or ethnographic is impossible to know—dramatically so at 1.2.1, where the poetic elements of Durkheim's argument that god concepts are not central to religion disappear. He no longer recounts the primeval sacrifice that created the dawn or the hymn that caused the waters to flow on Earth—"*and this despite the gods.*"[57] With lively British understatement, Jacqueline Redding summarized these goings-on as "legitimate," given the declared objective, but adds: "nonetheless one rather regrets interesting asides like the paragraph on the use of the word 'totem' missing from p. 88 of the new translation."[58] It is hard to imagine where such a paragraph belongs, if not in a book originally subtitled "The Totemic System of Australia." What a shame to chop and stitch and call the result "a new translation."

Issues and Answers

The Translator at Work: Medium or Artisan?

Literary translation is often called an undervalued art. Scholarly translation lives in a similar twilight. In both, the translator's active work of reconstruction is misimagined as a kind of mediumship that enables the text, itself, to move from one language to another. In the case of scholarly translation, one consequence is that the elementary norms of academic life tend to fade from view. Partly because the text itself is thought of as in charge of its own move, its new words somehow still those of the faraway or deceased author, few specific rules govern the work of translators. Thus, unlike other authors of scholarly interpretation, scholarly translators need not indicate their approach to the problems posed by their text. Again, they may, but need not, use notes to mark interpretive judgments, let alone stark incomprehension. The example of Swain's *Forms* giving generations of readers without French his whole-cloth manufacture for *l'étendu* and *l'inétendu* reminds us: even if specific norms were many and well conceived, most users of translations would have no way of knowing whether those norms have been violated or upheld. In that way, the predicament of scholarly translation becomes a predicament for scholarly collectivity.

One solution is to think more realistically about translators' work than is suggested by the notions of a traveling text and its medium-like conductor. As with the parlor mediums in Durkheim's day, the words originate inside the parlor, so to speak, not beyond it. The variations I have considered make that abundantly obvious. The less obvious next step is to recognize that a translated text contains not one thought process, the original author's, but two. Mediums are said to empty themselves; translators cannot. Who we are, what we know, and sometimes what we believe—all of that and more—stays put as we deal with an author's syntax, word choice, paragraph division, and so on. Conventional usage denies that. Typically, therefore, a competent introduction to Durkheim's work mentions elements of personal background such as his religious upbringing but is free to ignore such aspects of his translator's. I say: *Caveat lector.*

I resisted influences from my own religious upbringing, with mixed success.[59] For example, it was a hymn with the phrase "merciful and mighty" that bubbled up from childhood recollections, so that "moral yet mighty" just sounded right to me, diverting my attention from the key Durkheimian contrast at hand, "*moral* and at the same time . . ." I note too, in rereading, that I gave *en faute* as "in a state of sin" (305). In fact, Durkheim's subject—natural death interpreted as the consequence of sacrilege—neither requires nor invites such an expansion. Besides, ethnography and religious history caution against equating the notion of ritual tort with that of sin. Swain's "in fault" is better because more neutral.[60] Finally, why is it that Durkheim's gods, who *plânent,* "soar high above" for Swain (255), "look down from on high for Redding (133), and "loom" for Cosman and me (169, 225, respectively)? If I could have worked as a medium, I would have queried Durkheim: "Rap once if *faute* equaled *péché"* and "Rap once if those gods of yours were only high, twice if they also were menacing."

I would have set him rapping, too, about his evolutionist language—his phrase "les religions même les plus inférieures" (440), for example, which Swain rendered as "even the most inferior religions," or his *obscures consciences,* straightforwardly "obscure minds" for Swain. Since my own interpretive judgment was to make the first "even the simplest" (supplying no note, alas), my questions would begin this way: "Is your contrast "higher"/"lower" interchangeable with "simple"/"complex?" Then (if yes): "Is simple/complex the common core?"[61] And so on. I was (and am) passionately convinced that Durkheim affirmed the oneness of humankind, by seeking among stone tool–using peoples what is fundamental to *all* religious life.[62] Far from approaching *Forms* with a medium's emptiness, therefore, my mind was cluttered by the expectation of consistency.

Studying the phrase *obscures consciences,* I wondered where hung the obscuring cloudiness—inside the *conscience* of Durkheim's human Kangaroo (a member of that totem) or *between* the Kangaroo's *conscience* and Durkheim's own? If the first, Swain was right to say "obscure minds," full stop; and, using other meanings of *obscure,* he could have said "dark minds" or even "humble minds." All would have settled Durkheim among his many compatriots and contemporaries in Europe who considered the "primitive" to be mentally a child. But if the second, then the ambiguity of "obscure minds" should not stand. Imagining that Durkheim meant a cloud between his mind and the Australian's, I added "to us" and an explanatory note.[63] For unexplained reasons of her own, Cosman, too, wrote "simplest" for *les plus inférieures* and added "to us."[64]

But were we right? Consider this: Durkheim championed not only the oneness of humankind but also the Third Republic, whose soldiers carried an imperial *mission civilisatrice* to Africa and Asia. And this: The same dissonances recur in Durkheim's 1913 criticisms of Lucien Lévy-Bruhl's book *Les Fonctions mentales dans les sociétés inférieures* (which, as Pickering's note tells us, was translated with the indicative title *How Natives Think*). The word *inférieur* travels, like a barnacle on a boat, with his rejection of Lévy-Bruhl's thesis as to the "primitive's" innate illogic.[65] And so this: a perfect medium would have rendered the dissonances perfectly. In the end, my criticism of the spurious consistency Swain lent to the sacred/profane dichotomy applies to Cosman and me—and all the more whenever interpretive amendments proceed silently. Faithful translation includes the fault-lines and inconsistencies of the text translated.

Finally, here is a case in which a séance would have enabled me to ask Durkheim not what he meant, but how he intended what he meant to sound. Did he intend Swain's straightforward word choice or the physical metaphor I thought I saw in a passage about the ritual making of men? Here, first, is Swain's one-sentence version, which as usual preserves the underlying French structure:[66]

> On the other hand, the young initiate is submitted to a series of
> rites of particular severity; to give [*communiquer*] him the virtues
> which will enable him to enter into the world of sacred things, from
> which he had up till then been excluded, they centre [*on fait conver-
> ger*] an exceptionally powerful group [*faisceau*] of religious forces on
> him. (342)

I proceed by dividing the long sentence into two, rearranging the second, and translating certain key words differently from Swain:

> On the other hand, the young initiate undergoes an especially harsh
> set of rites. An exceptionally powerful *beam* of religious forces is *fo-
> cused* on him, so as to make it possible to *transmit* to him the virtues
> that will enable him to enter the world of sacred things, from which
> he had previously been excluded. (308)

The difference is not a question of accuracy. Swain's word choices convey the meaning and suit the context of initiation. *Communiquer* also means "hand down," "pass on," "hand over," and in that sense, "give." It need not go with "beam." For that matter, a *faisceau* is not necessarily a beam. According to the *Littré* (p. 1605) the etymology gives us "an assemblage of long things, bound together" (elegantly apropos, as I will show). Retain "assemblage." The *Petit Robert* gives first a "bundle," "stack," or "collection" of like things—Durkheim's sense when he calls society "the most powerful collection [*faisceau*] of physical and moral forces that we can observe in nature"[67] (Fields, 447, Durkheim, 637). Farther on, it gives us the bound bundle of reeds (often seen in public architecture) that symbolized public power in ancient Rome. "Beam," as in *faisceau lumineux* or *faisceau hertzien*, is among the meanings by analogy, down in the *Robert*'s fourth category. Nothing in the original required my image of radiation. Thinking that something drawn from early twentieth-century physics might fit what Durkheim had to say about force, I guessed at his intention, as one does with music known only from pages written by a long-dead composer.[68] Here finally is Cosman's version:

> In contrast, the young initiate is subject to a particularly harsh set of rites. An exceptionally powerful beam of religious forces is trained on him so as to transmit to him the power he needs to enter the world of sacred things from which he was previously excluded. (225)

Représentation: A Translator's Challenge

Anxious about this Durkheim translator's bugbear as I began working through *Forms*, I sought advice from a colleague, the late Lewis R. Beck. He told me that heavy weather surrounded *représentation* and the verb *se représenter* because of bad Kant translation. "All you need," he said, was "the idea of something present to the mind," and he made a graceful two-handed gesture around his head. So for *se représenter*, words like "conceive," "imagine," "picture," and so on were all *fine*. I took his advice, for translating the verb *se représenter* literally can lead to "represent to oneself." In my first reading of Swain's translation, "Religion is a system of ideas by which men represent to themselves the society of which they are members," I pictured men creating emblems. No. That does not fit. Plug in "imagine," and we have sense.

Se représenter, as "present to the mind," can also mean "remember" or "recall." That meaning gives us those "representative or commemorative rites" in which the Warramunga people recall their common history and common descent, back in the mists of time, from the giant snake Wollunqua. The non-reflexive form of the same verb, which denotes "standing for" something, gets us to the snake-like movements they make, howling *Yrrsh! Yrrsh! Yrrsh!* Beware, however, of applying that last idea—of something "standing for" something—

across the board, especially to the noun "representation." Though that idea may pop into mind first for an English speaker, it cannot give us the performance and the commemoration, with Wollunqua as centerpiece, that this example of "representation" puts before us. The Warramunga make their time immemorial present to the senses, and to the mind, by enacting it ritually. In summary: no single translation works in all contexts; and none of the foregoing meanings is applicable indiscriminately. Armed with this much, the reader can hope to meet Durkheim halfway when he uses the term *représentation* in the passage Swain accidentally dropped (see p. 61)—"the sacred beings exist only in and through their representations" ("present to the mind")—and in the footnote, where he adds:

> In a philosophical sense, the same is true of anything, for things exist only through representation. But as I have shown . . . this proposition is doubly true of religious forces, because there is nothing in the makeup of things that corresponds to sacredness. (Fields, 349)

With that last statement about sacredness, we arrive at a *collective* representation, and at workings of the *conscience collective* ("collective consciousness" or "conscience"), for we know that sacredness cannot be sacredness if present to only one mind, a single *conscience*. And we know, furthermore, that the faithful all witness it together, because they witness it as inherent in things around them. Accordingly, it is not that they form a "group mind," the captive of collectivity, but that they have and inhabit the same real world. When T. S. Eliot wrote about *Forms*, the big issue was not so much the untranslatable meaning of "representation" (no italics yet) as its being linked with "collective." He and his audience apparently thought they understood "collective representation" well enough to dislike it: "M. Durkheim talks far too much about 'society'; everything is ascribed to its influence. And Mr. Webb [another critic] has our sympathy in his stand for the rights of 'individual' religion."[69] That sort of objection must still be taught against, if students are to be wide-awake visitors to the intellectual foreign country that is *Forms*—but taught against undogmatically.[70] As visitors to Durkheim's country, they need not stay.

None of this means to deny the complexity of "representations," as signaled by the traditional italics. In the quotation just cited, Durkheim indicates the concept's location in philosophers' territory. Some in his milieu were reworking Kant's accounts of what goes on in the mind, when we encounter things outside the mind, and of what we can legitimately say about those things and about the mind. Having pointed to that difficult, philosophers' territory from afar, I leave the rest to their competence. The truth is that I worked without much focused concern for the conceptual apparatus that was being used by Octave Hamelin, who is cited in *Forms*, and by Durkheim's teacher Charles Renouvier, who is not cited. If I had to do the work again, I would scrutinize my choices whenever this family of terms came up, to see whether

I could keep better faith with meanings that might have been important to Durkheim the philosopher.

A convention that has developed over the years since Swain's translation of *Forms* prescribes keeping the word *représentation* in italics. In *Durkheim on Religion*, recall, Pickering tagged it as one of those Durkheimian concepts that "defy translation."[71] He then directed the reader forthwith to a twelve-page exposition in a different book.[72] As a translator, I fully understand that solution, but as a teacher, I know it to be a nonstarter for many students. Besides, it effectively shifts the burden of translation from the Durkheim translator to a teaching assistant who may be new to Durkheim and a stranger to French. Finally, italics convey two contradictory messages: needless anxiety on the one hand and unfounded confidence on the other. To italicize "representation" alone, or nearly so, is to announce that its meaning is both singularly important and uniquely incomprehensible (and *will* be on the test). On the other hand, to keep those italics while leaving everything else alone is to promote unfounded confidence that all other problems are solved or insignificant—like feeling reassured because flickering fires in the surrounding dark every now and then expose *only one* rearing tyrannosaurus rex.

Things Elementary

One of the neglected other monsters stands concealed in full view on the title page: "elementary." For some readers, the book stops there. *Forms* seems very nearly discredited in advance, not because of understood arguments rejected, but because "elementary" appears to be aligned with words like "primitive" and "simple." Those words belong to our discredited past, and stand indicted before the bar of the present. Fixed in a dated old classic, they cannot be censored or replaced with euphemisms. So, for some students and teachers, they create awkwardness as they come up in *Forms*. Not long ago, I found myself in a hot disagreement the core of which was precisely that awkwardness turned active. I could not make myself heard when I said that the notion of collective representations helped me pose the question of how "race" exists in America (for example, resisting scientific proof of its biological unreality) or that the example of "race" eases movement past individualist objections to Durkheim's concept. Race would not exist if held in only one mind, or in minds taken one at a time. It does exist "only in and through its representations." No use. No getting beyond "elementary," "simple," and "primitive" in *Forms*. "How on earth," my interlocutor demanded, "could you ignore the Victorian evolutionist and racist assumptions behind Durkheim's idea that the Australians were 'simple'?" So what can be done by the translator of *Forms* from English to English? I conclude with some thoughts.

"Primitive" is easily disposed of. Durkheim wrote that "man is man only because he is civilized"—in 1912, when champions of the *mission civilisatrice* were saying different things. What is more, he returned repeatedly to the technical and other flaws of "primitive." The following statement opens the chapter on animism: "Even the crudest religions that history and ethnography make known to us are already so complex that they do not fit the notion people sometimes have of primitive mentality."[73] If "primitive" is readily disposed of, however, "elementary" is a different matter. "Elementary" is there in the title, made by Joseph Ward Swain forever part of the life of *Forms* in English, and impossible to change now without doing violence to that life. But I would have preferred "elemental"—*élémentaire* expresses both.[74] The issue is not right or wrong translation but the scope each alternative leaves for right or wrong understanding. The term "elemental" would escape the diminutive and sometimes faintly pejorative sense of "elementary" and move onto the terrain of the positive science to which Durkheim was a passionate contributor.

He thought the stone-age cultures of Australia brought twentieth-century science as close as it could get to human origins (not in a directly chronological sense). He dreamed of incorporating what could be learned from them into the new science of sociology whose subject, scope, and methods he and his colleagues were working to define. That is why he said, on the very first page of *Forms*, that he had made a "very archaic religion" his topic. He thought it "better suited than any other to help us understand the religious nature of man, that is, to reveal a fundamental and permanent aspect of humanity." To advance, it was necessary to find "the simplest and most primitive" religion that could be observed. But here is the point. Durkheim's "simplest" referred not to people but to social organization based on totemic clans—that is, collectivity deriving not from natural givens like blood or soil but from the ordinary working of those extraordinary mental capacities that distinguish humankind. He assumed that what was discovered through the study of that "simplest" form of social organization would be indispensably part of the most complex. Think in terms of modern science in his day, the discoveries about atoms and about the chemical substances that make up chemists' periodic chart, the elements. Conceived of that way, Durkheim's "elementary" forms necessarily belong to the makeup of the religions he thought of as more complex or as "higher" in the evolutionary sense.

Whether he was right or wrong to think the study of Australians could yield religion in *elemental* form is a valid but separate question. What is important is to grasp the scientific exploration Durkheim attempted. The burden of the book as a whole is that an aspect of humanity's "fundamental and permanent" nature is to be found in humanity's social nature. For him, that human social nature is nothing other than its *vie religieuse*. He offers his study based on Australian ethnographies as a "single, well-conducted experiment." He intends his findings to reveal the fundamental building blocks of all that is religious, its ever-present source and natural resource in the mentality of humankind. So the "elementary" in *Forms* is not "other" but us.

NOTES

1. Emile Durkheim, *The Elementary Forms of the Religious Life*, trans. Joseph Ward Swain (New York: Free Press, 1965), 88. Originally published by Allen and Unwin, New York. Hereafter Swain.

2. Emile Durkheim, *Les Formes élémentaires de la vie religieuse: Le système totémique d'Australie* (Paris: Alcan, 1912), 99. Hereafter Durkheim.

3. That is, book 1, chapter 2, section 5, thus abbreviated for easy reference in differently paginated editions.

4. I borrow this phrase from W. H. Werkmeister's instructive essay "What Did Kant Say and What Has He Been Made to Say?" in *Interpreting Kant,* ed. Moltke S. Gram (Iowa City: University of Iowa Press, 1982), 133–145.

5. *Le Robert Petit: Dictionnaire de la langue française* (Paris: Dictionnaires Le Robert, 1992) provides these examples and is my reference throughout.

6. W. S. F. Pickering, ed., and Jacqueline Redding, trans., "The Elementary Forms of the Religious Life," in *Durkheim on Religion,* ed. Pickering and trans. Redding (Atlanta, Ga.: Scholars Press, 1994 [1975]). Hereafter Pickering-Redding.

7. Emile Durkheim, *The Elementary Forms of Religious Life*, trans. with an introduction by Karen E. Fields (New York: Free Press, 1995). Hereafter Fields.

8. Emile Durkheim, *The Elementary Forms of Religious Life*, trans. Carol Cosman and abridged with an introduction and notes by Mark S. Cladis (New York: Oxford, 2001). Hereafter Cladis-Cosman.

9. Werkmeister, "What Did Kant Say?" 133.

10. As quoted in Philip Smith and Jeffrey C. Alexander, "Review Essay: Durkheim's Religious Revival," *American Journal of Sociology* 102, 2 (September 1996): 589.

11. Ibid.

12. Sir Baldwin Spencer and Francis James Gillen, *Northern Tribes of Central Australia* (London: Macmillan, 1904), starting at 231.

13. Jean de Lannoy, "Le Style de *Les Formes élémentaires de la vie religieuse* d'Emile Durkheim," *Durkheimian Studies* 2, n.s. (1992): 73–75. My translation.

14. Ibid., 73.

15. W. S. F. Pickering and Jacqueline Redding, "Notation," in Pickering-Redding, x.

16. Swain's mistranslating *l'inconscient* as "the background" is understandable if we realize that, as a noun with a psychological meaning, "the unconscious" entered French only in the late nineteenth century. The *Petit Robert* gives the adjective's coining as 1820. For more on this passage, see Fields, liii.

17. Pickering-Redding, 108. See Fields, 6–7, and Cladis-Cosman, 9.

18. See Fields, 121, 127, 129, 133, 333.

19. See Fields, lxx n. 101, 121 n. Pickering-Redding omits all of book 3.

20. See Fields, 230 n. 43. Actually, he was pleased enough with that discovery to reuse it, 334, 336.

21. Pickering-Redding includes Durkheim's 1899 piece "Concerning the Definition of Religious Phenomena," 74–99, which has no sacred/profane dichotomy.

22. Pickering's excerpts omit all of book 3. In book 3 of the Oxford edition, the

pruning of ethnographic material omits Durkheim's mention of the Tree Louse and Crab Louse totems.

23. W. S. F. Pickering, introduction, in Pickering-Redding, 4.

24. T. Stearns Eliot, review of *Group Theories of Religion and the Religion of the Individual* (London: Allen and Unwin, 1916) by Clement C. J. Webb, *International Journal of Ethics* 27, 1 (1916): 115–117.

25. Unsigned, *Monist* 28 (1918): 158.

26. Fields, 349, other omissions appear at 315 n. 64, and 446. Translator's notes mark them all.

27. See also Pickering's book-length interpretation, published a decade later: *Durkheim's Sociology of Religion: Themes and Theories* (London: Routledge and Kegan Paul, 1984).

28. Pickering-Reading, "Notation," ix. For a systematic discussion of the term *representation*, see Pickering, *Durkheim's Sociology of Religion*, 279–283.

29. Pickering-Reading, "Notation," ix.

30. In a translator's note (4), I suggest that Swain possibly confused Durkheim's *prescrit* with *proscrit*.

31. Correspondences: intact paragraphs in Swain, 15–16, 255–256, 262–263, 338–339, and in Pickering-Redding, 104–105, 133–134,——,——; divided paragraphs in Cladis-Cosman, 5–6, 169, 175–177, 222–223, and in Fields, 3–4, 225–226, 231–232, 304–305. The dashes indicate passages that are absent from the excerpted *Forms*.

32. See, for example, W. E. B. Du Bois, the chapter titled "Of Our Spiritual Strivings," in *The Souls of Black Folk* (New York: Norton, 1999). One of that chapter's very few short paragraphs—the one about "double-consciousness"—is quite famous and constantly quoted out of context. Du Bois studied with William James, whose writing about multiple consciousness may be reflected not only in Du Bois's famous concept but also in Durkheim's remarks about notions of multiple personhood in modern psychology. See note hereafter.

33. Sir Arthur Conan Doyle, Durkheim's contemporary, offers in *The Hound of the Baskervilles* a sustained and powerful example of this usage. Carefully drawn, discrete impressions (darkness on the moor, shadows in Baskerville Hall, firelight, phosphorescence) build until they momentarily displace the positivistic outlook of even Sherlock Holmes, when the hound rushes out of the foggy night, toward him and John H. Watson. He regains it when (and because) his own and Dr. Watson's pistol shots reveal that the hellish hound can be wounded, and therefore killed.

34. Pickering, introduction, 7.

35. For example, we hear from the ethnographer W. E. H. Stanner (277–304) how Durkheim's ideas stood up in the field.

36. Pickering, introduction, 7.

37. Emile Durkheim, "Concerning the Definition of Religious Phenomena," in Pickering-Redding, 74.

38. Fields, li–lxi.

39. Ibid., lviii–lix.

40. See Fields, 242 n.; also Karen E. Fields, "Durkheim and the Idea of Soul," *Theory and Society* 25 (1996): 193–203. I acknowledge Andrée Douchin for illuminating suggestions.

41. Fields, 272 n. 127. Steven Lukes, *Durkheim, His Life and Work: A Critical Study* (New York: Harper and Row, 1972), 433 n., found "no evidence" that Durkheim had read Freud (though Freud cited *Forms* in "Totem and Taboo"). Still, since we know he read William James attentively (he quotes from *The Varieties of Religious Experience* in the conclusion of *Forms*), I suspect he is referring not to Freud but to James's notion of consciousness as multiple.

42. To become acquainted with that family is not necessarily to embrace it. See Nancy Jay's contribution toward a feminist theory of blood sacrifice, *Throughout Your Generations Forever: Sacrifice, Religion, and Paternity* (Chicago: University of Chicago Press, 1992), 135–137.

43. Durkheim, 298, and often elsewhere in *Forms*, but first elaborated in his book *De la division du travail social: etude sur l'organisation des sociétés supérieures* (Paris: Alcan, 1893).

44. Correspondence from Terry F. Godlove, July 9, 1993.

45. Jacqueline Redding, review of Emile Durkheim, *The Elementary Forms of Religious Life*, trans. Carol Cosman, abridged with an introduction and notes by Mark S. Cladis (Oxford: Oxford University Press, 2001), in *Durkheimian Studies* 8, n.s. (2002): 117.

46. Pickering, introduction, 6–9.

47. Cladis-Cosman, 177. See Fields, 233.

48. Cladis, "Note on the Text," in Cladis-Cosman, xxxvi.

49. Cladis, ibid., xxxvi. We are further informed that the Oxford edition incorporates corrections of the typos that, while absent from the 1912 edition, have multiplied from the second edition on and still infect the Poche to some degree.

50. Cladis-Cosman, 163; see Swain, 248, and Fields, 219.

51. E. E. Evans-Pritchard, *Witchcraft, Oracles and Magic among the Azande*, with a foreword by C. G. Seligman (Oxford: Oxford University Press, 1937). The list of philosophers and social scientists who have worked in this vein is long, and that work continues up to the present. See, for example, "Old Gods, New Worlds," by the philosopher Kwame Anthony Appiah, in *In My Father's House: Africa in the Philosophy of Culture* (Oxford: Oxford University Press, 1992), 107–136. See my answer to him, "Witchcraft and Racecraft: Invisible Ontology in Its Sensible Manifestations," in George C. Bond and Diane Ciekawy, eds., *Witchcraft Dialogs* (Athens: Ohio University Press, 2001).

52. For the importance of this point to Durkheim, see his own quick summary of *Forms*, "Lévy-Bruhl—*Les Fonctions mentales dans les sociétés inférieures*," and "Emile Durkheim—*Les Formes élémentaires de la vie religieuse Le système totémique d'Australie*, in Pickering-Redding, *Durkheim on Religion*, 171. It was first published in *L'Année Sociologique*, the year after *Forms* was published.

53. On Mauss, compare Cladis-Cosman, 260, Swain, 392, and Fields, 354, and on Durkheim's directive notes, compare Cladis-Cosman, 40–41, Swain, 55, 56, and Fields, 38, 39.

54. Compare Cladis-Cosman, 106 with Swain, 160, and Fields, 137.

55. Compare Cladis-Cosman, 233, with Fields, 319, and Swain, 354.

56. Compare Fields, 387 n. 32, 408, Swain, 428n., 451, and Cladis-Cosman, 285 (with deletions unmarked) and 301.

57. Durkheim's italics, 48. All mention of Abel Bergaigne (1838–1888), the great French scholar of the Vedic hymns, disappears from *Forms*.

58. Jacqueline Redding, review, 117.

59. See Fields, xxix–xxxi.

60. Compare Durkheim, 429, with Swain, 339, and Cladis-Cosman, 222 (which also says "in a state of sin"). In Evans-Pritchard's classic *Witchcraft, Magic, and Oracles among the Azande*, we encounter a religious logic in terms of which there can be no such thing as a "natural" death, so that the fact of death opened the way to an inquiry into who did (or failed to do) what.

61. Swain, 347 and 219; Fields, 312 and 193. Compare Durkheim, 440 and 272.

62. His justly famous 1898 article setting forth this position, "Individualism and the Intellectuals," is included in Pickering-Redding, 59–73.

63. Fields, 193 n. Compare Durkheim, 272, Cladis-Cosman, 143, and Swain, 219. The word *indistinction*, referring to a quality of mind, posed a similar problem, which I solved with a negative verb phrase, "not to make distinctions" (Fields, 240), and Cladis-Cosman (182) has "refusing to make distinctions." Swain (271) uses the nearly obsolete English equivalent, "indistinction."

64. Cladis-Cosman, 229, 143, respectively.

65. Emile Durkheim, "Lévy-Bruhl—*Les Fonctions mentales dans les sociétés inférieures* and Durkheim—*Les Formes élémentaires de la vie religieuse*," in Pickering-Redding, 169–173.

66. Compare Durkheim, 434.

67. "Une société, c'est le plus puissant faisceau de forces physiques et morales dont la nature nous offre le spectacle." In this sentence, "beam" will not work and *faisceau* must be rendered by something like "group" or "collection."

68. See Fields, xli and liv.

69. Eliot, review, 116.

70. An attempt to do just this occupies much of my introduction to *Forms*, xl–li.

71. Pickering, introduction, ix.

72. Those pages are well worth reading. See Lukes, *Durkheim*, 4–16.

73. Fields, 45.

74. I here draw on my introduction to *Forms*.

REFERENCES

Alexander, Jeffrey C., and Philip Smith. 1996. "Review Essay: Durkheim's Religious Revival." *American Journal of Sociology* 102, 2: 589.

Appiah, Kwame Anthony. 1992. *In My Father's House: Africa in the Philosophy of Culture*. Oxford: Oxford University Press.

de Lannoy, Jean. 1992. "Le Style de *Les Formes élémentaires de la vie religieuse* d'Emile Durkheim." *Durkheimian Studies*, 2, n.s.: 73–75.

du Bois, W. E. B. 1999. *The Souls of Black Folk*. New York: Norton.

Durkheim, Emile. 1994 [1975]. "Concerning the Definition of Religious Phenomena." In Pickering, ed., *Durkheim on Religion*.

———. 1912. *Les Formes élémentaires de la vie religieuse: le système totémique d'Australie*. Paris: Alcan.

———. 1994 [1975]. Review, "Lévy-Bruhl—*Les functions mentales dans les sociétés inférieures* and Durkheim—*Les Formes élémentaires de la vie religieuse*." In Pickering, ed., *Durkheim on Religion*.

———. 1965 [1915]. *The Elementary Forms of the Religious Life*, translated by Joseph Ward Swain. New York: Free Press.

———. 1995. *The Elementary Forms of Religious Life*, translated with an introduction by Karen E. Fields. New York: Free Press.

———. 2001. *The Elementary Forms of Religious Life*, translated by Carol Cosman and abridged with an introduction and notes by Mark S. Cladis. New York: Oxford.

Eliot, T. Stearns. 1916. Review of Clement C. J. Webb, *Group Theories of Religion and the Religion of the Individual*. *International Journal of Ethics* 27, 1: 115–117.

Evans-Pritchard, E. E. 1937. *Witchcraft, Oracles, and Magic among the Azande*, with a foreword by C. G. Seligman. Oxford: Oxford University Press.

Fields, Karen E. 2001. "Witchcraft and Racecraft: Invisible Ontology in Its Sensible Manifestations," in George C. Bond and Diane Ciekawy, eds., *Witchcraft Dialogs*. Athens: Ohio University Press.

Pickering, W. S. F., ed., and Jacqueline Redding, trans. 1994 [1975]. *Durkheim on Religion*. Atlanta, Ga.: Scholars Press.

———. 1994 [1975]. "The Elementary Forms of the Religious Life." In Pickering, ed., *Durkheim on Religion*.

Pickering, W. S. F. 1984. *Durkheim's Sociology of Religion: Themes and Theories*. London: Routledge and Kegan Paul.

Redding, Jacqueline. 2002. Review of Emile Durkheim, *The Elementary Forms of Religious Life*, trans. Carol Cosman, abridged and with an introduction and notes by Mark S. Cladis. *Durkheimian Studies* 8, n.s.: 117.

Spencer, Baldwin, and James Gillen. 1904. *Northern Tribes of Central Australia* London: Macmillan.

Werkmeister, W. H. 1982. "What Did Kant Say and What Has He Been Made to Say?" In Moltke S. Gram, ed., *Interpreting Kant*. Iowa City: University of Iowa Press.

5

Putting Durkheim's Texts to Work

Robert Alun Jones

In a variety of different contexts—for example, sociology, history, and most recently religious studies—Durkheim has been a central focus of my teaching for more than thirty years. As a graduate student during the late sixties, I had the good fortune to be introduced to Thomas Kuhn's *Structure of Scientific Revolutions* (1962), which dramatically changed the way many of us thought about the history of ideas. Since then, my approach to teaching intellectual history has remained largely the same—that is, historicist, nominalist, and neopragmatist—albeit with minor adjustments and repairs along the way. Since this defines so much of what I do in the present, it will be useful to take a brief look at the past.

The Pragmatist's Progress

Before 1960, the history of sociological theory was undeniably ripe for revision. There was substantial agreement on a canon of classic writers and texts—for example, Marx and Engel's *German Ideology*, Weber's *Protestant Ethic and the Spirit of Capitalism*, Durkheim's *Suicide*, so on. But the study of these texts was bound to a particular justification—that is, that they contain certain recurrent themes, ideas, or truths of ongoing relevance to the present—which in turn dictated a largely ahistorical approach to the way they were taught. Since the justification for their study was based on the premise that they contained certain recurrent themes—for example, alienation and anomie, egoism and altruism, positive and negative freedom, and so on—students were taught to read them in search of some kind of pronouncement on or contribution to these ideas.

It is easier to ridicule this approach than to identify precisely what is wrong with it. For we can understand what is unfamiliar only in terms of what is familiar, and thus we must find some kind of similarity between the vocabulary of these texts and our own, or we would be unable to describe them as instances of "sociological theory" in the first place. The problem was that these preconceptions about what Marx, Weber, and Durkheim must have been saying—especially in the absence of any knowledge of the social and historical context of their writings—often led sociologists to ascribe to them meanings and intentions that they could not have meant or intended. Even this kind of anachronism is unobjectionable so long as it is self-conscious; but in the absence of self-awareness—as well as the requisite knowledge of historical context—the result was an account of writers like Marx, Weber, and Durkheim that was very largely mythological.

Resources that could—and would—be used to challenge this approach were available well before the 1960s. In *The Whig Interpretation of History* (1931), for example, Sir Herbert Butterfield had already denounced the tendency of historians to write history on the side of Protestants and Whigs rather than Catholics and Tories, to praise revolutions (assuming they have been successful), and to emphasize "progress" in the past so as to ratify (if not glorify) the present. During the same year, J. L. Austin's book *How to Do Things with Words* (1931) encouraged us to understand past utterances not just as instances of people *saying* things but also of their *doing* things—that is, performing actions whose meanings were bound up with an often complex set of intentions and contexts. In his *Autobiography* (1939), R. G. Collingwood insisted that we can understand the arguments of past philosophers only if we first know the questions to which these arguments were answers, simultaneously observing that these questions change significantly over time, and must thus be studied historically. And in *Philosophical Investigations* (1953), of course, the later Wittgenstein taught us to relate the rules of language games to concrete forms of social life.

But the history of science—and, by implication, the history of social science—was resistant to such arguments. For however disillusioned we had become with the idea of progress in other areas, the development of science still seemed to be a cumulative record of reason comprehending nature.[1] Kuhn's *Structure of Scientific Revolutions* (1962) thus presented us with a new way of thinking about—and teaching—the history of science. Our conception of the nature of scientific practice, Kuhn observed, is learned primarily from scientific textbooks, which typically contain either an introductory chapter on the history of the discipline or scattered references to the giants of an earlier day. The purpose of these chapters and references is to provide students with a sense that they are participating in a distinguished scientific tradition; but precisely because textbooks are thus pedagogical vehicles for perpetuating of what Kuhn called "normal" science—not for understanding past scientific knowledge—the "scientific tradition" they describe is largely mythological.

The implications of this argument for teaching the history of the social sciences were drawn rather quickly. In a series of seminal essays on the history of anthropology, George W. Stocking, Jr., argued that Kuhn, as well as Butterfield and Collingwood, encourage us to read past texts together with the questions they were meant to answer, to try to grasp the "reasonableness" of points of view that have since been superseded, to see historical change not as a simple progressive sequence but as a complex process of emergence—in short, to understand the writings of the past "in their own terms."[2] Rather than searching the classic texts of past social science for their "contribution" to the canonic themes or theories of the present, Stocking urged us to focus on the *context* of past texts, to understand how they related to the social and cultural settings within which they emerged. As a graduate student at the University of Pennsylvania during this period[3]—not insignificantly one in which authority of every kind was being questioned—I quite naturally embraced both Kuhn and Stocking, and anticipated a career teaching and writing as a revisionist historian of social science.

At roughly the same time Stocking was applying Kuhn's ideas to the history of anthropology, a parallel development was taking place at Cambridge University, where three historians—Quentin Skinner, John Dunn, and J. G. A. Pocock—were sharing their dissatisfaction with the secondary literature in the history of political thought. Gradually their objections took the form of a series of critical methodological essays—for example, Dunn's essay "The Identity of the History of Ideas" (1968), Skinner's "Meaning and Understanding in the History of Ideas" (1969), and Pocock's "Languages and Their Implications: The Transformation of the Study of Political Thought" (1971)—as well as exemplary studies of writers including Machiavelli, Hobbes, and Locke.[4] Skinner's essay in particular made a powerful impression on me, and I used it as the model for a revisionist essay of my own—that is, "On Understanding a Sociological Classic" (1977)—which, in effect, proposed a different way of reading, teaching, and writing about Durkheim.

Like Kuhn and Stocking, Skinner insisted that we study the contexts of past texts; but he was also highly critical of Marxists who rather mechanically treated classic texts as the epiphenomenal reflection of underlying modes of production, as well as the followers of Lewis Henry Namier, who treated texts as the mere rationalization of concrete economic or political interests. Instead, drawing heavily on Collingwood and Austin, Skinner urged us to ask what a classic writer was *doing* in saying what he said, and thus to concentrate on the writer's intentions, and to view classic texts as the embodiments of concrete social actions. Since the very existence of these texts presumes the author's initial intention to be understood, whatever additional intended actions he performed must have been in some sense conventional—that is, must have fallen within the range of things that people in a society of that kind would have understood by someone doing and saying the sorts of things the author did and said. In short, we should read the author's contemporaries in the effort to reconstruct the linguistic contexts of his texts, on the ground that it was only within these contexts that his texts became meaningful utterances in the first place.

To me, Skinner's argument was particularly attractive because it provided a vocabulary for treating classic texts in social contexts, but without compromising their status as complex and intentional intellectual performances. But my experience teaching in a sociology department forced me to acknowledge that most treatments of the classic texts of sociological theory would continue to be ahistorical and anachronistic, and also that most students and teachers of sociology simply didn't care; and I was troubled by the fact that I possessed no satisfactory description of what these sociologists (by contrast with historians) were doing when they talked about Marx, Weber, and Durkheim—a deficiency that left me vulnerable to the (quite justifiable) charge that I was insensitive to their interests. Fortunately at about this time I stumbled on a famous article by Richard Rorty that seemed to provide me with an answer.

In "The Historiography of Philosophy: Four Genres" (1984), Rorty proposed that we think of the study of classic texts as an activity in which we imagine and reconstruct different kinds of "conversations," sometimes between ourselves and the classic writers of the past, and sometimes among the classic writers themselves.[5] In "rational reconstructions," for example, we imagine and then converse with an "ideally reasonable and educable Durkheim"—for example, the Durkheim who speaks *our* language, who might be brought to describe himself as having overstated the "objectivity" of social facts, the "normality" of crime, or the "pathology" of the forced division of labor. Once our concepts and language are thus imposed on Durkheim, and he has— in our imaginary conversation—been brought to accept such a new description of what he meant or did, he becomes one of us, our contemporary, a fellow-citizen, even a colleague in our disciplinary matrix.[6] The goal or purpose of such reconstructions, Rorty observes, is *reassurance* or *self-satisfaction*—that is, our quite natural and reasonable desire to understand the history of sociological theory as in some sense progressive, as employing a fairly stable idiom, and to see ourselves as disagreeing with our ancestors on grounds that our ancestors might in principle have been led to accept.

This, of course, is the kind of reconstruction in which most sociologists are engaged when they teach courses on Marx, Weber, or Durkheim; and it is also the kind of ahistorical, anachronistic way of approaching classic texts that had been criticized by Skinner, Dunn, and Pocock and that I had resolutely avoided in my classes on the history of sociological theory. Dunn, for example, once referred to "the weird tendency of so much writing, in the history of political thought especially, to be made up of what propositions in what great books remind the author of what propositions in what other great books"⁷—a tendency that seemed weird to me as well. But to Rorty, this tendency didn't seem weird at all; on the contrary, he described it as a part of the natural, even indispensable conversation in which philosophers engage when they are thinking and speaking ahistorically. In the classroom, for example, when sociologists say that Durkheim anticipated or adumbrated ideas of which he cannot have been aware, they presumably mean that, in an imagined conversation with themselves about whether or not he should have held certain other views, Durkheim would have been driven back on a premise that he never formulated—one that might have to be suggested to him by a friendly rational reconstructor. Despite their anachronism, therefore, rational reconstructions serve an important purpose—that is, they expand the circle of what Rorty has called "edifying conversational partners," embracing the dead as well as the living; and as long as sociologists are aware that Durkheim is thus being described as holding beliefs he never held, and performing actions he never performed, this kind of imaginary conversation seems unobjectionable.⁸

But there is still a second, more genuinely "historical" type of reconstruction, in which we are less interested in the Durkheim who might converse with us than with imagined conversations between Durkheim and his contemporaries. These conversations take place in a different context, and thus in an entirely different idiom; and as we reconstruct them, we find ourselves encountering vocabularies that are not our own, and realizing linguistic possibilities that have either been forgotten or not yet conceived. It is with the reconstruction of these kinds of conversations, of course, that Skinner, Dunn, and Pocock were concerned; and their value, Rorty observed, lies not in reassurance or self-justification but in *self-knowledge* or *self-awareness*—that is, in the fact that

> instead of supplying us with our usual and carefully contrived pleasures of recognition, [the classic writers] enable us to stand back from our own beliefs and the concepts we use to express them, perhaps forcing us to reconsider, to recast or even . . . to abandon some of our current beliefs in the light of these wider perspectives.⁹

Whether "rational" or "historical" reconstructions, I was attracted to Rorty's notion of reading as a kind of "imagined conversation." For as I had begun to teach, I had soon realized that most of our students are interpretive *essentialists*—that is, they are convinced that there is something that the text is Really About, and also that there is some hidden "code" to be broken, so that its meaning and truth will be revealed. They are also certain that we, as faculty, possess or at least have access to these codes, a dangerously flattering notion that indulges our self-image as academic "priests" whose prestige derives from the power to dispense the intellectual sacraments. Finally, they are equally certain that education is largely a matter of passively receiving these sacraments in the traditional liturgical environment of the lecture hall. But as Rorty insisted in his critique of Umberto Eco's "Intentio lectoris" (1988), there simply isn't anything that the text is Really About, and thus there is no "code" to be broken in order to discover it. "Reading texts," he insisted, "is a matter of reading them in the light of other texts, people, obsessions, bits of information, or what have you, and then seeing what happens." What happens may be too weird and idiosyncratic to bother with, or it may be exciting and convincing; and it might even be *so* exciting and convincing that one "has the illusion that one now sees what a certain text is *really* about." But what excites and convinces, Rorty insists, "will always be a function of the needs and purposes of those who are being excited and convinced."[10] In short, it will be a matter of the discursive contexts within which the text is placed, and of the imagined conversations—more or less useful to ourselves—that result.

Rorty's critique was inspired by Eco's distinction between *interpreting* texts and *using* texts, which Rorty took as parallel to E. D. Hirsch's famous distinction between *meaning* and *significance*—that is, between getting "inside" the text itself, as opposed to relating it to something else.[11] Rorty understood that the point of such distinctions is to preserve the integrity of the "internal coherence of the text itself" against the "willful imposition by a subjectivity [that is, the reader] of a theory on the texts." But for a pragmatist like Rorty, all anyone ever does with anything—including a text—is *use* it; and the parallel distinction between inside and outside the text, between its nonrelational and relational features, is equally unattractive, for pragmatists don't believe in essential, intrinsic, nonrelational properties. "Interpreting something, knowing it, penetrating to its essence, and so on," Rorty insisted, "are all just various ways of describing some process of putting it to work."[12] Rorty thus provided me with a succinct description of what I had long wanted to do with my students—that is, engage in "edifying conversations" by putting texts to work; and I began exploring whatever tools there might be for this purpose.

From Theory to Practice

Although trained as a historian, I had settled in a sociology department, teaching undergraduate survey courses on the history of social thought and graduate courses on classical sociological theory (primarily Marx, Weber, and Durkheim), with occasional forays into other departments to teach European intellectual history or "Religion, Science, and Society." Regardless of the course, the level of the students, or the departmental setting, my pedagogical practices have been generally consistent with the approach I've just described. Because I want students to read classic texts without preconceptions about what they are supposed to contain—at least so far as this is humanly possible—I avoid textbooks and other secondary sources almost entirely. My lectures typically begin not with observations about the text but rather with a discussion of some of the more salient aspects of its social, cultural, and intellectual context. When I turn to the text itself—even in very large classes—I begin by asking the students what they think the author is saying; and since this is frequently followed by a period of excruciatingly painful silence, I sometimes resort to preparing a slide with a passage from the text, projecting it before the class as a whole, and inviting them to work collectively on its possible meanings.

Teaching *Suicide*, for example, I often begin by asking students—as Durkheim had asked himself—what constitutes "a suicide" in the first place. The point here is not to introduce Durkheim's definition or compare it with those of later writers but rather to destabilize students' widely held assumption that suicide, like other things, can be defined by a set of necessary and sufficient conditions. After several minutes of trying out definitions and being confronted with cases—for example, the overzealous soldier, the spurned lover, and so on—that are not intrinsically suicides or nonsuicides, most students are ready to at least entertain the more nominalist view that defining suicide is a matter of social convention rather than a fact of nature. From there, I have often moved on to an account of the "suicide epidemic" in nineteenth-century France—that is, the fact that the proportion of the population committing suicide roughly doubled in each generation throughout the century; and then I ask students if they think Germans, Italians, Protestants, Catholics, or Jews, or married people or their single counterparts, were more likely to participate in this epidemic. And before we turn to the famous discussion of anomic suicide, I make certain that students are aware that even as late as 1897, France—a country whose subsistence technology was still primarily agricultural—had recently experienced an extended period of economic prosperity, allowing many people to rise into the middle class higher and more rapidly than they had ever anticipated.

Following Skinner and Pocock, I also try to focus on the way languages change, so that the classic text might be understood not simply as a set of propositions but as a vocabulary—a way of speaking and thinking about certain ideas or institutions—that could prove useful to concrete interests and purposes. Consider, for example, the case of Durkheim's social realism—that is, the view, epitomized in *The Rules of Sociological Method* (1895), that social phenomena should be studied *comme des choses*, as real, concrete things, subject to the laws of nature and discoverable by scientific reason. Social realism is discussed in almost every introductory sociology textbook; but since Durkheim was a sociologist, and a commitment to the "reality" of social phenomena seems an almost unquestioned article of faith in that discipline, there has been almost no discussion of *why* Durkheim was committed to this view in the first place—an instance of what Skinner has called "insufficient puzzlement" about the questions these classic texts were written to answer.[13]

What was Durkheim *doing*, I ask my students, between the early 1880s and and the appearance of *Suicide* (1897)—the period during which he developed his famous argument that social facts should be treated *comme des choses*? At least a part of the answer clearly lies in his ambivalent but ultimately hostile attitude toward Cartesian metaphysics (a selection from the *Discourse on Method* is required reading). For if Durkheim always described himself as in some sense a "rationalist" and considered Cartesianism "one of the characteristic traits of the French mind," he also considered the conceptual apparatus of Descartes—in which complexity was consistently reduced to simplicity, the concrete to the abstract, observation and experience to logic and reasoning, and things to ideas—deeply problematic. Admirably suited to the mechanical, mathematical certainties of the seventeenth century, Durkheim observed, Cartesianism was completely inadequate when applied to the social and moral needs of advanced industrial societies. In an age of individualism, egoism, and anomie, it was essential that the institutions of the Third Republic become the primary focus of a citizen's duties and obligations; and no mere "mental construct," no Cartesian *idée claire et simple* could ever become the object of such unconditional devotion. This is why Durkheim insisted that social phenomena must be studied *comme des choses*, as things resistant to human will, identified by their properties of externality and constraint. In sociology textbooks, of course, this is described as a methodological injunction, for this has been its significance in the discipline; but if we examine Durkheim's context and intentions, it's clear that his purposes were at least as much moral and political—that is, to construct a normative vocabulary, a new way of speaking about duties, obligations, and ideals that would take the place of the more traditional, Cartesian idiom.

If we think of Durkheim this way—that is, as someone cobbling together a language rather than discovering something about Nature—his social realism seems less a coherent doctrine or theory than an extraordinary assortment of rhetorical strategies. On the one hand, he described society not just as *similar* to nature but as itself a *real, natural* thing, a part of nature and subject to its laws; on the other hand, he emphasized that society is a *particular, distinctive* part of nature, a reality *sui generis*, irreducible to the laws discovered by psychology or biology. So there was always a precarious tension between these two metaphors—the former vulnerable to the criticism that it explained social phenomena by referring to nonsocial (for example, psychological, and biological) causes, and the latter to the charge that sociology is not a "science" at all. Durkheim's description of society as an external, regulative force—epitomized in his treatment of anomic suicide—thus had to be balanced with his depiction of society as the source of positive, collective ideals—exemplified in his treatment of aboriginal religion; and if Durkheim spoke like an empiricist when attacking Descartes in *Moral Education*, he could also sound like a rationalist when criticizing Mill in *The Rules of Sociological Method*. But all of this, of course, makes no sense whatever unless we assume—as I urge my students to do—that Durkheim was trying to serve the very real, concrete interests and purposes of the Third French Republic.

Most important, I emphasize to my students that this is only one interpretation of Durkheim's text, one way of describing its meaning. For what a text "means" is never something to be settled by the "essential nature" of the text, or what the text is Really About; rather, it is always a question of how the text fits into some larger context of thought and action. As a result, any text will have as many meanings as there are contexts in which it might be placed, and the particular contexts we favor will necessarily reflect our own interests and purposes. This means that our answer to the question "What did Durkheim mean when he said, in the second chapter of *The Rules of Sociological Method*, that 'the first and most basic rule is *to consider social facts as things*'" will differ according to the range of discursive contexts—of imagined conversations—in which we can imagine Durkheim participating.

Finally, the more "interesting" the text, the more contexts there will be— perhaps the most defensible distinction between "classic" texts and their presumably "nonclassic" counterparts. If my students begin as essentialists, therefore, my hope is that their subsequent development is one where their effort to discern the "essential" meaning is gradually replaced by their realization that meaning is something that *happens* to a text when it is placed in some larger context, which in turn gives way to their recognition that to "understand" *Suicide* is simply to approach it with a certain interpretive flexibility, giving it as many descriptions as are useful to their purposes. The final stage in this process is reached when the students realize that intellectual growth itself is a matter not of getting our language to "correspond" or "match up" with some external reality, textual or otherwise, but rather a matter of learning how to inhabit some more interesting, useful, and rewarding vocabularies and thus participating in an ongoing, edifying philosophical discourse.[14]

A Brief Digression on Electronic Texts

As I embraced the work of Kuhn, Stocking, Skinner, and Rorty and tried to apply these principles in my classes in the seventies and eighties, I became aware that there was a second, apparently unrelated revolution taking place in the realm of information technologies. By many accounts, this second revolution began in July 1945, when Vannevar Bush published an article in the *Atlantic Monthly* entitled "As We May Think." As President Franklin D. Roosevelt's science advisor, Bush was concerned over the staggering and still rapidly increasing amount of information scientists were required to master, and his proposed solution was the Memex, "a device in which an individual stores his books, records, and communications, and which is mechanized so that it may be consulted with exceeding speed and flexibility."[15] The medium was to have been microfilm, with several projection systems producing multiple "windows" for the comparison and analysis of multiple files on the user's desktop. Data in these files were to have been linked together to form trails of associative, informational webs, built and browsed through by manipulating a system of pulleys and levers.

Bush of course had no notion of the microcomputer, and in fact the Memex was never built. But his vision inspired later pioneers like Douglas Engelbart, and Ted Nelson, who in 1965 coined the word "hypertext" to refer to the kind of intuitive, nonlinear reading and writing the Memex would, in theory, have made possible. Experiments at Brown University produced the first working hypertext systems in the late 1960s, and twenty years later yielded Intermedia, a powerful prototype of the computerized information systems of the future. For reasons not entirely clear to me at the time, I became fascinated with hypertext, making a number of trips back to Brown and eventually building a computer laboratory of my own to experiment with Intermedia as a tool for teaching intellectual history; somewhat later, I was especially fortunate to be at the University of Illinois when Mosaic—which eventually became Netscape, the first graphic hypertext browser for navigating the internet—was developed there.

As this technology advanced, writers like Jay David Bolter and George Landow began to point to a convergence between technology and our understanding of the problems of textual interpretation. In *Writing Space* (1991), for example, Bolter emphasized that electronic texts are the first in which "the elements of meaning, of structure, and of visual display are fundamentally unstable." The aspirations of writers like Wittgenstein, Barthes, and Derrida, which are frustrated by conventional, hierarchical structures, are arguably realized in the networked, hypertextual medium. The "figurative text" emphasized by Stanley Fish—that is, the intertextual structure of sounds, images, and ideas formed in the mind of the reader—is actively constructed as the reader navigates among nodes, links, webs, and networks.[16] Similarly, in *Hypertext: The Convergence of Contemporary Critical Theory and Technology* (1992), Landow insisted that "we must abandon conceptual systems founded on the ideas of center, margin, hierarchy, and linearity and replace them with ones of multilinearity, nodes, links, and networks." Hypertext is the realization of Barthes's *readerly* (by contrast with *writerly*) texts, and of Derrida's focus on the intertextuality, multivocality, and decentering of texts. Rorty is the "philosopher of hypertext," Landow argued, because the hypertextual dissolution of centrality and authority is potentially democratic, a model of that "society of conversations" in which no one voice dominates or preempts the others.[17]

Despite the formidable language of interpretive theory, the point that Bolter and Landow are trying to make is really quite simple—that is, hypertext is a technology with enormous potential for putting texts in contexts, for generating imagined conversations, and thus for putting these texts to work in the way suggested by Rorty. Consider the following scenario, which I have paraphrased from an article on hypertext and literary theory written by Landow in 1989.

> It is 8:00 P.M., and, after having helped put the children to bed, Professor Jones settles into his favorite chair and reaches for his copy of Durkheim's *Suicide* to prepare for tomorrow's class. Having taught and written about Durkheim for more than twenty years, he returns to the book as one turns to meet an old friend. Glancing through the dog-eared pages, he once again encounters allusions to the political insecurities of the Third French Republic, to Rousseau's notion of *la volonté générale* as a constraint on the individual will of the rising *bourgeois*, the growing "epidemic" of suicide rates in nineteenth-century France, which Durkheim considered a serious social problem, Frazer's notion of *taboo*, anticipations of Isaiah Berlin's distinction between "positive" and "negative" liberty, the economic prosperities of the Second Empire, and so on.
>
> Meanwhile Jane Smith, one of the most conscientious students in Professor Jones's survey of Western social thought, begins to prepare for class. What kind of text does she encounter? Where Professor Jones experiences Durkheim's classic study of suicide within a field of relations and connections, his student encounters an eviscerated, isolated, and significantly reduced text, most of whose allusions go unrecognized and almost all of whose challenges pass by unperceived. An unusually mature student, she pauses in her reading to check footnotes for the meaning of unfamiliar words and allusions, a few of which she finds explained.
>
> Suppose one could find a way to allow Smith to explore some of the connections so obvious to Professor Jones. Suppose she could touch the opening lines of *Suicide*, for example, and the relevant passages from Rousseau, Frazer, and Berlin would appear, or that she could touch another line and be presented with a brief history of the Third Republic—or, for that matter, interpretations and critical judgments made since the first appearance of *Suicide* in 1897—and that she could then call up any or all of them.[18]

Professor Jones is using *Suicide* to participate in an imagined conversation with Durkheim, as well as a variety of other writers before and since. The allusions he recognizes in the passages of the text is neither internal nor external to anything; rather, it is simply an interesting way of describing that part of the text, by placing it in a context and thus using it to satisfy his interests and purposes. But in her relative ignorance, Jane Smith lacks access to these contexts and is thus unable to imagine the conversations in which Professor Jones comfortably participates. The conscientious Smith clearly has interests—not least to pass Jones's survey of Western social thought. But deprived of many contexts, Smith is unable to ascribe any meaning to the passages of the text and thus to put it to work.

In sum, hypertext is a technology for putting texts to work—that is, for placing them in contexts and giving them meaning—and thus for using texts to serve our own concrete interests and purposes. In the case of the hypothetical Jane Smith (as with my less hypothetical students), it's a tool for participating in imagined conversations to which they otherwise have difficult and infrequent access, and thus giving meaning to texts that might otherwise seem meaningless. There is even an interesting body of psychological theory—as well as a smaller body of empirical evidence—suggesting that hypertext encourages the kind of "cognitive flexibility" necessary to the mastery of "ill-structured knowledge domains."[19] If to read a classic text is indeed to engage in "imagined conversations," this is a tool we should not deny ourselves.

Sociology and Irony

At the beginning of this essay I noted that before the 1960s, the study of classic texts in sociological theory was tied to a particular justification—that is, that they contain certain recurrent themes, ideas, or truths of ongoing relevance to the present—which in turn dictated a largely ahistorical approach to the way they were taught. I then proceeded to describe the growing call—in the work of writers like Kuhn, Stocking, Skinner, Pocock, Dunn, and Rorty—for a more historicist, nominalist, and pragmatist approach to these texts. But this in turn leaves us with a problem. For by insisting on this alternative approach to the study of classic texts—that is, that these texts should be understood within their own time, as the answers to their own, nonperennial questions—I seem, at least implicitly, to be suggesting that these texts lack such recurrent themes and thus to be denying the traditional justification for reading them in the first place. The value of "historical" reconstructions, as I have shown, lies not in reassurance or self-justification but in *self-knowledge* or *self-awareness*; but in the absence of a more complete description of precisely what this entails—and thus an alternative justification for the historicist approach to classic text— what we have come to call "historical reconstructions" may appear to be nothing more than "scholarly antiquarianism."[20] This in turn could only have a deleterious effect on our students' learning, for the one question they are always prepared to ask is: "What is the practical utility of our historical studies?"

Fortunately, Rorty has provided us with such a description, and thus with an alternative justification.[21] Each of us, he suggests, carries around something he calls a "final vocabulary"—that is, a set of words (for example, "true," "good," "right," "beautiful," "progressive," "professional," "rigorous," and so on) we use to justify our actions, our beliefs, and our selves. These are the words we use to praise our friends, condemn our enemies, express our deepest self-doubts and our highest hopes—in short, to tell, whether prospectively or retrospectively, the stories of our lives. Such a vocabulary is "final" in the sense that if doubt is cast on the value of these words, we have no noncircular argumentative recourse. Whatever arguments we might present to defend the value of these words must be constructed from the words themselves. This vocabulary, therefore, is "final" in the sense that it is as far as we can go with language, and beyond it lies only resignation or the resort to force.[22]

The "ironist" is someone who has radical, continuing doubts about the final vocabulary she uses. This is because she's encountered other final vocabularies with which she's been impressed, either by meeting other people or by reading lots of books. The ironist recognizes that arguments phrased *within* her present vocabulary cannot underwrite or dissolve these doubts, for these arguments would be circular; she also recognizes that nothing *beyond* her vocabulary—no "foundation," natural or supernatural, physical or metaphysical—can justify, verify, or certify her own way of thinking and speaking. For the ironist, therefore, there are simply multiple, final vocabularies, and there is no neutral, metavocabulary within which universal criteria for the choice among other vocabularies might be formulated. Rorty's ironist is thus "meta-stable" in the sense intended by Sartre—that is, never quite able to take herself seriously, because she is always aware that the terms in which she describes herself are fragile, contingent, and thus subject to change.[23]

By contrast to the ironist, a "metaphysician" is someone who assumes that the presence of a word in *his* final vocabulary ensures that it actually refers to something more essential or more real. The metaphysician, in short, doesn't question the platitudes that encapsulate the use of a particular final vocabulary, especially the platitude that says there is a single permanent reality to be found behind the many temporary appearances. This point is often made by saying that the metaphysician believes that the world is "really out there." But simply to say that the *world* is "out there"—that is, that it is not our own creation but rather the product of other causes—is to say something that the ironist also believes. The significant difference between the ironist and the metaphysician is thus that the latter makes the additional assertion that the *truth* is "out there"—that is, that there is a nonhuman language that the world wants to speak. The ironist, by contrast, is persuaded that nature doesn't speak, that only people do, and that people cannot step outside their language in order to compare their sentences with something more basic, intrinsic, essential, or foundational.[24] The ironist thus resists speaking of any "essential reality"—natural or social—to which her utterances might be said to correspond.

Rorty adds that this confusion—that is, between the notion that the *world* is out there and the notion that the *truth* is out there—is exacerbated by the focus on individual sentences rather than whole vocabularies. As long as we

limit our attention to sentences like "Protestants commit suicide more frequently than Catholics or Jews," or "the members of central Australian clans
are forbidden to kill or eat the totemic animal except at an annual feast called
the Intichiuma," for example, it is easy to confuse (1) the undeniable fact that
the world contains the causes of our feeling justified in holding such beliefs
with (2) the quite different, and thoroughly deniable, claim that some nonlin-
guistic state of the world makes these beliefs true by "corresponding" to them.
Such confusion is less frequent, however, when we turn from individual,
criterion-governed sentences *within* language games to language games *as
wholes* (that is, games we do not choose between by reference to criteria at all).
Does the world speak Aristotelian or Copernican? Does the language of Kant
or that of Nietzsche more adequately correspond to reality? Does nature prefer
to be described by St. Augustine or by Freud?

But this observation—that is, that the world does not tell us what vocabulary to use—does *not* mean that the choices we make about which language
games to play are arbitrary or subjective. It simply means that, when it comes
to changes from one vocabulary to another, the notions of "decision," "criteria,"
and "choice" are no longer useful. Europeans, Rorty observes, did not "decide"
to adopt the idiom of Romantic poetry, or socialist politics, or Galilean mechanics; on the contrary, they just gradually lost the habit of playing some
language games, and gradually acquired the habit of playing others. It was not
on the basis of telescopic observations, Kuhn argues in *The Copernican Revolution*, that Europeans "decided" that the heliocentric theory was correct, or
that macroscopic behavior could be explained on the basis of microscopic motion, or that prediction and control should be the goal of scientific theory;
rather, after a hundred years of inconclusive debate, Europeans found themselves speaking "Galilean" rather than "Aristotelian," and took the intercon-
nected theses of the former for granted.[25]

By now the distinction between metaphysicians and ironists should be
clear. The metaphysician, for example, will see Durkheim as having made a
discovery "about the world"—that is, that social forces are natural forces, distinguished by their characteristics of externality and constraint. The ironist will
see Durkheim as someone who, frustrated with the language that he and his
contemporaries had inherited from the seventeenth and eighteenth centuries,
managed to cobble together a normative vocabulary that worked better for
nineteenth- and twentieth-century purposes; and once sociologists found out
what could be done with a Durkheimian vocabulary, few were interested in
doing the things that had been done with its Cartesian predecessor. The metaphysician still seeks to fulfill the pre-Kantian, Enlightenment dream of "getting
the world right," of describing societies in Nature's Own Language. The ironist,
by contrast, has embraced the notion shared by French revolutionaries, Hegel,
the Romantic poets, Nietzsche, Heidegger, Derrida, Dewey, James, Davidson,
Rorty, and others—that is, that language is solely a human creation, that any-

thing can be transformed simply by being redescribed, and that to change how we talk is to change who we are.

How is this relevant to teaching the history of social thought? Recall my earlier suggestion that the confusion between the notion that the *world* is out there and the quite different notion that the *truth* is out there tends to be exacerbated when the focus is on individual sentences rather than whole vocabularies. Such confusion, I observed, is less frequent when we turn from individual, criterion-governed sentences *within* language games to language games *as wholes* (that is, games we do not choose between by reference to criteria at all). Where intellectual history turns its attention from individual sentences to the larger vocabularies in which sentences are formulated—for example, in works like Kuhn's *Copernican Revolution* or Skinner's *Foundations of Modern Political Thought*—the notion that "the world" somehow decides how it wants to be described becomes less tenable and persuasive. The reader begins to see Copernicus and Galileo, Hobbes and Descartes, Durkheim and Weber not as people who "got the world right," but as writers casting about for a redescription, a metaphor, or a vocabulary that might tempt the rising generation to embrace it, and then see it embodied in their institutions.

In this way, self-consciously "historical" reconstructions—that is, imagined conversations between Durkheim and his contemporaries, in their own language rather than ours—have the potential to encourage an ironist perspective. Like Plato in the early Socratic dialogues, Durkheim was pointing to a state of conceptual incoherence in the moral vocabulary of his culture, one he sought to replace with what he sometimes called "the new rationalism"— that is, a vocabulary more suitable to his own interests and purposes. Unlike the rationalism of Descartes, with its emphasis on *idées claires et simples*, Durkheim's vocabulary emphasized that social phenomena were real *things*, concrete and complex, to be studied *comme des choses*. For the ironist, however, to speak of social facts in this way is simply to describe, and then redescribe, according to one's pragmatic interests and purposes. Similarly, to say that society is "essentially" anything at all is itself a survival of the metaphysical error of thinking that Nature prefers to be spoken of in one way rather than another. Since the ironist rejects the notion that true sentences are true because they in some sense "correspond" to reality, the seemingly endless debate between rationalism and empiricism—that is, over *what kind* of reality a given sentence corresponds to—is over. For the ironist, there is not even a standard by which we can say that Durkheim's "new" rationalism was *better* than its Cartesian antecedent. We can only say that it has come to *seem* better to subsequent generations of sociologists.[26]

Allan Bloom once insisted that the single conviction held in common by almost all university students was the belief that truth is relative.[27] My own experience has been very different—that is, my students combine an excessive commitment to a variety of dubious religious, moral, and political goods with a staggering ignorance of history, philosophy, and social theory. My problem isn't that my students believe too little but rather that they believe too much—with scarcely any discernible reason for doing so. Far from being ironists, they are budding metaphysicians, and interpretive essentialists as well. And this is where intellectual history can play an important part in their education. What we learn from the nominalist, historicist, and pragmatist way of redescribing past sociological thought is that what were once regarded as undeniable truths—scientific propositions that were "true" because they corresponded to some putative social "reality"—were in fact the merest contingencies of a particular history, biography, language, or social structure. Ironically, to learn this is surely to learn a more general truth, not just about the past but about ourselves.

NOTES

1. Even here, Kuhn's arrival wasn't quite unprecedented. In the introduction to *Structure*, he himself pointed to the work of Hélène Metzger, Emile Meyerson, Ludwik Fleck, Alexander Koyré, and Anneliese Maier as among those who wrote about "what it was like to think scientifically in a period when the canons of scientific thought were different from those current today." Thomas S. Kuhn, *The Copernican Revolution: Planetary Astronomy in the Development of Western Thought* (Cambridge, Mass.: Harvard University Press, 1962), vi.

2. George W. Stocking, Jr., *Race, Culture, and Evolution: Essays in the History of Anthropology* (New York: Free Press, 1968), 8; Kuhn, *Copernican Revolution*, 4, 5, 13, 52. Stocking's application of these methodological arguments to the history of Victorian anthropology can be found in Stocking, *Victorian Anthropology* (New York: Macmillan, 1987).

3. Like Stocking ten years earlier, I was a student in the graduate program in American Civilization, where I was not only encouraged to read Kuhn but literally required to read Stocking's monumental doctoral dissertation.

4. See, for example, John Dunn, *The Political Thought of John Locke* (Cambridge: Cambridge University Press, 1969); Quentin Skinner, "The Ideological Context of Hobbes's Political Thought," *Historical Journal* 9 (1966): 286–317, and *The Foundations of Modern Political Thought*, vol. 1, *The Renaissance*, vol. 2, *The Reformation* (Cambridge: Cambridge University Press, 1978; and J. G. A. Pocock, *The Machiavellian Moment: Florentine Political Thought and the Atlantic Republican Tradition* (Princeton: Princeton University Press, 1975).

5. The discussion that follows is developed in greater detail in the introduction to my recent book *The Development of Durkheim's Social Realism* (New York: Cambridge University Press, 1999), 1–8.

6. Richard Rorty, "The Historiography of Philosophy: Four Genres," in *Philosophy in History*, edited by R. Rorty, J. Schneewind, and Q. Skinner (Cambridge: Cambridge University Press, 1984), 51–52.

7. Dunn, *Political Obligation in Its Historical Context* (Cambridge: Cambridge University Press, 1980), 15.

8. Rorty, "Historiography of Philosophy," 59 n. 5, 53.

9. Rorty, "Historiography of Philosophy," 202, 197–198; see also Robert Alun Jones and Douglas A. Kibbee, "Durkheim, Language and History: A Pragmatist Perspective," *Sociological Theory* 11 (1993): 156.

10. Rorty, "The Pragmatist's Progress," in *Interpretation and Overinterpretation*, edited by Stefan Collini (Cambridge: Cambridge University Press, 1992), 103, 105–106.

11. See E. D. Hirsch, *The Aims of Interpretation* (Chicago: University of Chicago Press, 1976).

12. Rorty, "Pragmatist's Progress," 93.

13. See Skinner, "A Reply to My Critics," in *Meaning and Context: Quentin Skinner and His Critics*, edited by James Tully (Princeton, N.J.: Princeton University Press, 1988), 282–283.

14. See Rorty's discussion of "edifying philosophy," in *Philosophy and the Mirror of Nature* (Princeton, N.J.: Princeton University Press, 1979), 377; see also Stefan Collini, "Interpretation Terminable and Interminable,"in Collini, *Interpretation and Overinterpretation*, 11; and George Landow, *Hypertext: The Convergence of Contemporary Critical Theory and Technology* (Baltimore: Johns Hopkins University Press, 1992), 182.

15. Bush, "As We May Think," *Atlantic Monthly*, July 1945, 106.

16. Jay David Bolter, *Writing Space: The Computer, Hypertext, and the History of Writing* (Hillsdale, N.J.: Erlbaum, 1991), 30–31, 157–158.

17. Landow, *Hypertext*, 2–3, 11–13; Rorty, *Philosophy and the Mirror of Nature*, 377.

18. Landow, "Hypertext in Literary Education, Criticism, and Scholarship," *Computers and the Humanities* 23 (1989): 173; see also *Hypertext*, 176.

19. See Robert Alun Jones and Rand Spiro, "Imagined Conversations: The Relevance of Hypertext, Pragmatism, and Cognitive Flexibility Theory to the Interpretation of 'Classic Texts' in Intellectual History," in *The ACM European Conference on Hypertext* (Milan, Italy: Publications of the Association for Computing Machinery, 1992).

20. Skinner, "A Reply to My Critics," 107.

21. See Rorty, "Private Irony and Liberal Hope," in *Contingency, Irony, and Solidarity*, edited by Richard Rorty (Cambridge: Cambridge University Press, 1989). This argument is developed in greater detail in the conclusion of Jones, *Development of Durkheim's Social Realism*, 302–308.

22. Rorty, "Private Irony and Liberal Hope," 73.

23. Ibid., 73–74.

24. Ibid., 74–78.

25. Ibid., 6; see Kuhn, *Copernican Revolution*.

26. Rorty, introduction to *Consequences of Pragmatism* (Essays: 1972–1980), edited by Richard Rorty (Minneapolis: University of Minnesota Press, 1982), xiii–xlvii.

27. Allan Bloom, *The Closing of the American Mind: How Higher Education Has Failed Democracy and Impoverished the Souls of Today's Students* (New York: Simon and Schuster, 1987), 25.

REFERENCES

Austin, J. L. [1931] 1975. *How to Do Things with Words*. Cambridge, Mass.: Harvard University Press.

Bloom, Allan. 1987. *The Closing of the American Mind: How Higher Education Has Failed Democracy and Impoverished the Souls of Today's Students.* New York: Simon and Schuster.

Bolter, Jay David. 1991. *Writing Space: The Computer, Hypertext, and the History of Writing.* Hillsdale, N.J.: Erlbaum.

Bush, Vannevar. 1945. "As We May Think." *Atlantic Monthly,* July 1945, 101–108.

Butterfield, Herbert. 1931. *The Whig Interpretation of History.* Harmondsworth, England: Penguin.

Collingwood, Robin George. 1939. *An Autobiography.* Oxford: Oxford University Press.

Collini, Stefan. 1992. "Interpretation Terminable and Interminable." In *Interpretation and Overinterpretation,* edited by Stefan Collini. Cambridge: Cambridge University Press.

Dunn, John. 1968. "The Identity of the History of Ideas." *Journal of the Royal Institute of Philosophy* 43: 85–104.

———. 1980. *Political Obligation in Its Historical Context.* Cambridge: Cambridge University Press.

———. 1969. *The Political Thought of John Locke.* Cambridge: Cambridge University Press.

Durkheim, Emile. 1915. *The Elementary Forms of the Religious Life.* Translated by J. W. Swain. New York: Free Press.

———. 1961. *Moral Education: A Study in the Theory and Application of the Sociology of Education.* Translated by Everett K. Wilson and Herman Schreurer. New York: Free Press of Glencoe.

———. 1938. *The Rules of Sociological Method.* Translated by S. A. Solovay and J. H. Mueller. Chicago: University of Chicago Press.

———. 1951. *Suicide: A Study in Sociology.* Translated by John A. Spaulding and George Simpson. Glencoe, Ill.: Free Press of Glencoe.

Eco, Umberto. 1988. "Intentio Lectoris: The State of the Art." *Differentia* 2: 147–168.

Hirsch, E. D., Jr. 1976. *The Aims of Interpretation.* Chicago: University of Chicago Press.

Jones, Robert Alun. 1999. *The Development of Durkheim's Social Realism.* Cambridge: Cambridge University Press.

———. 1977. "On Understanding a Sociological Classic." *American Journal of Sociology* 83, 2: 279–319.

Jones, Robert Alun, and Douglas A. Kibbee. 1993. "Durkheim, Language and History: A Pragmatist Perspective." *Sociological Theory* 11: 152–170.

Jones, Robert Alun, and Rand Spiro. 1992. "Imagined Conversations: The Relevance of Hypertext, Pragmatism, and Cognitive Flexibility Theory to the Interpretation of 'Classic Texts' in Intellectual History." In *The ACM European Conference on Hypertext.* Milan, Italy: Publications of the ACM.

Kuhn, Thomas S. 1957. *The Copernican Revolution: Planetary Astronomy in the Development of Western Thought.* Cambridge, Mass.: Harvard University Press.

———. [1962] 1970. *The Structure of Scientific Revolutions.* Chicago: University of Chicago Press.

Landow, George. 1989. "Hypertext in Literary Education, Criticism, and Scholarship." *Computers and the Humanities* 23: 173–198.

———. 1992. *Hypertext: The Convergence of Contemporary Critical Theory and Technology*. Baltimore: Johns Hopkins University Press.

Pocock, J. G. A. 1971. "Languages and Their Implications: The Transformation of the Study of Political Thought." In *Politics, Language, and Time: Essays on Political Thought and History*, edited by J. G. A. Pocock. Chicago: University of Chicago Press.

———. 1975. *The Machiavellian Moment: Florentine Political Thought and the Atlantic Republican Tradition*. Princeton, N.J.: Princeton University Press.

Rorty, Richard. 1984. "The Historiography of Philosophy: Four Genres." In *Philosophy in History*, edited by R. Rorty, J. Schneewind, and Q. Skinner. Cambridge: Cambridge University Press. Minnesota Press.

———. 1982. "Introduction: Pragmatism and Philosophy." In *Consequences of Pragmatism* (Essays: 1972–1980), edited by Richard Rorty. Minneapolis: University of Minnesota Press.

———. 1979. *Philosophy and the Mirror of Nature*. Princeton, N.J.: Princeton University Press.

———. 1992. "The Pragmatist's Progress." In *Interpretation and Overinterpretation*, edited by Stefan Collini. Cambridge: Cambridge University Press.

———. 1989. "Private Irony and Liberal Hope." In *Contingency, Irony, and Solidarity*, edited by Richard Rorty. Cambridge: Cambridge University Press.

Skinner, Quentin. 1978. *The Foundations of Modern Political Thought*. Vol. 1. The Renaissance. Vol. 2. The Reformation. Cambridge: Cambridge University Press.

———. 1966. "The Ideological Context of Hobbes's Political Thought." *Historical Journal* 9: 286–317.

———. 1998. *Liberty before Liberalism*. Cambridge: Cambridge University Press.

———. 1969. "Meaning and Understanding in the History of Ideas." *History and Theory* 8: 3–53.

———. 1988. "A Reply to My Critics." In *Meaning and Context: Quentin Skinner and His Critics*, edited by James Tully. Princeton, N.J.: Princeton University Press.

Stocking, George W., Jr. 1995. *After Tylor: British Social Anthropology, 1888–1951*. Madison: University of Wisconsin Press.

———. 1968. *Race, Culture, and Evolution: Essays in the History of Anthropology*. New York: Free Press.

———. 1987. *Victorian Anthropology*. New York: Macmillan.

Wittgenstein, Ludwig. [1953] 1958. *Philosophical Investigations*. New York: Macmillan.

6

Teaching the Critics

One Route through The Elementary Forms

Terry F. Godlove, Jr.

My aim here is to give a sympathetic portrayal of Durkheim's "theory of religion" in the *Elementary Forms of Religious Life* (*EF*) in light of some of the major criticisms of that work. I have not aimed at complete coverage, nor have I mounted anything like a full-scale defense; the former would require book-length treatment, and I am not sure the latter is possible or even desirable.[1] Rather, I have tried to chart one path among many through some of the more contested parts of the text, one that brings out what I think of as its best face, in conversation with the critics.

My main theme is that the *EF* houses two largely independent approaches to its subject. One approach is functionalist. It tries to account for the existence and persistence of religion by appealing to the cohesion it supplies to society; it tries to account for the behavior and beliefs of individuals by appealing to the needs of the whole. The other approach posits a causal mechanism by which religious ideas and symbols are generated in the very act of assembly—the theory of collective effervescence, what William Pickering calls "effervescent assembly," and Randall Collins "ritual solidarity."[2] Both theories are going to implicate causes and effects, but for shorthand I will refer to the first as functional and the second as causal.

I will be focusing on this duality for two reasons—first, because I think the functionalist line has been emphasized to the detriment of the causal one. On what has become an increasingly standard picture, Durkheim is presented as a founder of functionalism in the study of religion.[3] Part of my purpose here is to disentangle the causal theory from the functionalist one, and to urge that we broaden the standard picture of the *EF* that we present to our students so as to include it. Second, my experience in teaching the *EF* has led me to see this tendency as worse than one-sided; I shall also be arguing that the causal theory is better equipped to meet some of the standard criticisms we associate with Durkheim's work on religion.

My interpretation will emerge in the course of working through these five familiar criticisms:

1. The theory distorts the participant's experience.
2. The definition of religion suffers from a vicious circularity,
3. and so does the eventual explanation.
4. The theory reduces belief in God to belief in society,
5. and is based on bad ethnographic data.[4]

The issues raised in one lead to those in the next, each discussion providing resources to be drawn on later.

1. *The theory distorts the participant's experience.* Thus an early French critic, Gaston Richard (1923): "The very object of *Les Formes élémentaires* is to reduce . . . religious experience to that of the collective life."[5]

To assess this criticism, one must help one's students to distinguish descriptive from explanatory moments in the *EF*. The main point has been made by Wayne Proudfoot, who notes that Durkheim does indeed appeal to the social order to explain the origin of the religious experiences that interest him, but only after he thinks he has provided careful and accurate descriptions of those experiences.[6] In fact, Durkheim does not turn to his sociological explanation of those experiences until book 2, chapter 7, nearly the midpoint of this large book. In the introduction, he announces his epistemological ambitions. In book 1, he tries to undermine competing theories of religion. And even when he finally turns to the Australian materials in book 2, he spends the first six chapters not explaining but merely reporting on the participants' experiences. In these pages one reads that the native feels this or that, that the totem is experienced in this or that way, and so on. Here Durkheim is of course relying on what he terms the "remarkably astute observations" (*EF*, 88–89) of recent ethnographers of Australian totemism, most importantly Baldwin Spencer, Francis James Gillen, and Alfred William Howitt.[7]

In 2.7 Durkheim will argue that the participants wrongly identify the cause of their experience. The participants think their experience of power and moral superiority comes from the totemic object, typically a plant or an animal, in the same straightforward way that we may think that the sour taste comes wholly from the lemon or the impression of blue from the cloudless sky. Durkheim thinks he can show otherwise—that the experience of power and moral superiority *in fact* comes from that which the totem has come to represent, the social order. Each of us is authoritative about how his or her experience feels—about its subjective character. And it is a sufficient answer to the criticism I am now considering to note that Durkheim never calls that authority into question. But we are not fully authoritative about what causes us to feel this or that, or to seem to see or to experience this or that.[8] It is this asymmetry in our first-person authority that legitimizes Durkheim's basic methodological stance.

William Paden puts the emphasis in the right place when, following Proudfoot, he comments that "it is at a second, causalistic level that Durkheim tries to *explain* the data of the sacred by exposing its origins in the chemistry of collective power and symbols."[9] This second move

> represents a shift in the level of discourse. It does not deny the fact that Durkheim has first, on another level, presented a set of data about sacrality. The famous reducer just happens to have been the one to have given us a phenomenology of the irreducible character of the sacred—penultimate to his ultimate act of explanatory reduction.

Where in the text are these "levels" to be found? With Paden, I would emphasize two main instances. First, the one I have already mentioned—the discussion of the "elementary beliefs" in 2.1–6, followed by the sociological explanation of them in 2.7; second, the discussion of the negative cult and ascetic practices in 3.1 (the first chapter on ritual), which concludes with an explanation consistent with that of 2.7. Each of these pairings is composed of descriptions of religious experience and practice—of descriptions that Durkheim takes to be accurate enough that they would be endorsed by the agents themselves were they made aware of them—followed by explanations of those experiences in terms that they would presumably (though, as I will show, not necessarily) reject.

I note that Paden, Giovanni Paoletti, and others use the language of phenomenology to describe the first element in each pairing;[10] Durkheim is attempting to be descriptively accurate—in Proudfoot's terms, there is no "descriptive reductionism." Though Durkheim will later deny that the totem has all of the properties the participant takes it to have (that the participant experiences), that denial does not by itself prevent an accurate description of how the totem is experienced.

But while there is no descriptive reductionism, there are plenty of descriptive errors in the ethnography that finds its way into the *EF*. These errors are of two sorts. First, recent studies have documented what any student of human nature might have surmised, that Durkheim is far from a passive reporter. From the vantage point of his armchair, he feels free to play his ethnographic sources off against one another, to emphasize those reports that favor his theoretical standpoint over those that do not, and even to smuggle in a key term from Oceanic sources, *mana*, which is not to be found in the Australian ones.[11] And from the start Durkheim's reviewers have raised questions about the empirical adequacy of the sources themselves. Indeed, Steven Lukes has cataloged eight distinct "ethnographic criticisms" of the *EF*.[12] I will return (criticism 5) to assess what damage there may be from these to Durkheim's wider project. But this first criticism alleges a deeper, more systematic distortion than that introduced by ordinary empirical error. Richard and many others are alleging that Durkheim's basic explanatory stance somehow distorts the participant's experience from the start. This criticism rests on a confusion about the extent of first-person authority.

> *2. Durkheim's definition of religion suffers from a vicious circularity.*
> Thus Daniel Pals (1996): "If, already at the start of the discussion, Durkheim envisions the sacred as the social, is it not quite easy— rather too easy—to reach the conclusion that religion is nothing more than the expression of social needs? The inquiry would seem to begin at the very place where Durkheim wants to finish. The sacred is the social, he writes, and the religious is the sacred; therefore the religious is the social."[13]

Pals is focusing on what we have come to think of as Durkheim's signature "definition" of religion, which comes at the end of 1.1.[14] Taken by itself, it does indeed make for a small circle: religious beliefs and practices are aimed at sacred objects, and these are inextricably tied to social contexts. No surprise, then, that "religion must be an eminently collective thing" (*EF*, 44).

The question, however, is what place does the definition hold in the larger work? And here the pedagogical problem is that the *EF* is such a large work. It is often impractical to assign it all in a standard "theory and methods" course. On the other hand, Pals's criticism illustrates nothing so much as the danger in focusing too much on the preliminary material. For Durkheim could hardly be clearer that the circle enshrined in his definition is precisely what he intends to vindicate in the remaining four hundred pages. He prefaces the definition with the cautionary remark that all the base-level questions—"what religion is, of what elements it is made, from what causes it results, and what function it performs"—are "questions whose answers cannot be preordained, for we have not crossed the threshold of research" (*EF*, 44).

Durkheim puts off that crossing for another 150 pages, focusing in the meantime, as I have said, on description. Then, suddenly, in 2.7, comes the explanation: he portrays "the social gathering as a kind of machinery for charging [certain] objects with sacredness."[15] That is, Durkheim will begin with group interaction and argue that, under favorable circumstances, participants come to treat as sacred certain objects that have come to represent the group. On this line of reasoning, the conferring of sacrality is the effect of group dynamics. Here, at least, there is no threat of circularity—rather, the positing of a causal mechanism, the details of which I will turn to in a moment. My point here is that the definition of religion in 1.1 does not unfairly prejudice the direction of the subsequent inquiry; rather, it is a promissory note, a single-sentence summary of the "research" to come.

> 3. *Even putting aside the preliminary definition of religion, the mature theory itself suffers from a vicious circularity.* Thus E. E. Evans-Pritchard (1965): "The rites create the effervescence, which creates the beliefs, which cause the rites to be performed; or does the mere coming together generate them?"[16]

This allegation of circularity cuts deeper than the first one. Though Evans-Pritchard does not cite particular passages, his charge does find legitimate targets in the *EF*. In this section I will frame the central issues as follows. The circularity rightly detected by Evans-Pritchard is itself an artifact of a functionalist line of thought running throughout the *EF*. While the issues are not quite clear-cut, Durkheim's functionalism is deeply flawed. But the book also houses the more promising explanatory strategy, to which I have just alluded—one that depends on answering Evans-Pritchard's pointed question in the affirmative.

To begin, consider these two examples of the kind of circularity that seems to trouble Evans-Pritchard, one from 2.7 and one from the conclusion.

First:

> Take away the name and the symbol that gives [the clan] its tangible form, and the clan can no longer even be imagined. Since the clan was possible only on condition of being imaginable, both the institution and the emblem and its place in the group's life are thus explained. (*EF*, 235)

By "the institution" Durkheim has in mind totemic religion, in which, he claims, can be seen the elemental forms of religious life. The initial claim is that (totemic) religion has an unintended, beneficial effect: it provides the clan with a tangible form, thereby making it imaginable. The extended claim is that this effect in turn explains the origin and persistence of its cause—thus the circularity.

Second:

> There is something eternal in religion that is destined to outlive the succession of particular symbols in which religious thought has clothed itself. There can be no society that does not experience the need at regular intervals to maintain and strengthen the collective feelings and ideas that provide its coherence and its distinct individuality. This moral remaking can be achieved only through meetings, assemblies, and congregations in which the individuals, pressing

close to one another, reaffirm in common their common sentiments. Such is the origin of ceremonies that, by their object, by
their results, and by the techniques used, are not different in kind
from ceremonies that are specifically religious. (*EF*, 429)

As before, Durkheim is claiming both that certain ceremonies produce and
strengthen social integration and solidarity and that this effect explains its own
cause, that is, explains the origin and persistence of these ceremonies.

Anyone who has grappled with the *EF* knows that these examples could
be greatly multiplied. In instance after instance, Durkheim seems to assume
that, having shown that religion has unintended, unrecognized, and beneficial
effects for society, he has thereby explained its existence and persistence.[17]

But, as many critics have argued, it is not at all clear that he has. We may
agree that Durkheim has given evidence that religion produces the effect that
interests him. But the deeper question is whether, to engage Evans-Pritchard's
objection, Durkheim needs to give some account of *how*—rather than merely
to assert *that*—these effects manage to maintain their own causes. It seems
very plausible that he needs at least to sketch what has become known in the
literature as a "causal feedback loop." The notion of a causal feedback loop
finds its natural home in evolutionary biology, where such concepts as fitness,
survival, reproduction, and inheritance have been made to take up the sort of
explanatory slack facing Durkheim. Thus, the biologist first theorizes that a
certain trait is a caused by a certain gene, and then describes the process by
which genes are inherited. If the trait is thought to be adaptive, then the story
will depend on the further concept of differential reproduction—on the idea
that "individuals with this trait were able to leave more offspring than individuals without it."[18] On this line, prosecuted in religious studies by Hans Penner
and in the philosophy of the social sciences by Jon Elster, Michael Root, and
many others, the question of whether Durkheim can muster a direct answer
to Evans-Pritchard depends on whether these concepts or their analogues can
be legitimately imported from biology into the social sciences.[19]

While I know of no general consideration blocking this move, neither am
I aware that anyone has plausibly sketched how to proceed.[20] Certainly Durkheim himself is no help, for, as Root observes, he says nothing about "how
adaptive traits are passed on or maintained."[21] The problem goes deeper than
Durkheim's (or anyone's) failure to translate the notion of differential reproduction into the social sciences: if we have no idea how to connect the cause
back up with itself, what reason do we have to think that *it*, rather than something else, is actually at work? Again: even if we agree that Durkheim presents
evidence in the *EF* that collective, ritual practices often have beneficial effects
for society, which effects are neither intended nor recognized by the actors
themselves—and even if we help our students to see this as a genuine and
important discovery—still, we ought to resist the urge to conclude, with Durk-

heim, that he has thereby explained the continued existence of the practices in question.

A more promising line of thought avoids the question of circularity altogether. In 2.7.3, Durkheim relies heavily on Spencer and Gillen's description of the Arunta *corroboree* celebration, but, as he proclaims on the first page of the book, he is looking well beyond Australia. At stake is a claim about what tends to happen when people get together and engage in common activities—in this example, such things as dancing, singing, eating. Durkheim first emphasizes the physical proximity of the participants: "The very act of congregating is an exceptionally powerful stimulant. Once the individuals are gathered together, a sort of electricity is generated from their closeness and quickly launches them to an extraordinary height of exaltation" (*EF*, 217). But beyond physical proximity, Durkheim requires common activities: "It is by shouting the same cry, saying the same words, and performing the same action in regard to the same object that they arrive at and experience agreement" (*EF*, 232). Later in the book he combines these two elements: "What matters most is that individuals are assembled and that feelings in common are expressed through actions in common" (*EF*, 390).

Surely Durkheim is wagering that his readers will have felt something like this, and surely we have. As teachers, we may ask our students to reflect on their own experience, just as we find members of the professional guild doing the same. Thus Nick Allen: "I suspect Durkheim was right to emphasize the emotions generated simply by assembling. I have felt something similar."[22] And, writing of Durkheim's handling of the Arunta celebration, Collins pauses to remark parenthetically: "(Think of the noise level at a party going up as the festivities get going.)" and then continues: "the excitement is heightened and focused by carrying out activities in common: chants, dances, ritual gestures."[23] Karen Fields has recently asked whether, in Durkheim's own case, he may have been influenced by his own experience as a youth in Alsace with anti-Semitic mobs.[24]

The trick, both for Durkheim and for the classroom teacher, is to move from the descriptions of single events to the level of empirical generalization. Put differently, in the service of what general rule is Durkheim's discussion of collective effervescence?

Here is Collins's attempt to capture the regularity that Durkheim has in view: "Humans have a physiological propensity to respond to social interaction with contagious emotional arousal, to a degree that varies with the social density of activities."[25] This strikes me as exactly right, as far as it goes. Focusing on social density allows us to accommodate under the Durkheimian tent the sort of large-scale examples Durkheim favors in the text (the Crusades, the French Revolution, and so on ones in which a person spends lots of time engaged in lots of common activities with lots of other people), but also, as Collins points out, allows us to extend Durkheim's analysis to the micro level:

to, for example, an act of simple, individual politeness. Whether in Riefenstahl's *Triumph of the Will* or in an ordinary handshake, we have the creation and intensification of a common emotional state.[26]

But equally crucial for Durkheim is the fact that sometimes the upshot, the distillate, of this process is partly conceptual. Thus, in the macro-scale cases that most interest him, participants are caused to believe they are in contact with a being superior to themselves, to whom they owe respect and on whom they depend, one that requires sacrifice and even servitude (*EF*, 208–209). In such cases the arousal is both emotional and conceptual, and results in representations that are strikingly religious in content.

I have portrayed, and tend to portray to my students, the causal story as more promising than the functional one. If it is, it is partly because its goal is more narrowly defined. In introducing 2.7, Durkheim says that we will have explained the origin of totemic religion when we have explained the origin of the totemic belief—and that is the immediate goal of the theory of effervescent assembly. Why do people hold these representations of a divine realm for which there is strikingly little evidence? Because at work is a causal mechanism and not a cognitive weighing of the evidence—because the participants are not sizing up evidence at all. Or, to draw on a different vocabulary, we are in the space not of reasons but rather of causes.

At this point a charge of inconsistency may arise, for at the outset Durkheim had said he would be using the participants' religious beliefs to explain their actions, their rites (*EF*, 34)—a strategy that seems to put belief squarely in the cognitive realm. The key, I think, is that while Durkheim does (in book 3) treat religious belief as providing the participant with reasons to engage in ritual practices, he does so only after (in book 2) he has given a causal, noncognitive account of the origin of those beliefs. Thus, the explanatory order of the full "theory of religion" takes a noncircular, linear form: first an appeal to group dynamics to explain the (causal, noncognitive) origin of religious belief, and then, *once the beliefs have been given content*, an appeal to them to explain the motivation for and nature of the associated rites.

Here the instructor may wish to address fundamental issues in the philosophy of social sciences, including causation and reductionism. I have been confidently referring to Durkheim's discovery of a "causal mechanism," but clearly it is not at all well worked out in the *Elementary Forms*.[27] The basic thought is that Durkheim has formulated a macro-level empirical generalization—that (Collins again) we have "a physiological propensity to respond to social interaction with contagious emotional arousal, to a degree that varies with the social density of activities." No doubt Durkheim's most detailed supporting instances, his descriptions of the Arunta festivals, are not especially fine-grained; other candidates, the French Revolution, the Crusades, and so on, are merely mentioned. Still, he is calling attention to a certain regularity, one heretofore unnoticed and, for the student of religion, of great importance. There is of course the question whether one takes such regularities, even suitably refined, to exhaust the metaphysical facts about causation, or whether— as did Durkheim himself—one takes them merely as clues to the discovery of natural laws "rooted in [the objects'] nature" (*EF*, 239). There is little consensus about this even today. But neither uncertainty about this point of metaphysics nor doubts about the coarseness of his descriptions are grounds to deny that Durkheim is offering us a causal explanation of the generation of religious belief.[28] The pursuit of regularity is, after all, the stuff of science, social or other.

To be sure, one expects that with additional inquiry our descriptions of these regularities will become more fine-grained, and will be supported by more fine-grained examples than those Durkheim offers in the *EF*. Though I cannot pursue the point here in any detail, I think this is in fact what we see when we look back over the near-century since the book's publication. I will mention two sorts of examples. First, in the area of statistical sociology, there is the ongoing debate over Guy Swanson's claim, first articulated in *The Birth of the Gods* (1968), to have established a correlation between the degree of abstraction of the local gods and the complexity of the local political and social hierarchy. Swanson claims that his survey of fifty societies supports his hypothesis that monotheism will exist where "there are three or more types of sovereign groups ranked in hierarchical order."[29] This claim and others like it have generated their own effervescence, with some authors claiming to have replicated Swanson's basic findings, others not.[30] I have found it very instructive for students—especially for those in theory and methods courses that otherwise emphasize more qualitative, methodological materials—to see the empirical issues debated in the literature. Second, a survey of recent work in evolutionary biology would quickly redeem Evans-Pritchard's forward-looking remark that "it is not a long jump from Durkheim's theory . . . to a biological explanation of religion"—Walter Burkert's *Creation of the Sacred: Tracks of Biology in Early Religions* and David Sloan Wilson's book *Darwin's Cathedral: Evolution, Religion, and the Nature of Society* are conspicuous items in a rapidly expanding literature.[31] We may think of these as efforts to expose the biological basis of the "physiological propensity" that Collins sees at work in effervescent assemblies. From Durkheim's point of view, this multidisciplinarity would be good and bad news: On the one hand—and this is Evans-Pritchard's point— it violates Durkheim's methodological stricture against explaining a sociological fact nonsociologically. On the other hand, once we have explicated the finer structure of one of his basic principles, we will have gained further confidence in its use.[32]

To sum up my discussion of this objection: Evans-Pritchard is right to allege an unredeemed circularity running through the explanatory heart of the

EF. It is fallout from Durkheim's functionalism, whereby effects are asked to reproduce their causes, we know not how. But sharing the stage is a linear, causal story, one that deserves a much better claim on our attention.

Finally, since I have distinguished so sharply between Durkheim's functional and causal stances, how did Durkheim understand their relationship? How should we?

Perhaps the most natural thought has the causal story supplying the mechanism missing from the functional one, thereby remedying its central flaw. But in fact this helps with neither of our questions. As to Durkheim: despite repeated readings (and teachings) of the *EF*, I find no hint of this move or, for that matter, any attention whatever to the larger issue of the relationship between the functional and causal arguments. While the two are, as I have argued, quite distinct, Durkheim moves silently between them.[33] Nor can the causal argument be made to shore up the functional one. For suppose we succeed in tracing the causal mechanism whereby religion-cum-social cohesion gets differentially reproduced (again, a process into which we now have no insight). Then we will have replaced a functional explanation with a causal one. The causal mechanism promises not to so much repair its functional host as to replace it.[34]

4. *Durkheim reduces belief in God to belief in society.* Thus D. Z. Phillips (1976): Durkheim holds that "religion is in fact the worship of society. This is an extremely odd claim and it is not at all easy to understand why anyone would want to make it."[35]

The first criticism alleged that Durkheim's theoretical stance in the *EF* distorts the participant's experience. In reply, I noted that Durkheim tries faithfully to convey the subjective "feel" of the experience—and to preserve it even as he later offers his sociological explanation of it. As Proudfoot says (replying specifically to Phillips), Durkheim eschews a descriptive reductionism even as he pursues an explanatory one. I now turn from the subjective to the objective— roughly, from how the experience *feels* to what aspect of the world it is *about*. Here Phillips and many others have accused Durkheim of making a puzzling mistake about the object of religious belief and practice.

Two of Durkheim's best known claims are relevant here, either of which could, at first glance, qualify as "odd." One claim is metaphysical and the other interpretive. First, he says that, as a matter of fact, "God and society are one and the same" (*EF*, 208). Then, so armed, he argues that "the faithful are not mistaken when they believe in the existence of a moral power to which they are subject and from which they receive what is best in themselves" (*EF*, 226– 27). How shall we understand these claims?

In discussing the third criticism, I emphasized Durkheim's discovery of a causal mechanism whose output is, in the cases that interest him, both affective and conceptual. In assessing the fourth criticism, the conceptual element takes center stage. I have said that what mainly interests Durkheim is the extent to which the local *concept* of divinity matches up with the *actual* nature of the local community. At this point, in turning from the subjective to the objective, Durkheim turns from reliance on others' ethnography and engages in the evidential balancing act that characterizes real-world linguistic interpretation.

How well, then, do the two match up? Here I have found it useful to write out on the board a list of relevant properties culled from the *EF* (208–209; see also 421):

"a being that man conceives of as superior to himself"
"on whom he believe he depends"
one that imposes "certain ways of acting" on "the faithful"
"fosters a sense of perpetual dependence"
"pursues its own ends by working through us"
"categorically demands our cooperation"
"requires us to make ourselves its servants"
"subjects us to restraints, privations, and sacrifices"
"is the object of genuine respect"

I then ask the class whether these properties are more accurately applied to "the divine" or to "society" (Durkheim's terms). My experience is that most classes divide up more or less evenly, a result that would, I take it, warm Durkheim's heart.

Many students will want to pursue the tightness of fit between various conceptions of God and society. Those with some background in what we think of as the monotheistic traditions, especially those with some philosophy or theology, may see the more metaphysical attributes and doctrines as obstacles—eternity, infinity, perfection, omnipotence, omniscience, *creatio ex nihilo*, and the like. This in turn allows the instructor to remind the class that the God of medieval and early modern Western philosophy is not the God of sacred scripture, whether Hebrew, Christian, or Muslim. On this point it is hard to improve on Durkheim himself: "A philosophical and abstract conception that has never been realized as such in any historical religion; it is without interest for the science of religions" (*EF*, 80). A better question is whether a less metaphysically demanding doctrine of God can be plausibly superimposed over a Durkheimian conception of community. I have suggested elsewhere that the Jewish conception of Shekhinah, the Christian conception of the salvific community, and the Muslim notion of Ummah[36] might all be candidates—but whether to pursue such issues will obviously depend on the goals of the course and the interests of the instructor.

Comparing concepts in this way can be a useful exercise. It is certainly Durkheimian in spirit. But by focusing too narrowly on the conceptual point, one invites the conclusion that Durkheim intends it to be self-supporting. Thus, Malcolm Hamilton has recently complained that "even if the parallel between the character of society and the divine were as close as Durkheim makes it out to be . . . it does not follow that it is society that *is* the source of religious conceptions or the object of religious concern."[37] Agreed. But Durkheim does not argue this way. Rather, he makes the conceptual claim—the closeness of the two concepts—work in tandem with the causal mechanism discussed in the previous section.

This point comes out clearly in his treatment of the Australian material. The situation Durkheim has before his armchair is roughly this. We have people believing the claims just listed and apparently believing them about an object, the totem, which answers to none of them (which makes none of them true). This much Durkheim accepts from what he reads. At the same time, he notices something extraordinary: that these claims are reliably occasioned (prompted) by contact with an aspect of the world to which they *do* correspond and which *does* make them true: society. It is only in this context—the confluence of the conceptual *and* the causal—that the issues raised by the fourth criticism are fully and fairly considered.[38]

Notice that Durkheim does not use the causal element to supply the conceptual one. But, equally, notice that this stratagem is an indispensable part of our everyday, interpretive tool kit, domestic or foreign. Suppose I have no idea what my friend means when he talks about "cilantro." I may begin to remedy my ignorance just by noticing that cilantro-talk tends to come up while he is chopping the leafy green vegetable I had taken to be parsley. Again, if I am wondering how to understand someone's "Il pleu," and I notice that she regularly makes these sounds when it is raining close by, I may try out the interpretation "It is raining." Had Durkheim taken this route, he would have interpreted the participant's utterances as about the thing that reliably prompts them, as *about* society. We might want to call *that* an "extremely odd claim," though we would know perfectly well why Durkheim had made it. We would recognize that he had made a kind of mistake to which presumably all of us finite interpreters are liable—that of putting too much weight on what turns out to be the wrong pairing of word and object.

Why are we so sure about "wrong"? Because all parties, including the real Durkheim, are assuming, apparently with good reason, that the participant intends to be speaking and believing about the totem and not about society, and thinks he or she is experiencing the totem and not society. This confidence in turn motivates Durkheim to hold meaning, belief, and experience steady (to take the ethnographers at their word) and so to take them as the things to be explained rather than interpreted. Thus, Durkheim asks: Why do the Arunta say and believe these interestingly false things about this plant or animal, and why do they think *it* conveys the experience they are having? Recall that my reply to the first criticism depended on this strategy of "holding steady." Durkheim is not trying to reinterpret the Arunta's words or the content of their beliefs or experience—even though he now discovers that they assert and believe truths about the aspect of the world that reliably prompts these very assertions and beliefs. Having rightly resisted the temptation to use it as a guide to reinterpret, what, now, shall we make of this extraordinary discovery?

We might well be ambivalent. We do not want to put words in anyone's mouth (with Phillips, we do not want to say they are "worshipping society"), but we do want our discovery to make a difference in how we understand what is being said and believed. (With an eye toward the first criticism, we must not add "and felt" to this list.)

I read the *EF* as reflecting just this ambivalence. It finds two expressions in the text. First, a theory of totemism—one that tries to show how and why representations of society get transferred to an object that bears no resemblance to it.[39] Second, an oscillation between finding the participant in error and correct. My way of making sense of the second is to see Durkheim as sometimes holding meaning and belief steady (as intended by the participants—as intended about the totem) and at other times focusing on the literal truth of the utterances and beliefs (as in fact true of society). In the former mood he finds the participants in error; to think that the totem has the powers claimed for it is an "illusion" (*EF*, 351). In the latter mood, "the faithful are not mistaken" (*EF*, 226)—their beliefs and utterances are literally true when and where they are caused to be held and made. This, I think, is also the way to take Durkheim's puzzling talk of religion as "true, practically" or "symbolically." Practical, symbolic truth results when descriptions of the divine and the nature of society overlap substantially but not fully. In such cases, the former "express *correctly enough* the manner in which [the latter] affect us" (*EF*, 77, italics added). Ambivalence, yes—but never do we find Durkheim attempting to use his remarkable discovery as a way of fixing meaning and belief.

For purposes of thinking through the criticism as applied to Durkheim's treatment of Australian totemism in the *EF*, this strikes me as sufficient. But the objection speaks of "religion" more generally, and of course in most cases it is essential to get one's students to think about cases that do not involve totemism and, in particular, about cases in which the conceptual gap between society and divinity is narrower, for such cases sometimes invite a very different analysis. Take, for example, the British classicist Jane Harrison, who, having recently read Durkheim, comments as follows on the *Iliad*.

We no longer wonder why in Homer Themis convenes the assembly. She is no herald like Hermes, no messenger like Iris, she is the very spirit of the assembly incarnate. Themis and the actual concrete Agora are barely distinguishable. Patroklos comes running to the ships of godlike Odysseus, [and asks]
"Where were their agora and themis?"

Here the social fact is trembling on the very verge of godhead. She is the force that brings and binds men together, she is the "herd instinct," the collective conscience, the social sanction.[40]

Once again we are in the position of noticing that a speaker says something true about the thing that prompts his utterance—the question is whether Homer or Patroklos intend it to be about Themis the Titan or about "the very spirit of the assembly."

The difference between the two cases is the fact that, whereas Themis and the spirit of the assembly are "barely distinguishable," the Arunta's totem diverges from it in nearly all respects. And whereas the Arunta were unaware of the causal history of their beliefs and practices, Homer or Patroklos are "on the very verge" of self-understanding. Perhaps, then, we should take the objection head-on, and say that Patroklos's utterance is about the spirit of the assembly, that he is "worshipping society"? Surely neither the slight conceptual gap nor the incremental lack of self-understanding should stop us—we do not ask for a perfect fit in ordinary cases, why should we in this one? That is, we often tolerate a measure of each of these if an otherwise satisfying interpretation is on offer.[41]

The more general point is that, because she is reassessing what Homer or Patroklos means by his words, Harrison is engaged, as Durkheim is not, in the everyday work of linguistic interpretation, using stratagems familiar to us all—in this case, matching (reports of) vocalizations with causes in the hope that reference will emerge—sifting, balancing evidence, and finding more or less conceptual clarity about that very cause. We may agree that she has found a lot—but, again, has she found enough to license interpreting Patroklos's utterance as about the spirit of the assembly?

The point is made if the difficulty of the question is apparent. Probably the thing to say is that nothing much turns on the answer. In fact, in an article published six years before the *EF*, Durkheim makes just this point. He says he is "indifferent" to the choice between God and society.[42] I have always been attracted to this remark; it is what he ought to say. The context makes clear that he is imagining a case like Harrison's, one in which the two candidates in view answer to nearly the same description. What difference could it make for the purposes of interpretation? After all, our underlying duty is to make the best sense we can of the speaker at hand. If we come out with him "worshipping society," then so be it.

5. *The argument of the EF is based on bad ethnographic data.* Thus Arnold van Gennep (1913): "In ten years the whole of [Durkheim's] analysis of the Australian material will be completely rejected, as will the generalizations based on the most unsound group of ethnographic facts I have come across." Related criticisms have been

made by many others, including Evans-Pritchard, A. A. Goldenweiser, Lukes, and W. H. Stanner.[43]

The main thing is to separate out the various charges and predictions. I have no wish to defend the underlying ethnography—though it is noteworthy that two recent reappraisals of Spenser and Gillen's work are strikingly appreciative.[44] As to Durkheim's handling of this material, we have already recognized the presence of theoretical bias and descriptive error. But even if his treatment of Australian totemism should be "completely rejected," surely the interest in the book on the part of the student of religion does not depend on it.

The question is in what sense the theory of effervescent assembly is "based" on the Australian ethnography? If by this we mean the theory as presented in the *EF*, then no doubt it stands or falls with the Australian material. To separate them would require, as Stanner says, "an act of violence."[45] Following Collins, I have portrayed that theory as resting on an empirical generalization that pegs emotional and conceptual arousal to the degree of social density. If that generalization gets any empirical support in the *EF*, it is from the Australian data. But in putting forward this generalization, Durkheim was confident that a wide variety of supporting evidence would be forthcoming from other researchers looking at similar cultural phenomena from around the world. In particular, I am with Hans-Peter Mueller, when he remarks that "there is no doubt that Durkheim had the understanding of modern society in mind when he formulated his theory of archaic religion" and continues, "thus, the decisive critiques of Goldenweiser, Lukes and Stanner are in some sense irrelevant to Durkheim's main project."[46] They are irrelevant in the precise sense that they leave untouched the question of the extent to which the empirical generalization at the heart of the *EF* has been or will be supported.

As van Gennep's comment illustrates, the debate over the ethnographic foundations of the *EF* began immediately on its publication. Over this issue, probably Durkheim's most influential defender has been Talcott Parsons. In *The Structure of Social Action* (1937), Parsons enlists Durkheim in the cause of his own emerging functionalism—indeed, he was influential in erecting what at the outset I called the "standard picture" of Durkheim's theory of religion. But on this issue, the extent to which Durkheim is hostage to his Australian "facts," Parsons points us in the right direction: It is not

> that facts do not matter in general or that facts are unimportant. . . .
> It is rather that the facts which are important to this discussion are
> not among those which are controversial. Only certain very broad
> contentious facts are involved. The really crucial ones are . . . (1) that
> there is a basic distinction of attitude toward the classes of things
> which Durkheim designates as "sacred" and as "profane" and (2)
> that sacred things have a symbolic significance.[47]

I think Parsons gets the first bit exactly right but then does not go deep enough for the "very broad contentious facts." Objects become sacred and profane as the result of a deeper mechanism, one that tags certain objects with an emotional and conceptual "surplus." Thus, I would say that the "really crucial" and "very broad contentious" claim on which Durkheim's project depends is that emotional and conceptual arousal is tied to the degree of social density.

So is it? Our answer will partly depend on how we assess the research legacy of the *EF*, a task that is of course beyond the scope of this essay. Jeffrey Alexander has argued persuasively that, at least in the Anglophone world, the key development was, ironically, dissatisfaction with Parsons's functionalist reading of the book. This dissatisfaction made possible Robert Bellah's concept of civil religion and its subsequent exploitation in religious studies by Martin Marty, John F. Wilson, and many others.[48] I have already mentioned Goffman's work at the micro level—the emotional solidarity created by bits of conversation, acts of politeness, and the like. At the macro level, one might point to Collins's work on American election campaigns, Alexander on Watergate, Lynn Hunt on the French Revolution, and Eric Rothenbuhler on mass labor strikes, not to mention the work of many of the authors in this book.

I have shown that Durkheim himself entertained a range of cases. On the nonconceptual end of the spectrum are instances of effervescent assembly that express nothing more than "pleasure" and the need for "play" (*EF*, 385). No need to "go beneath" the surface, no need for a fancy theory of symbolism, totemic or other. In these cases the question of truth, symbolic or other, does not arise because nothing is being asserted, nothing believed (see note 38 herein). Arranged in the middle of the spectrum are cases in which the causal mechanism is generating emotional solidarity and, now, conceptual output as well, but where the conceptual element takes a detour—as, for example, the one described in Durkheim's theory of totemism. These middle cases, the ones that occupy Durkheim for most of the *EF*, are ones in which group activity prompts utterances and beliefs most of which are literally false as applied to the object of worship but some of which are literally true of society. And, as I have shown, the conceptual point itself admits of degrees: as "some" shades into "most," we are on the way to "symbolic" or "practical" truth. Finally, anchoring the other extreme are cases, if there are any, in which we may want to say that the participants "are not deluded"—that their religious beliefs are true, full stop. These would be cases in which the causal mechanism is accompanied by a large measure of conceptual clarity.

If, indeed, there are any. Self-applied, Durkheim's mature theory of religion seems to have issued in his "indifference" as between the divine and society. But we may wonder how many religious persons, having once achieved Durkheimian clarity, would react with his equanimity, let alone with Harrison's enthusiasm. Ironically, these reactions were probably only possible for them because each lacked an affiliation with a recognizable religious community! Durkheim's identification of god and society may well strike the occupant of an unaffiliated armchair as of a piece with the discovery that the morning star is the evening star or that heat is mean molecular motion. Startling, perhaps, and suggestive of new research programs—but not requiring the large-scale revision of belief and practice that one would expect to find elsewhere.

It appears, then, that Durkheim leaves us with a sharp distinction between the study of religion and religious thought and practice. But our readiness to draw this conclusion depends, of course, on what we take the point of religious thought and practices to be. In a series of recent articles, Proudfoot has been emphasizing *inquiry into causes* as an enterprise common to both religious studies and to religious inquiry:

> Religious practices in many traditions are intended to clear the mind of illusion and deceit, and to prepare conditions for genuine awareness, including awareness of desires and fears that are difficult to acknowledge. Such practices can be used to support illusion and to avoid acknowledgment, but they can also be instruments for increasing self-awareness.

And

> Religious belief and commitment should be compatible with an understanding of the causes and the effects of that belief and that commitment. Continuing inquiry into those causes and effects is not something external to religion, but should be a central concern of religious inquiry itself. There should be no sharp separation between religious inquiry and the study of religion.[49]

Proudfoot has James and Nietzsche in view, but I take it that Durkheim's work on the causal mechanism underlying religious representation places him squarely in this conversation. Paoletti suggests that Durkheim's slogan in 2.7 might be "Less effervescence and more awareness"[50]—but this undersells the underlying connection between social density and religious representation. At the heart of the *EF* is a story about a nonrational, causal mechanism that triggers religious affective and cognitive output; true, Durkheim expected the telling of this story in turn to trigger a noncausal, rational process by which persons are led to revise their beliefs, attitudes, and practices in the light of what the causal story has revealed. But self-awareness is not the enemy of effervescence, nor, for social animals, could it be.

NOTES

My thanks to Dan Varisco for detailed comments on this essay. Tony Dardis, Warren Frisina, Hans Penner, and Kevin Reinhart all prompted improvements, as did a faculty colloquium at Hofstra University.

1. For more complete coverage, see Steven Lukes, *Emile Durkheim, His Life and Work: A Historical and Critical Study* (New York: Penguin, 1973), 497–529, and William Pickering, *Durkheim's Sociology of Religion* (Boston: RKP, 1984).

2. The extent of my debt to Collins's recent work will be clear throughout, but I am glad to record it at the outset; see, especially, "The Durkheimian Tradition in Conflict Sociology," in *Durkheimian Sociology: Cultural Studies*, edited by Jeffrey C. Alexander (New York: Cambridge University Press, 1988), 107–128, and "Stark and Bainbridge, Durkheim and Weber: Theoretical Comparisons," in *Rational Choice Theory and Religion: Summary and Assessment*, edited by Lawrence A. Young (New York: Routledge, 1997), 161–180.

3. One measure of the strength of the standard picture is the extent to which it holds sway across a spectrum of critics who otherwise have little in common. It is, for example, common to Catherine Bell, *Ritual: Perspectives and Dimensions* (New York: Oxford University Press, 1997), 23; Stewart Guthrie, *Faces in the Clouds: A New Theory of Religion* (New York: Oxford University Press, 1993), 17; Bruce Lincoln, "Conflict," in *Critical Terms for Religious Studies*, edited by Mark C. Taylor (Chicago: University of Chicago Press), 55; Robert A. Nisbet, *The Sociological Tradition* (New York: Basic Books, 1966), 226; Daniel L. Pals, *Seven Theories of Religion* (New York: Oxford University Press, 1996), 114.

4. Because of lack of space, I have not treated criticisms of Durkheim's theory of religion that are so general as to apply to many other sociological approaches. For example, I pass over the common complaint that the theory represents a sociological reduction of the individual, that, as A. A. Goldenweiser puts it, it "permits individual factors to become altogether obscured"; "Emile Durkheim—*Les Formes élémentaires de la vie religieuse: Le système totémique en Australie. 1912*," *American Anthropologist* 17 (1915): 719–735, reprinted in Durkheim, *Durkheim on Religion: A Selection of Readings with Bibliographies and Introductory Remarks*, ed. W. S. F. Pickering, trans. Jacqueline Redding (Atlanta, Ga.: Scholars Press, 1994), 219. And I have not commented on Durkheim's fundamental claim that society exists, that it has properties that its constituent parts (persons) do not have when taken as a mere collection of individuals. This is the debate over methodological holism. While any Durkheimian view of religion will of course be holistic, the defense of holism does not draw on issues in the study of religion. I am also ignoring criticisms of scope—for example, the Marxist complaint that a Durkheimian approach fails to expose class oppression, and Stark and Bainbridge's claim that it fails to take into account the element of rational choice.

5. Gaston Richard, "Dogmatic Atheism in the Sociology of Knowledge," in *Durkheim on Religion*, 267.

6. Wayne Proudfoot, *Religious Experience* (Berkeley: University of California Press, 1985), 200–201.

7. Unless otherwise noted, references will be to Emile Durkheim, *Elementary Forms of Religious Life* (New York: Free Press, 1995). Baldwin Spencer and Francis James Gillen, *The Native Tribes of Central Australia* (London: MacMillan, 1899), and *The Northern Tribes of Central Australia* (1904); Alfred Howitt, *Native Tribes of South-East Australia* (New York: MacMillan, 1904).

8. Not *fully* authoritative, because there are apparently limits to how far wrong we can go about what prompts our utterances, if those utterances are to be interpretable (if they are to be utterances and not mere sounds); see Donald Davidson, "First Person Authority," and "Knowing One's Own Mind," in *Subjective, Intersubjective, Objective* (New York: Oxford, 2001).

9. William Paden, "Before 'The Sacred' Became Theological: Rereading the Durkheimian Legacy," in *Religion and Reductionism: Essays on Eliade, Segal, and the Challenge of the Social Sciences for the Study of Religion*, edited by Thomas A. Idinopolis and Edward A. Yonan (New York: Brill, 1994), 200; next reference, 207.

10. Giovanni Paoletti, "The Cult of Images: Reading Chapter VII, Book II, of *The Elementary Forms*," in *On Durkheim's Elementary Forms of Religious Life*, edited by N. J. Allen, W. S. F. Pickering, and W. Watts Miller (New York: Routledge, 1998), 79.

11. Thus, he complains that Spenser and Gillen mar their "translation" with "an unwarranted interpretation" (*EF*, 199 n. 35). In this instance, Durkheim is taking as authoritative Carl Strehlow, *Die Arand-und Loritja-Stämme in Zantral Australien*, vol. 2 (Frankfurt: Baer, 1907), 76 n. See *EF*, 107 n. 40, for a similar "correction" of Howitt. For documentation of Durkheim's selective emphasis, see Howard Morphy, "Spenser and Gillen in Durkheim: The Theoretical Construction of Ethnography," in Allen, Pickering, and Miller, *On Durkheim's Elementary Forms of Religious Life*, 13–28; for Durkheim the smuggler, see Jonathan Z. Smith, "Manna, Mana Everywhere and /./././," in *Radical Interpretation in Religion*, edited by Nancy K. Frankenberry (New York: Oxford, 2002), 202.

12. Lukes, *Durkheim*, 477–478.

13. Pals, *Seven Theories of Religion*, 115. For discussion, see William Pickering, *Durkheim's Sociology of Religion* (Boston: RKP, 1984), 380–381.

14. "A religion is unified system of beliefs and practices relative to sacred things, that is to say, things set apart and forbidden—beliefs and practices that unite into one single moral community called a Church, all those who adhere to them" (*EF*, 44).

15. Collins, "Durkheimian Tradition in Conflict Sociology," 111.

16. Evans-Pritchard, *Theories of Primitive Religion* (New York: Oxford, 1965), 68.

17. According to Jon Elster, this fallacy plagues "virtually all" functionalist explanations in sociology; *Ulysses and the Sirens: Studies in Rationality and Irrationality*, rev. ed. (New York: Cambridge University Press, 1984), 28.

18. Michael Root, *Philosophy of Social Science: The Methods, Ideals, and Politics of Social Inquiry* (New York: Blackwell, 1993), 85.

19. Though he does not mention Durkheim in particular, Penner argues that functional explanations in the study of religion founder over their inability to provide a causal feedback loop; "What's Wrong with Functional Explanations?" in *Language, Truth and Religious Belief: Studies in Twentieth-Century Theory and Method in Religion*, edited by Nancy K. Frankenberry and Hans H. Penner (Atlanta, Ga.: Scholars Press, 1999), 254. I have benefited here from his discussion.

20. I am tentative here and in the previous paragraph in deference to what are still unsettled issues in the literature. Two items in particular. First, Elster describes a case in which economists seem to have successfully explained profit-maximizing behavior as a result of the "natural selection" of firms by the market (*Ulysses and the Sirens*, 31). The analogy to religion strikes me as weak but not unrecognizable. Second, G. A. Cohen and others have argued that, as Cohen puts it, "it is sometimes rational to have confidence in a functional explanation in advance of having a good idea of what the mechanism may be"; "Functional Explanation: Reply to Elster," *Political Studies* 28, 1 (1982): 131. For example, suppose we have ruled out, or nearly ruled out, possible competitors—then our functional explanation begins to look like an argu-

ment to the best explanation, an argument-type whose credentials in the history of science and elsewhere are widely respected. But Cohen's appeal to "good idea" in the context seems clearly question-begging.

21. Root, *Philosophy of Social Science*, 82.

22. Allen, "Effervescence and the Origin of Human Society," 157.

23. Collins, "Durkheimian Tradition in Conflict Sociology," 111.

24. Fields, "Individuality and the Intellectuals: An Imaginary Conversation between W. E. B. Du Bois and Emile Durkheim," *Theory and Society* 31 (2002): 435–462.

25. Collins, "Stark and Bainbridge, Durkheim and Weber," 167.

26. For the extension to the micro level, Collins credits Erving Goffman, *Interaction Ritual* (New York: Doubleday, 1967), and *The Presentation of the Self in Everyday Life* (New York: Doubleday, 1959); see Collins, "Durkheimian Tradition in Conflict Sociology," 108, and "Stark and Bainbridge, Durkheim and Weber," 163.

27. For discussion of the development of Durkheim's views on effervescent assembly, see Pickering, *Durkheim's Sociology of Religion*, chaps. 21, 22; in particular, for Durkheim's large and largely unacknowledged debt to his nephew Marcel Mauss, see N. J. Allen, "Effervescence and the Origin of Human Society," in Allen, Pickering, and Miller, *On Durkheim's Elementary Forms*, 157, and Evans-Pritchard, *Theories of Primitive Religion*, 69.

28. Gaston Richard seems to have inaugurated a line of criticism that finds Durkheim arguing on extraempirical grounds: "*A priori*, to some extent, Durkheim deduced from his idea of solidarity that religious ideas are the products of the social environment" ("Dogmatic Atheism in the Sociology of Religion," 240). However it stands elsewhere in Durkheim's authorship, the *EF*'s theory of collective effervescence clearly depends on an empirical generalization.

29. Swanson, *The Birth of the Gods: The Origin of Primitive Beliefs* (Ann Arbor: University of Michigan Press, 1968), 64–65.

30. See Peter Peregrine, *The Birth of the Gods* Revisited: A Partial Replication of Guy Swanson's (1960) Cross-Cultural Study of Religion," *Cross-Cultural Research* 30, 1 (February 1996): 84–112.

31. Evans-Pritchard, *Theories of Primitive Religion*, 68. Burkert, *Creation of the Sacred: Tracks of Biology in Early Religions* (Cambridge, Mass.: Harvard University Press, 1996); Wilson, *Darwin's Cathedral: Evolution, Religion, and the Nature of Society* (Chicago: University of Chicago Press, 2002). It is of course not obvious that either Burkert or Wilson is wise, or even entitled to count Durkheim as a friend. Daniel Dennett, for one, thinks Burkert ought to have turned to Dawkins, not Durkheim; "The Evolution of Religious Memes: Who—or What—Benefits," *Method and Theory in the Study of Religion* 10, 1 (1998): 120.

32. In *Genetics and Reductionism* (New York: Cambridge University Press, 1998), Sahotra Sarkar makes the point that this consideration is sometimes made to serve in arguments against eliminative reductionism—reduction with replacement (61).

33. Durkheim's failure to mark this distinction in the *EF* is all the more puzzling in that he had made it so explicitly seventeen years earlier in the *Rules of Sociological Method*: "The determination of function is . . . necessary for the complete explanation of the phenomena. . . . To explain a social fact it is not enough to show the cause on which it depends; we must also, at least in most cases, show its function in the estab-

lishment of social order"; trans. W. D. Halls (New York: Free Press, 1982), 97. Durkheim is apparently suggesting that the functional somehow completes the causal. Most contemporary writers reverse this order, holding that functional "explanations" are provisional, heuristic devices, sometimes useful in the eventual identification of underlying causal mechanisms. For this view, see Robert N. McCauley and E. Thomas Lawson, "Functionalism Reconsidered," *History of Religions* 23 (1984): 380. For the claim that Durkheim fails to make this distinction in his wider corpus, see Warren Schmaus, "Explanation and Essence in *The Rules of Sociological Method* and *The Division of Labor in Society*," *Sociological Perspectives* 38, 1 (1995), 120–122; for the same claim as confined to the *EF*, see William Ramp, "Effervescence, Differentiation and Representation in *The Elementary Forms*," in Allen, Pickering, and Miller, *On Durkheim's Elementary Forms*, 145. Pickering is more charitable: "Durkheim indeed saw, as simplistic functionalists in later generations failed to realize, that a nonfunctional factor has to be introduced" (*Durkheim's Sociology of Religion*, 381).

34. Writing in this spirit, Root comments that "functional explanations seem to be incomplete in sociology and unnecessary in biology," *Philosophy of Social Science*, 86.

35. D. Z. Phillips, *Religion without Explanation* (Oxford: Blackwell, 1976), 90.

36. Godlove, "Interpretation, Reductionism and Belief in God," *Journal of Religion* 69, 2 (1989): 196.

37. Malcolm B. Hamilton, *The Sociology of Religion: Theoretical and Comparative Perspectives* (New York: Routledge, 1995), 104.

38. Though they come together in this context, I have found that, in the classroom, it is important to keep the causal and conceptual claims separated, as I have in this essay. Useful devices in this regard are primatological accounts of so-called chimp carnivals. Thus, Vernon Reynolds describes the result of a meeting between two groups of chimpanzees: "All of them began the wildest screaming and hooting, swinging about, running along branches at top speed, leaping down branch by branch to the ground, climbing up again, shaking branches wildly, and occasionally coming up close to each other to meet briefly and part again, stamping on branches and slapping them, and behind all this confusion a steady undercurrent of drumming resounded" *Budongo: An African Forest and Its Chimpanzees* (New York: Garden City Press, 1965), 158. Elsewhere Reynolds compares these events to the carnivals of hunter-gatherers; *The Apes, the Gorilla, Chimpanzee, Orangutan and Gibbon: Their History and Their World* (London: Dutton, 1967), 271. With Reynolds's work in mind, Nick Allen draws the Durkheimian conclusion: "one need not regard [effervescent assemblies] as a distinctively human innovation" ("Effervescence and the Origins of Human Society," 158). Strategically, chimp carnivals have the advantage of ruling concepts out from the start—particularly effective with those students who want to think of religion in abstract philosophical or theological terms. This ploy is thoroughly Durkheimian, for he is quite aware that not all effervescent assemblies among *homo sapiens* involves concept-mongering.

39. For discussion, see Paoletti, "Cult of Images." Officially, 2.7 aims at a theory of totemism, though it receives explicit treatment only in the second half of 7.3 and all of 7.5. Unfortunately, Pickering and Redding omit these sections from *Durkheim on Religion*, an otherwise invaluable collection of primary and secondary sources.

They include everything else from 2.7, including the central passages having to do with collective effervescence.

40. Jane Ellen Harrison, *Themis: A Study of the Social Origins of Greek Religion* (New York: Meridian Books, 1912), 484–485 (quoting *Iliad*, chap. 11). Harrison cites three essays in which Durkheim is developing the positions that eventually surface in the *EF*: "Représentations Individuelles et Représentations Collectives" (1898), "De la Définition des Phénomènes Religieux" (1899), and "Sociologie Religieuse et Théorie de la Connaissance" (1909).

41. As Hilary Putnam notes, "often" understates the case: "All interpretation depends on charity, because we always have to discount at least *some* differences in belief when we interpret"; *Representation and Reality* (Cambridge, Mass.: MIT Press, 1989), 13.

42. "La Détermination du fait moral" (1906), cited by W. E. H. Stanner, "Reflections on Durkheim and Aboriginal Religion," in *Durkheim on Religion*, 287.

43. A. van Gennep, "Review of *Les Formes élémentaires de la vie religieuse*, by E. Durkheim," in *Durkheim on Religion*, 206; see also Gaston Richard, "Dogmatic Atheism," 257; Evans-Pritchard, *Theories of Primitive Religion*, 67; A. A. Goldenweiser, review of *Les Formes élémentaires*, by Emile Durkheim, in *Durkheim on Religion*, 214; Lukes, *Durkheim*, 477; Stanner, "Reflections on Durkheim and Aboriginal Religion," 280.

44. "Gillen was able to work in the Aranda language and recent linguistic research has tended to confirm the accuracy of his and Spencer's translations. They were meticulous in cross-checking their data and in seeking clarification of things that they failed to understand. They pioneered the use of film, photography and sound recording in the field, and used these to further document ritual performances that they had observed. Their ethnography has stood the test of time and continues to be cited by current researchers to an almost unparalleled extent"; Morphy, "Spencer and Gillen in Durkheim," in Allen, Pickering, and Miller, *Durkheim's Elementary Forms*, 18. See also L. R. Hiatt, *Arguments about Aborigines: Australia and the Evolution of Social Anthropology* (New York: Cambridge University Press, 1996).

45. Stanner, "Reflections on Durkheim and Aboriginal Religion," 280.

46. Hans-Peter Mueller, "Social Structure and Civil Religion: Legitimation Crisis in a Later Durkheimian Perspective," in Alexander, *Durkheimian Sociology*, 143, 151.

47. Talcott Parsons, *The Structure of Social Action*, vol. 1 (New York: Free Press, 1937), 410 n. 1.

48. Alexander, introduction to *Durkheimian Sociology*, 7. See also Alexander, introduction, for references to Bellah, Marty, and Wilson, and Alexander, *Durkheimian Sociology*, for the essays by Collins, Hunt, and Rothenbuhler.

49. Wayne Proudfoot, "William James on an Unseen Order," *Harvard Theological Review* 93, 1 (January 2000): 65–66. See also "Religious Belief and Naturalism," in Frankenberry, *Radical Interpretation in Religion*, 78–92.

50. Paoletti, "Cult of Images," 90.

REFERENCES

Alexander, Jeffrey C., ed. 1988. *Durkheimian Sociology: Cultural Studies*. New York: Cambridge University Press.

Allen, N. J., W. S. F. Pickering, and W. Watts Miller, eds. 1998. *On Durkheim's Elementary Forms of Religious Life*. New York: Routledge.

Bell, Catherine. 1997. *Ritual: Perspectives and Dimensions*. New York: Oxford University Press.

Cohen, G. A. 1982. "Functional Explanation: Reply to Elster." *Political Studies* 28, 1: 129–135.

Davidson, Donald. 2001. "First Person Authority." In *Subjective, Intersubjective, Objective*. New York: Oxford University Press.

———. 2001. "Knowing One's Own Mind." In *Subjective, Intersubjective, Objective*. New York: Oxford University Press.

Dennett, Daniel. 1998. "The Evolution of Religious Memes: Who—or What—Benefits," *Method and Theory in the Study of Religion* 10, 1: 115–128.

Durkheim, Emile. 1994. *Durkheim on Religion: A Selection of Readings with Bibliographies and Introductory Remarks*. Edited by William Pickering. Atlanta, Ga.: Scholars Press.

———. 1995. *Elementary Forms of Religious Life*. Translated by Karen E. Fields. New York: Free Press.

———. 1982. *Rules of Sociological Method*. Translated by W. D. Halls. New York: Free Press.

Elster, Jon. 1984. *Ulysses and the Sirens: Studies in Rationality and Irrationality*. Rev. ed. New York: Cambridge University Press.

Evans-Pritchard, E. E. 1965. *Theories of Primitive Religion*. New York: Oxford University Press.

Fields, Karen. 2002. "Individuality and the Intellectuals: An Imaginary Conversation between W.E.B. Du Bois and Emile Durkheim." *Theory and Society* 31: 435–462.

Frankenberry, Nancy K., and Hans H. Penner, eds. 1999. *Language, Truth and Religious Belief: Studies in Twentieth-Century Theory and Method in Religion*. Atlanta, Ga.: Scholars Press.

Frankenberry, Nancy K., ed. 2002. *Radical Interpretation in Religion*. New York: Oxford University Press.

Godlove, Terry F., Jr. 1989. "Interpretation, Reductionism and Belief in God." *Journal of Religion* 69, 2: 184–198.

Guthrie, Stewart. 1993. *Faces in the Clouds: A New Theory of Religion*. New York: Oxford University Press.

Hamilton, Malcom B. 1995. *The Sociology of Religion: Theoretical and Comparative Perspectives*. New York: Routledge.

Harrison, Jane Ellen. 1912. *Themis: A Study of the Social Origins of Greek Religion*. New York: Meridian Books.

Hiatt, L. R. 1996. *Arguments about Aborigines: Australia and the Evolution of Social Anthropology*. New York: Cambridge University Press.

Idinopolis, Thomas A., and Edward A. Yonan, eds. 1994. *Religion and Reductionism: Essays on Eliade, Segal, and the Challenge of the Social Sciences for the Study of Religion*. New York: Brill.

Lincoln, Bruce. 1998. "Conflict." In *Critical Terms for Religious Studies*, edited by Mark C. Taylor. Chicago: University of Chicago Press.

Lukes, Steven. 1973. *Emile Durkheim, His Life and Work: A Historical and Critical Study.* New York: Penguin Books.

McCauley, Robert N., and E. Thomas Lawson. 1984. "Functionalism Reconsidered." *History of Religions* 23: 372–381.

Nisbet, Robert A. 1966. *The Sociological Tradition.* New York: Basic Books.

Pals, Daniel L. 1996. *Seven Theories of Religion.* New York: Oxford University Press.

Parsons, Talcott. 1937. *The Structure of Social Action.* Vol. 1. New York: Free Press.

Peregrine, Peter. 1996. "*The Birth of the Gods* Revisited: A Partial Replication of Guy Swanson's (1960) Cross-Cultural Study of Religion." *Cross-Cultural Research* 30, 1: 84–112.

Phillips, D. Z. 1976. *Religion without Explanation.* Oxford: Blackwell.

Pickering, William. 1984. *Durkheim's Sociology of Religion.* London: Routledge and Kegan Paul.

Proudfoot, Wayne. 1985. *Religious Experience.* Berkeley: University of California Press.

Proudfoot, Wayne. 2000. "William James on an Unseen Order." *Harvard Theological Review* 93, 1: 65–66.

Putnam, Hilary. 1989. *Representation and Reality.* Cambridge, Mass.: MIT Press.

Reynolds, Vernon. 1967. *The Apes, the Gorilla, Chimpanzee, Orangutan and Gibbon: Their History and Their World.* London: Dutton.

———. *Budongo: An African Forest and Its Chimpanzees.* New York: Garden City Press, 1965.

Root, Michael. 1993. *Philosophy of Social Science: The Methods, Ideals, and Politics of Social Inquiry.* New York: Blackwell.

Sarkar, Sahotra. 1998. *Genetics and Reductionism.* New York: Cambridge University Press.

Schmaus, Warren. 1995. "Explanation and Essence in *The Rules of Sociological Method* and *The Division of Labor in Society.*" *Sociological Perspectives* 38, 1: 57–75.

Strehlow, Carl. 1907. *Die Arand-und Loritja-Stämme in Zantral Australien.* Vol. 2. Frankfurt: Baer.

Swanson, Guy. 1968. *The Birth of the Gods: The Origin of Primitive Beliefs.* Ann Arbor: University of Michigan Press.

Young, Lawrence A., ed. 1997. *Rational Choice Theory and Religion: Summary and Assessment.* New York: Routledge.

7

Durkheim as a Teacher
of Religion

Warren Schmaus

Durkheim taught courses that dealt with religious topics throughout his entire career. When he was a lycée professor of philosophy, he lectured on the nature and existence of God and the soul. As a university professor of pedagogy and social science, first at Bordeaux and then at Paris, he only rarely taught courses that dealt specifically with the sociology of religion. However, he also touched on issues relating to religion in a sociology course that he called "Physics of Morals and Law," in his pedagogy courses on moral education and the history of educational thought, and in a philosophy course on pragmatism that he taught near the end of his career.

Teaching was serious business for Durkheim. He made disparaging remarks about public lectures that were offered merely as entertainment for high society, although he was in favor of the new "public universities" founded to bring about the intellectual improvement of the working classes.[1] In the published opening lecture of his course on the history of education, he expressed deep concerns about what ought to be the current goals of secondary education. For Durkheim, the humanistic, literary education that secondary schools had offered for the last several centuries was no longer appropriate for the contemporary world (1906a). Durkheim put much work into his courses and appears to have been admired, respected, and valued as a teacher by his students. One piece of evidence from his early career that supports this claim concerns André Lalande (1867–1962), who was a student in Durkheim's philosophy course at the Lycée de Sens during the academic year 1883–84. Durkheim was transferred to the Lycée de Saint-Quentin in February 1884. For the remainder of the course, Lalande copied the notes taken the previous year by another of Durkheim's students. This indicates that the students valued Durkheim's teaching to such an extent that they were circulating notes from his classes, trusting Durkheim to get them through the philosophy section of the baccalaureate examination.[2]

Durkheim taught the sociology of religion only three times in his career, in the academic years 1894–95, 1900–1901, and 1906–7. Through preparing his lectures for this course, he developed many of the views on religion that would receive their ultimate expression in *The Elementary Forms of Religious Life* (1912). He put a great amount of effort into this course each time he taught it. In a letter he wrote to Henri Hubert in February 1900, he explained how he was devoting at least four days each week to preparing for his sociology of religion course, titled "The Elementary Forms of Religion," for the following year. As Philippe Besnard points out, the course was not even entirely new, as Durkheim had already taught a course in 1894–95 on the "original forms of religion."[3] Durkheim was again deeply concerned about his sociology of religion course six years later. As he wrote to Hubert again in May 1906, this course was more difficult for him to prepare than his education courses.[4]

Durkheim's nephew, Marcel Mauss, reported that his uncle regarded his education courses as an onerous chore, one he resented, as they took him away from his preferred subjects of study.[5] William Pickering and Geoffrey Walford claim that his lectures on education are not based on extensive empirical research.[6] Indeed, there was little empirical work in education on which he could draw at the time. The situation was quite unlike the one he faced when writing such works as *Suicide* (1897) and *The Elementary Forms*, where there was much empirical work by others for him to use. Pickering and Walford's claim appears to be especially true for the course on moral education (1925), in much of which Durkheim appears simply to have been drawing consequences for education from his sociological theorizing. However, in his introduction to the French edition of *The Evolution of Educational Thought in France*, Maurice Halbwachs said that Durkheim did a lot of reading in preparation for this course. The majority of these lectures were accompanied by bibliographies that Halbwachs and his associates unfortunately decided not to publish, saying that they were now "out of date."[7] What Halbwachs reported is actually consistent with what Pickering and Walford say, because this was in effect a history course, and the empirical sources on which Durkheim drew were no doubt historical works, not empirical studies of education.

In this chapter I trace the development of Durkheim's thinking about religion through courses in philosophy, sociology, and education that dealt with religious topics. I interpret his sociological views about religion as a natural outgrowth of the metaphysical views he expressed in his earliest teaching about religion as a lycée philosophy professor, and I argue that it was through his teaching that he developed the sociology of religion of *The Elementary Forms of Religious Life*. The first part of this chapter deals with the metaphysical and theological lectures from his philosophy course at the Lycée de Sens in 1883–84. Given the seemingly atheist implications of Durkheim's subsequent sociology of religion, the reader may be surprised to find the young Durkheim endorsing the argument for God's existence as the living moral law. He also defended a metaphysical view he called "spiritualist realism," according to which all that is real is spirit. The second part of the chapter deals with the development of Durkheim's sociological thinking about religion during his years in Bordeaux. It draws on his sociology course on the "physics" of morals and law, as well his course on moral education. I argue that many of the important sociological concepts that characterize this period of his thought, such as his notions of collective forces and the collective consciousness, can be interpreted as outgrowths of his earlier spiritualist realist metaphysics. Even the fundamental idea of his sociology of religion, that God is society, appears to have this metaphysical source. Finally, I look at how his mature views on religion are reflected in his teaching in Paris, including his courses on the history of educational thought and the origins of religion, and how he defended some of these views in his course on pragmatism.

Durkheim's Early Career: Philosophy at the Lycée de Sens

French academic philosophy in the nineteenth century was dominated by the eclectic spiritualist tradition initiated by Victor Cousin (1792–1867). Cousin followed the Cartesian tradition of grounding philosophy in an introspective inquiry into the human mind. This philosophical psychology was then supposed to provide a foundation for logic, ethics, and metaphysics, in that order. Metaphysics included proofs for the existence of God and related theological issues. Cousin placed metaphysics after ethics because he held that ethics did not rest on religion or theology, a philosophical position that did not sit well with some religious authorities. Despite these disagreements, Cousin at the height of his career was the director of the École Normale Supérieure, which was the leading institution in France for the training of academics, and minister of public education. Although he retired from public life under the Second Empire, his influence on French academic philosophy continued through a network of colleagues and former students who had also achieved prominent positions in the academy.[8]

Cousin's posthumous influence on the philosophical curriculum is reflected in the syllabi published by the Ministry of Public Instruction in 1874 and 1880, which laid out the philosophical topics that all lycée students needed to cover in order to prepare for the baccalaureate examination.[9] In Durkheim's day, teachers of philosophy were still expected to follow Cousin's order of presentation of philosophical topics, although they at least enjoyed an increasing degree of freedom with respect to their positions on these topics. The 1880 syllabus was drafted by a committee that included Paul Janet (1823–99), a former secretary of Cousin and a member of Durkheim's dissertation committee at the École Normale.[10] Janet was also the author of a standard philosophy text used in the lycées, the *Traité élémentaire de philosophie à l'usage des classes*, first published in 1879 and reissued in a new edition in 1883 that reflected the syllabus of 1880.

The recently discovered notes taken by Lalande as a student in Durkheim's philosophy class at the Lycée de Sens in 1883–84 closely follow the syllabus of 1880. In this syllabus and in Lalande's notes, proofs for the existence of God come after ethics, not before. It also appears that Durkheim used Janet's text in this course. Lalande wrote in his notes that Durkheim said that Cousin's division of philosophy was the simplest and the best, "and we will adopt it" (1884, 25–26).[11] These notes also give some insight into what Durkheim was like as a teacher. They show that he used a very formal style of lecturing. At the end of each class he outlined his lecture on the blackboard.[12] Lalande copied this outline dutifully as the first page of each day's notes, which was then followed by an average of about six handwritten pages in which each of the points on the outline is clearly developed. Durkheim followed the dialectical method of presentation familiar from his subsequent published works, in which he presented the various theories and arguments relevant to a topic, criticized them, and then defended his own position as not subject to these criticisms.

Durkheim defined philosophy as the study of our internal conscious states and the conditions on which they depend. Psychology provides a description, enumeration, and classification of the different types of mental states. Logic differs from psychology in that it concerns only those mental states connected with our intellect. In addition, logic is not merely descriptive but explains "the rules that the mind ought to follow to arrive at the truth" (282). Logic, like moral philosophy, is an art as well as a science. Moral philosophy concerns those mental states that are relevant to our active lives and the laws to which we should submit. It is based on the Kantian principle that one should always treat others as ends in themselves, never as means (26–27, 285–86). Metaphysics, finally, is concerned with the conditions on which our mental states depend, that is, whether they depend on the existence of the soul, the body, or God (493). Durkheim devoted the last twelve lectures to metaphysics. Lecture 69 deals with preliminaries, defining metaphysics as the study of the conditions of states of consciousness. The next four lectures concern the spirituality and immortality of the soul and the relation of the soul to the body. Finally, lectures 74 through 80 are about theological issues, including the existence and nature of God. These lectures are worth discussing in some detail because they are still relatively unfamiliar and because some of the metaphysical positions expressed in these early lectures shed light on his more mature theories of religion and society.

Durkheim began his discussion of the spirituality of the soul by reminding his students of his earlier discussion of this metaphysical question in his lectures on psychology. In lecture 14, Durkheim had defended a position he called "spiritualist realism." This term was not unique to Durkheim but was used by other philosophers, including Félix Ravaisson-Mollien (1813–1900) and Jules Lachelier (1832–1918).[13] Spiritualism has its historical antecedents not in Descartes's dualism or Berkeley's idealism but in Leibniz's metaphysics of monads of varying degrees of consciousness (1884, 101–102). For the spiritualist philosophy, nothing exists except either as a spirit or, presumably, as an object of representation. The very idea of extension is contradictory, and what we call extended matter is only an ensemble of appearances, according to Durkheim (496, 503). But spiritualism, unlike idealism, does not deny the existence of the external world. Rather, it says that external reality consists in forces or spirits analogous to ourselves but with perhaps with less consciousness (101, 496). Hence, Durkheim concluded, there is no point in asking whether the states of consciousness are material, since nothing is (496).

Nevertheless, in lecture 70 Durkheim proceeded to give three more Cartesian arguments for the spirituality of the soul. By Cartesian arguments, I mean arguments that are based on the assumption that contradictory properties cannot inhere in the same substance. These arguments are (1) that spirit is one while matter is multiple and infinitely divisible; (2) that spirit remains identical to itself while matter changes; and (3) that matter is inert while spirit is active (496–498). He then added a fourth argument: that conflicts between body and soul indicate the existence of two separate principles (498). Although spiritualism may be supported by Cartesian arguments, he thought that spiritualism is superior to Cartesian dualism, insofar as it is a monist realism that is not faced with the problem of how two essentially different sorts of substance, mind and matter, are able to interact with each other. For the spiritualist, there is no break in continuity between mind and matter. Spirit is found throughout the scale of being: everything is living, animated, and thinking to at least some degree (498). Durkheim also connected spiritualism with the vitalist philosophy that there is some sort of organizing or directing principle in living matter (509). The monistic philosophy that there is only one kind of stuff, which is neither Cartesian mind nor matter, was actually quite common in nineteenth-century thought. In addition to vitalism, it often took the form of energeticism, the view that all is energy.

In the next lecture, lecture 71, Durkheim proceeded to knock down the arguments for the alternative, materialist position. He explained that Occamite arguments against the unnecessary multiplication of entities are to no avail, since spiritualism as well as materialism is a monist philosophy. Furthermore, spirit has the advantage over matter insofar as it can think (500–501). The second argument concerns physiological influences, such as illness, age, and gender, on the mind. Durkheim responded by pointing out the influences that psychological states such as moods can have on the body (501). The third argument for materialism is that thought depends on the brain. Thought varies concomitantly with such properties of the brain as its volume, weight, and form and the circulation of the blood. In addition, experimentation has shown the localization of sensory and language functions. According to Durkheim, however, these arguments show that the brain is only a necessary and not a sufficient condition for thought, hence do not establish materialism (502). The following class, lecture 72, is then devoted entirely to the relation between the soul and the body and defends the vitalist position mentioned earlier. Lecture 73 turns to the arguments for the immortality of the soul, all of which Durkheim found wanting.

The spiritualist philosophy was not just something the young Durkheim was paid to teach but rather a position that continued to characterize his thinking even in his mature works. The view that three-dimensional extended matter exists only as the content of a mental representation is implicit, for instance, in both *The Elementary Forms*, where he said "nothing exists for us except through representation,"[14] and a published draft of the introduction to it, where he wrote that "the world exists for us only to the extent to which it is represented."[15] Views expressed in his earlier publications from the 1890s also reflect his spiritualist background. For instance, his claim that society is a collective consciousness that constrains the individual can be seen as an outgrowth of the philosophy that all of reality consists of spiritual forces of varying degrees of consciousness. A generation after his student years, Lalande continued to attribute a kind of spiritualism to Durkheim. Specifically, he attributed to his former teacher the position that the laws of mental and social life do not reduce to biology and physics. However, to insist too strongly that this is a methodological rather than a metaphysical position may be to impose a distinction on Lalande and Durkheim that they themselves did not make. In addition, as Lalande pointed out, Durkheim never expressly formulated his metaphysics.[16]

Durkheim then turned to theological issues in lecture 74. He divided the arguments for the existence of God into two types, the metaphysical and the moral. The metaphysical arguments are the traditional ones based on the ideas of perfection, causality, and finality. There are two arguments based on the idea of perfection. One, introduced by Aquinas and adopted by Descartes in the third *Meditation*, argues that the source of our idea of absolute perfection must itself be a perfect being. But as Durkheim pointed out, this rests on the doubtful assumption that there is at least as much reality in the cause as in the effect. The second, the ontological argument introduced by Anselm, in effect argues that God, as a perfect being, must exist by definition. Here Durkheim cited

Immanuel Kant's criticism that existence is not a property that can belong to the definition of a thing. Durkheim also drew on Kant's philosophy in his rejection of the argument that God must exist as a first cause. In lecture 75, Durkheim explained that the very idea of a first cause violates the principle of causality, according to which every event must have a cause. He then said that for Kant, the proper role of such principles of reason as the principle of causality is to regulate or organize our experience. Hence these principles apply only to the realm of phenomena, and any attempt to use these principles to demonstrate the existence of a being beyond experience will wind up in paralogisms.

Of the arguments based on the idea of final causes, the more important one is perhaps the design argument, according to which the order we experience in the world is evidence of its having been designed with certain ends in view by an intelligent being or beings. In lectures 76 and 77, Durkheim replied to this argument by pointing out that ever since Democritus and Epicurus, there have been thinkers who have questioned why the principle of order cannot be in things themselves. More recently, evolutionism has offered an alternative explanation of the appearance of order in things. Here Durkheim was talking about Herbert Spencer; Charles Darwin is not mentioned. He argued that Spencer's system nevertheless cannot actually dispense with the need for the principle of finality in explaining either how needs give rise to new organs or how the different parts of an organism achieve a systematic unity (538–542). Durkheim also had no truck with recent attempts by G. W. F. Hegel, Eduard von Hartmann, and Arthur Schopenhauer to replace a transcendent with an immanent finality, arguing that the notion of a nonconscious goal or purpose was incoherent (544). Ultimately Durkheim, along with Kant (and Hume, who is also never mentioned), rejected the argument from final causes because we cannot prove the existence of a perfect being from that of an imperfect world. In lecture 77 he also rejected the argument from universal consent, pointing out that even if it were true that everyone believed in God, this would not prove that God existed.

Finally, at the end of lecture 77, Durkheim turned to the moral argument for the existence of God, in which God is made the foundation of morality. God provides this foundation in two ways. First, God provides a basis for moral obligation. The moral law can bind us only if it is considered as something living. The moral law considered in this way is God. That is, God is the living moral law. God also provides the basis for moral sanctions. Reason requires a harmony between virtue and happiness that only God, as the living moral law, can assure. The moral argument for the existence of God thus fills the gap left by the metaphysical arguments, which were shown to be insufficient, and establishes the existence of an absolute being as the living moral law. In Durkheim's later thought, of course, it is society that provides the foundation for morality, and God is equated with society. None of that is mentioned here. In the remaining three lectures, Durkheim went on to discuss the attributes and nature of God and to argue that God is beyond our understanding. In the very last lecture, in a discussion of God's providence and the problem of evil, he defended a kind of Leibnizian optimism and rejected the pessimism of Hartmann and Schopenhauer.

The Bordeaux Years: The Transition to Durkheim's Sociology of Religion

Durkheim received his first university appointment in 1887, not long after he presented the philosophy lectures I have just discussed. He was hired to teach social science and pedagogy at the Faculty of Letters at Bordeaux. As Steven Lukes explains, Durkheim's interest in sociology began during his years as a student at the École Normale Supérieure.[17] This interest is reflected in his earliest publications, a series of reviews of sociological works that appeared in the *Revue philosophique* in 1885 and 1886. During this time as well Durkheim had begun work on the dissertation that was to become *The Division of Labor in Society* (1893), a sociological classic. Yet it was not until the academic year 1894–95 that he taught his first course on the sociology of religion. Somewhat later, Durkheim claimed that it was his reading of William Robertson Smith and his school of ethnographers in preparation for this course that led him to view religion as the basis for social life and hence to rethink his entire conception of sociology (1907b). However, as I will show, Durkheim's views concerning the relation of religion to the state and the institution of private property also reflect the influence of Numa Denis Fustel de Coulanges (1830–89), who had been one of his teachers at the École Normale Supérieure. Perhaps it was Durkheim's understanding of his teacher's thoughts on the social aspects of religion that made him receptive to the theories of ethnographers like Robertson Smith.

Unfortunately, at least according to Lukes, no account of Durkheim's first course on the sociology of religion remains.[18] Nor do I know of any account of his second course on this topic, titled "Elementary Forms of Religion" and given in the academic year 1900–1901, unless we assume that it is similar to the 1906–7 course he gave in Paris and for which we have Paul Fontana's published account (1907a). However, although we do not have records or notes from these two courses, I think we can safely assume that the theories he worked out in these courses are reflected in his comments on religion in his other courses from this period for which we do have published accounts. These include a sociology course with the Comtean-sounding title "General Physics of Morals and the Law" (Physique générale des moeurs et du droit) and a pedagogy course called "Moral Education" (L'Éducation morale).

The sociology course was first given in the academic year 1896–97, repeated the following year, expanded into a two-year course in the academic years 1898–99 and 1899–1900, and repeated as the "physiology" of morals and law several times in Paris.[19] Durkheim's lectures for this course were first published under the title *Leçons de sociologie: Physique des moeurs et du droit* in 1950 in Istanbul by Huseyin Nail Kubali, who had obtained the manuscript from Mauss, who told him that it had been written between November 1898 and June 1900. An English translation with the misleading title *Professional Ethics and Civic Morals* was published in 1957. At least parts of the text may derive from a draft earlier than the dates Mauss reported. For instance, Durkheim referred in these lectures to a discussion of the family "last year" (1950, 193, 195; 1957, 163, 165), which could refer to his sociology course of 1895–96.[20] Certainly Durkheim was very busy in the years 1898–1900 with his publications and the new journal *Année sociologique*, so it would not be surprising if did not have time to do a thorough revision of his lecture notes for this course.

Although many have accepted Paul Fauconnet's dating of 1902–3 for the lectures by Durkheim on moral education that were first published in 1925 and translated into English in 1961, Besnard has recently challenged that date and argued that these lectures were actually written much earlier. Lukes lists the course for the academic years 1889–90, 1898–99, and 1899–1900,[21] and Besnard says there are records of the course as early as 1887–88, the first year Durkheim taught in Bordeaux.[22] Besnard also provides evidence to the effect that the 1925 publication was actually based on notes from the course given in 1898–99 and repeated or continued in 1899–1900. First, all of Durkheim's bibliographic references predate 1899. Besnard also finds terminological and thematic affinities with Durkheim's *Suicide*, which was published in 1897, including the use of the concepts of anomie, integration, and regulation. Finally, the opening lecture for the 1902 course that Durkheim published (1903b) does not match up with the subsequent references to the opening lecture in the later lectures.[23] Hence it is safe to assume that Durkheim's lectures on moral education, as well as those on the sociology of morals and laws, represent the state of his thinking in the late 1890s in Bordeaux. Thus both courses can give us some insight into the early stages of the development of his sociology of religion.

Leçons de sociologie: Physique des moeurs et du droit

The sociology course published under this title is described as a "physics" of morals and law based on the study of moral and juridical facts. These facts consist of rules of conduct that have received sanctions (1950,5; 1957, 1).[24] Historically, morality has been closely connected with religion. Thus, it is to be expected that this course on the sociology of morals and the law would contain an early expression of many of Durkheim's main theories of religion.

Among the relevant themes of this course are the religious character of the state, the religious origins of property rights, and the religious origins of contracts. Perhaps most important, this work contains the earliest statement of Durkheim's thesis that the gods a society worships are nothing but the society itself. By some time in the 1890s, society had replaced God as the living moral law for Durkheim. There is also a change in the style or format of Durkheim's lectures, perhaps reflecting his move up from the lycée to the university level. Although we find here the same tightly reasoned, dialectical structure we find in his early philosophy lectures, at least the published version of these lectures contain no explicit outlines. In addition, with this course he began the practice of starting each lecture with a summary of the previous one, a practice he was to continue through the rest of his teaching career.

Durkheim's claim that the gods or god is nothing but society may be his most important thesis about religion in this work, insofar as it is fundamental to the rest. According to Durkheim, the very idea of gods is fictitious and imaginary (133/112): "The gods are nothing but incarnated collective forces, hypostasized in material form" (190/161).[25] However, he explained, religions are not totally illusory but have a basis in reality. It is through their religions that primitive societies become conscious of themselves as societies. Durkheim compared the role of gods, demons, and genies in the social realm to that of secondary qualities such as colors, tastes, and odors in the psychological. Both are things we add to what we perceive yet correspond to real differences in things (189–190/160–161).

> Doubtless they [namely, religions] do not express things in the phys-
> ical world such as they are; as explanations of the world, they are
> without value. But they translate, in symbolic form, social necessi-
> ties and collective interests. They represent the various relations that
> the society sustains with the individuals of which it is composed or
> with the things that make up part of its substance. And these rela-
> tions and these interests are real. Through a religion one may find
> again the structure of a society, the degree of unity it has attained,
> the degree of coalescence of the segments of which it is formed, the
> extent of the space that it occupies, the nature of the cosmic forces
> that play a vital role there, etc. (189/160).

The last sentence of this passage foreshadows his later thesis about the religious character of such fundamental categories of thought as space and force and the concepts of classification and hierarchy embedded in social structure. These ideas were to be developed more fully, first in the "Primitive Classification" essay (1903a), written with Mauss, and later in the *Elementary Forms.*

Durkheim went on to explain that the superiority of the gods to people is simply that of the society over the individual. But of course, society exists only in and through individual members. Hence people conceived of sacred beings as dwelling in individual people themselves. Every member of the clan carries a share of the totem whose cult is the religion of the clan. For example, every member of the Wolf clan is considered a wolf (190–191/161–162). In the same way that the gods are the embodiment of collective forces, the sacred objects of primitive societies, such as totemic images, "are nothing but the emblems of the collective being" (133/112). These ideas are reflected in one of his earliest articles on the sociology of religion, "On the Definition of Religious Phenomena" (1899). This was his earliest publication in which he proposed that the concept of the sacred was social in origin, with the dichotomy between the sacred and the profane reflecting that between society and the individual.

The religious character of society is reflected in that of the state as well. Durkheim speculated that in early times the destiny of the state was tied to that of the gods (68/55–56). As evidence, he cited the fact that in Rome, at least, but not Athens, religion was in the hands of the state (71/58). Religious sentiments had great authority and were connected to severe penalties. That is, crimes against the religious, political, and familial order were considered more serious than crimes against the individual (132/111). The individual was subservient to the ends of the state. His private concerns were of little importance, even to himself (68–69/55–56). All this changes with history. The modern state is no longer a religion but is more closely connected with a well-defined territory (54/44). The individual acquires greater rights, and thus crimes against the individual assume greater importance. The individual becomes a moral end in himself or herself, not just a means to society's ends (69–70/56–57). The cult of the individual replaces the religious cults of former times (84/69). Durkheim did not at all regret these changes: not only did he think that there was no turning back but he felt that there should not be.

The religious character of society and the state is also reflected in the law. According to Durkheim, both property rights and contracts were religious in origin. He argued for the hypothesis of the religious origins of property rights first by drawing analogies between private property and sacred things. He then adduced further evidence of the sacred character of private property and proposed a theory of how private property could have evolved from primitive religious beliefs and practices.

The first analogy Durkheim drew between private property and sacred things concerns the fact that private property is distinct from common property. It is withdrawn from general circulation. Only certain people have access to it or can even touch it. Durkheim compared this characteristic of private property to the Polynesian taboo, which is also a setting-apart. Taboos are closely connected with taking possession of property. In Tahiti, kings and princes are carried because if they touch the ground, they appropriate it and it is taboo for everyone else. Ordinary people then begin to protect their property through taboos as well, and the taboo becomes a title of possession (170–171/143–144). Taboos associated with things are of the same rank as the people who own these things. A second analogy concerns the contagiousness of the sacred. This contagiousness explains the ritual interdictions that separate the sacred from the profane, the purpose of which is to keep the sacred potency from dissipating itself into other things and disappearing. Property is contagious in a similar way. One owns the fruits or the harvests of one's fields, the offspring of one's female animals, the products of one's sons or slaves, alluvial deposits, and the buildings on one's land because all these things have touched one's property. In addition, in many societies, estates were inalienable, and this inalienability of the family's land carried over to the things that were connected with it, such as their animals. For Durkheim, that the family and its property could not be separated from one another indicated the sacred character of family estates (174–177/147–150).

According to Durkheim, landed property is the oldest known form of private property, having been established with the rise of agriculture. This property belonged to the family; individual ownership derives from the rise of the head of the family (195/165). Before the invention of agriculture, there was only a collective right of the members of a clan to the territory they occupied. The sacred character of landed property is revealed by certain customs. In Roman times, according to Fustel de Coulanges, fields were separated by a band of land a few feet wide that could not be cultivated. This narrow strip of land was considered sacred. To profane it with cultivation was a sacrilege, and anyone who committed this crime could be killed with impunity. Terminal or boundary stones that marked the edge of the property assumed a sacred character and were part of a yearly ritual involving sacrifices. With time, the sacred character of boundaries was personified in the god Terminus. The Hindu Law of Manu also describes rituals associated with boundaries. The gates, walls, and thresholds of houses also have a sacred character. Rituals accompany the process of building, with sacrificial victims left in walls or foundations. Hence, Durkheim thought, derives the custom of carrying the bride over the threshold: since she is not of the house or family, she would profane the threshold (177–179/149–152).

Durkheim was not suggesting that property owners merely used religious beliefs and practices as an expedient to protect their property. Indeed, these religious customs placed obligations on the owners, as well. The owner was not allowed to sell the property or to change the boundaries in any way. According to Fustel de Coulanges, the origin of such obligations lay in the cult of the dead, as the family's ancestors were buried on the property. However, Durkheim argued that there was little evidence that family members were actually buried on the property. In addition, this theory does not explain the sacred character of houses and boundaries. According to Durkheim, the family cult extends not just to the dead but to all things associated with the property, such as the harvest. Gods are everywhere and in everything. From this point of view, all sorts of ritual practices become intelligible. For instance, we can explain the sacrifice of the first fruits as due to their sacred character, which derives from the sacred character of the field. The sacrifice draws off some of the sacredness of the rest of the harvest so that it may be used. Boundary rituals are explained in a similar fashion. They draw the sacred character of the field to the boundary so that the field may be used. Rituals transform the deities of the land into protective powers for the house and field, and only those who participate in these rituals may use the house or field (181–186/ t.153–157).

That the primitive conceives of gods dwelling in all land and in all things suggests to Durkheim that the right of property derives from or is a substitute for that of these indwelling gods (186/157). Contrary to philosophers like Locke, property rights are not founded on the respect that we have for the individual's right to the fruits of his or her labor (200/169). Rather, property was inviolate in itself by virtue of its sacred character. However, this sacred character actually derives from the collectivity. If there are gods in the soil, it is because the soil is closely bound up with the life of the society. Individual appropriation of the land presupposes a collective one. Hence we can interpret the rituals associated with land in a new way. The sacrilege one thinks one is committing against the gods by tilling the land is actually a sacrilege against society. It is to society that one actually offers up one's sacrifice. Sacrifice is thus the earliest form of taxation, according to Durkheim. First there is a debt paid to the gods, then one paid to the priesthood, and finally one paid to lay authorities (191–192/ 162–163; 192/163).

Durkheim's theory of the religious origins of contracts develops dialectically through a critical examination of several possible origins, including Robertson Smith's theory that they began with the blood covenant, and ends with the suggestion that contracts have their origin in oath-taking. Robertson Smith had characterized the blood covenant or sharing of blood as a way of creating mutual obligations or forming a contract. Durkheim compared the blood covenant to breaking bread together or sharing a cup, since blood, after all, derives from food. Hence sharing food or drink is another way of binding individuals together. However, this bond is different from what Durkheim called a "real" contract, which is formed by the actual transfer of something with the receiving party thereby incurring an obligation. But even this is not a contract properly so-called, which, according to Durkheim, involves the mutual expression of the agreement of wills. This expression of wills occurs through words. When words are pronounced as part of a ritual, they acquire a sacred character. One way this can occur is through making an oath, in which the divine being invoked becomes the guarantor of the promises that are made. The words have to be said in the right order, and the proper ritual must be performed, or there is no contract. The solemn oath then represents the true origin of the contract for Durkheim. Of course, this is only the origin and not yet our current understanding of the contract (211–215/180–183). Much of the ritual has dropped out of the contract as people's lives have become busier (227/193).

As I mentioned earlier, Durkheim had claimed that it was his reading of ethnographers such as Robertson Smith that led him to appreciate the religious basis of social life. It is true that Durkheim discussed Robertson Smith's work on the religious origins of the contract in this course, and that his discussion of taboos also drew on ethnographies, much as did such important papers from this period as "Incest" (1898) and "Totemism" (1902b). However, this sociology course reflects Durkheim's reading of comparative law as much as his reading of ethnographies. His *Leçons de sociologie* brings to mind his book *The Division of Labor in Society* (1893), both through the way he uses of codes of law as evidence and in the way he speculates about the evolutionary development of social institutions. Indeed, he published a second edition of *Division* soon after this course, in 1902, as he never did with *Suicide*, which would seem to indicate that he still accepted the methodology of *Division*. *The Division of Labor in Society* also contains some of the same themes about religion that I have discussed in *Leçons*. In *The Division of Labor in Society*, he expressed the view that religion is not defined by a belief in gods. In defense of this view, he explained that there are many rules that have a religious character that do not relate to divine beings and that there are even religions such as Buddhism with no gods. He also equated religion with social life in this work (1902a, 142–143; 1984, 118–119). One could argue that the germs of this thesis predate his reading of comparative law as well as ethnography, as one can find a certain consistency among the identification of God with society in the *Leçons*, the identification of religion with moral and legal rules in *The Division of Labor in Society*, and Durkheim's position in the Sens lectures that God is the living moral law.

Moral Education

While Durkheim's *Leçons de sociologie* can be regarded as at least consistent with his philosophy in the Sens lectures, the relationship between this philosophy and his course on moral education is even stronger. Especially when one reads these lectures in the original French, one can see Durkheim's early spiritualist realist metaphysics reflected in the way he makes society a living moral force in place of God. In this course, Durkheim sought a secular moral education that is completely separate from religion. He grounded morality in what he took to be the more fundamental reality that underlies religion, which is society. Durkheim conceded that separating morality from religion is a very difficult task. Since morality has always been bound up with religion, if we simply try to eliminate everything religious from traditional morality without substituting something for it, we run the risk of leaving out "some essential moral ideas and sentiments" (1925, 21; 1961, 19).[26] The first half of the course is devoted to an analysis of these essential elements of morality. These include for him a spirit of discipline, a sense of attachment to a group, and the autonomy of the individual. Durkheim's alternative, sociological account of these elements of morality, especially the first two, draws on his spiritualist metaphysics. The second half of the course is devoted to the issue of how to introduce this secular moral education into the schools.

Durkheim explained the need for discipline in terms of spiritual forces. According to him, "every force not contained by any contrary forces necessarily tends to lose itself in the infinite" (46/40). Hence there is a need for something to constrain the power or force that is the mental life of the individual:

> Only a power that is equally spiritual is able to act on these wholly spiritual forces. This spiritual power is the authority inherent in moral rules.
>
> In effect, thanks to this authority that is in them, the moral rules are true forces with which our desires, needs, and appetites of all sorts come into collision when they tend to become immoderate. Doubtless, these forces are not material; but if they do not move bodies directly, they move the spirits. They have in themselves everything that is necessary to bend the wills, to constrain them, to contain them, to incline them in such and such a direction. And, consequently, one can say without metaphor that they are forces. (46–47/41)

For Durkheim, these moral forces quite literally constrain the will. We feel them every time we try to do something that goes against the dictates of morality, just as clearly as we feel it when we try to lift something that is too heavy for us (47/41).

It is easy to imagine some hard-nosed social scientist today being embarrassed by this passage and dismissing it as an example of Durkheim being carried away by his own metaphors. But Durkheim had perhaps anticipated this reaction in the last sentence when he said that the authority of moral rules can be called forces "sans métaphore." The metaphor interpretation has Durkheim's thought exactly backward. It is not that the notion of physical forces is being extended metaphorically to the social realm. Remember, for Durkheim in 1884, which was only three years before the first time he taught the course on moral education, even matter was nothing but spiritual forces analogous to our own spiritual force, but with less consciousness. Furthermore, metaphors do not constrain people, except perhaps in a metaphorical sense. Durkheim's notion that moral or social forces are literally forces that constrain the individual becomes intelligible against the background of his spiritualist realism. For Durkheim, people in coming together to form a collectivity create a new spiritual force or power—society—which constrains them and which they then mistakenly worship as a god or gods. This becomes clear in his discussion of the second element of morality, the attachment to social groups, and its relation to the first element, the spirit of discipline.

For Durkheim, discipline is good not because our natural inclinations are sinful and must be kept in check but because our very nature requires it. By nature, a person is part of a whole, both physically and socially, and may not supersede certain limits. Indeed, the very idea of a distinct individual implies that there are certain limitations (58/50–51, 77/68). Traditionally, religion has served as the foundation of collective life and thus fulfilled our need for attachment to social groups. However, religion is a social institution, and all religious ideas, including moral rules, are social in origin (79/69). It is society that has instituted rules of morality; hence it is also society that endows them with authority. It does not really matter whether the powers of authority as people conceive them are real or imagined. For Durkheim, "it suffices that they may be represented as real in the minds of individuals" (100/88). For example, the sorcerer is real for those who believe in him.

According to Durkheim, the entity that best fulfills the necessary conditions for constituting a moral authority is the collective being. First of all, it surpasses us in power and scope because it is the synthesis of all the individuals that go to make it up:

> Not only does it command incomparably more considerable forces, since it is due to the coalescence in a single bundle of all the individual forces, but it is in it that is found the source of that intellectual and moral life to which we come to nourish our mentality and morality. (100/88)

A second condition for moral authority is an element of mystery. This need for mystery explains why moral authority "achieves maximum impact" in religion, with its superhuman powers (101/89). Durkheim explained this sense of mystery as arising from the presence of unseen forces of which we can know only the effect. These forces are, at bottom, social forces:

> We perpetually have the impression that there are surrounding us a multitude of things in the course of happening, of which the nature escapes us. All sorts of forces are moving, meeting one another, colliding very close to us, nearly touching us in passing, without our being able to see them, until the time when some severe outburst makes us catch a glimpse of a clandestine and mysterious work that has occurred very close to us, of which we had no suspicion, and of which we perceive only the results. But there is above all one fact that perpetually maintains this feeling in us: it is the pressure that society exercises on us at every instant, and of which we cannot be unaware. (101/89)

These social forces are like a voice within us that tell us what our duty is and how we must act. However, because it feels odd to us for something that is not human to be telling us what our duty is, we imagine that this voice is that of some higher being (101–102/89). By associating morality with a transcendent power, religion makes it easy to represent the authority of moral rules. This authority is not an abstraction, but the emanation of the divine will. God also serves as an ideal that we try to realize by trying to emulate him. In addition, we think of our soul as coming from him (118–119/103–104). Nevertheless, the reason that people obey moral rules is that underneath them are genuine social forces: "But beneath the maxim, there are collective sentiments, the states of opinion of which it is only the expression, and which gives it its efficacity. Because this collective sentiment is a force, as real and as active as the forces that people the physical world" (104/92).[27]

In the end, according to Durkheim, we can express all the elements of morality in rational terms by substituting society for God (119/104). In modern times, the third element, personal autonomy, comes to the fore. The individual merits the respect formerly accorded to the gods. Humanity is now the end that is served by society (123/107). Finally, when Durkheim in the second half of the course turned to implementing this secular rational morality, he discussed the need for intermediate groups such as schools. Durkheim's emphasis on the moral role of intermediate groups brings to mind a similar discussion of the need for occupational groups in the preface to the second edition of *The Division of Labor in Society* (1902a, i–xxxvi/1984, xxxi–lix).

For Durkheim, the ultimate end of moral education is to inculcate the collective consciousness in the child:

> Society is not the work of the individuals that it includes at such and such a phase of history; it is no more the soil that it occupies; it is, above all, an ensemble of ideas and sentiments, of certain manners of seeing and sensing, a certain intellectual and moral physiognomy that is distinctive of the entire group. Society is, above all, a consciousness; it is the consciousness of the collectivity. It is thus this collective consciousness that it is necessary to make pass into the soul of the child. (318/277)

The collective consciousness was of course a key explanatory concept in Durkheim's major works from his time in Bordeaux, *The Division of Labor in Society* and *Suicide*. *Moral Education* resembles the latter work in another aspect as well. In *Moral Education*, religious minorities provide an interesting example for Durkheim of how a strongly cohesive group can temper the character of its members. Solidarity is stronger in religious minorities due to external resistance. Hence the lower suicide rate in religious minorities (274/239–240), as he explained in *Suicide* (1897a).

Durkheim's Mature Thought: The Paris Years

In 1902 Durkheim was hired to teach pedagogy in the newly reorganized university in Paris, in which the École Normale Supérieure was merged with the Faculty of Letters and Sciences (Clark 1972, 163). He dealt with religious topics in several of his courses here. He continued to present the lectures on moral education that I have just discussed, first in 1902–3, then in 1906–7 and 1907–8, and perhaps again in a similarly named course in 1913–14.[28]

Beginning with the academic year 1904–5, he also taught a course on the history of education in France, in which he revealed some of his thoughts about religion in discussing the role that the Church has played in education. Durkheim published the opening lecture for this course in 1906 (1906a), and the full set of lectures were published posthumously in 1938 as L'Évolution pédagogique in France (1938/1977). He also touched on religion in a lecture he gave at the École des Hautes Études in the academic year 1905–6. This lecture was part of a winter course of lectures on the nontheological teaching of morality, under the direction of Alfred Croiset, who gave the opening lecture on November 9, 1905.[29] Lalande wrote a resume of this talk from memory and included it in his article "Philosophy in France (1905)," in the second section, which dealt with ethics. This article was published in English in the American journal Philosophical Review (Durkheim 1906b). As I mentioned earlier, we also have Fontana's report of Durkheim's course on the origins of religion, given in 1906–7, on which to draw for the development of Durkheim's teaching about religion in this period (Durkheim 1907a). Finally, Durkheim offered some of his thoughts on religion in his critique of William James in his 1913–14 course on pragmatism, a published version of which has been compiled from student notes (1955/1983).

L'Évolution pédagogique en France

This course on the history of secondary education in France does not concern religion in general so much as Christianity in particular. Durkheim described the role of Christianity, specifically Roman Catholicism, in the development of teaching in France from about the fourth century to the present, with respect to both the setting up of educational institutions and the content of what was taught. However, he did raise some more general points about religion in his comparisons of Christianity with other religions. These comparisons illustrate several of his sociological theses, such as how religion provides the basis for society and how religion and the social institutions to which it gives rise can affect our thought, reflecting his new interest in the sociology of knowledge at this time. In addition, his interpretation in this course of the medieval theological and philosophical dispute between the realists and the nominalists over the status of universals bears a curious resemblance to and perhaps contains the germs of his interpretation of Australian totemism and religion generally in *The Elementary Forms*.

Durkheim discussed the differences between Christianity and paganism in his explanation of how Christianity depended on education and required the setting up of schools. "Paganism was above all a system of ritual practices backed up no doubt by a mythology, but vague, inconsistent, and without expressly obligatory force," he said (1938, 1:29/1977, 22).[30] Christianity, on the other hand, is an "idealistic" religion, that is, a system of ideas and a body of doctrine. To be a Christian is not so much to carry out certain prescribed rites as to adhere to certain articles of faith, to share certain beliefs, and to accept certain ideas.[31] It is precisely because of this emphasis on beliefs and ideas that Christianity depends on education. Christianity brings with it preaching, which is a form of teaching, which presupposes culture and learning. Teaching and preaching presuppose a certain knowledge of language, dialectic, humanity, and history. Where else, he asked, was this to be found except in the works of ancient authors? In addition, in order to understand the Bible, there is a need for a knowledge of ancient languages and of the things themselves expressed by the words. Rhetoric is also needed by the defender of the faith. Hence the Church found it necessary to open schools and create a place in them for pagan or classical learning. The first such schools were opened in the vicinity of cathedrals and were meant for the training of priests. But they also began to accept laymen (1:29–30/22–23).

A second difference between paganism and Christianity, according to Durkheim, concerns their relations to ethics. He argued that we owe our notion of moral duty to Christianity. According to Durkheim, pagan ethics, that is, the ethics of the classical authors of Greece and Rome, was strictly eudemonic. The ancients conceived the problem of ethics as one of determining what is the greatest good and how to live a life in accordance with this conception. They had no sense of duty, that is, of a categorical imperative that must be obeyed. Durkheim was talking not only about Aristotle here. He explained that even the Stoics linked virtue to a state of blessedness. For Christianity, on the other hand, considerations of personal happiness were irrelevant to morality (2.47/209). These claims are consistent with what he said elsewhere about Christian virtue having to do with inner states and not outer actions. For the Christian, a moral action is one that is done out of a sense of duty. This sense of duty is an inner, intentional state. The claim that we owe our sense of duty to Christianity appears to be one about which Durkheim must have subsequently changed his thinking. In *The Elementary Forms* he argued that the sense of moral obligation arose hand in hand with the sense of obligation to participate in religious rites (1912, 525/1995, 371). In addition, he clearly thought of the obligatory totemic rites of the Australians as representing an earlier form of religious life than Christianity.

Durkheim also contrasted Christianity with Hinduism, at least with respect to the monastic life. Christian monasticism, he said, was never purely contemplative. Christians are concerned not just with their own salvation but with that of humanity. Their role is to prepare for the reign of truth and of Christ, not just in their own minds but in the world. The truth that they possess is not to be jealously guarded but spread throughout the world. They must show people the light and recruit new Christians. Hence the Christian monk is a preacher and a missionary. The majority of the monasteries thus opened schools. These schools were not just for candidates for the monastic life but for children from different walks of life. Thus the earliest schools in France were the cathedral schools discussed earlier and the cloister schools (1.31/24). With respect to monastic schools, Durkheim discussed in particular the Benedictines, whose order was founded in the sixth century. When not working at various manual tasks, Benedictine monks were expected to spend their time reading, including both the Bible and commentaries on it by church fathers. However, in order to understand these commentaries and their controversies, the monks had to know the theories that these works were discussing and rejecting. In this way profane learning became necessary for them (1:45–46/ 34–35).

The founding of cathedral and cloister schools illustrates for Durkheim the way institutions can affect our thought. These early Christian schools imposed a unity on what had previously been diverse fields of study. In antiquity, students received instruction from different masters who had no connection with one another. They would have had one teacher for grammar, one for music, one for rhetoric, and so on. In Christian schools, all these subjects were taught in one place and directed toward the same moral end: to make good Christians. Even today in secular schools, we continue to conceive education as having to do with shaping character (1:33–39/26–30).[32] Christianity unifies our thought and knowledge in another way as well. For the Christian, the truth must be one, because the truth is the word of God and God is one (1:60/46). Durkheim also discussed how Christianity gave Europe a common culture and unified it, reflecting his developing ideas about how religion provides the basis of society (1:51–52/39). Especially around the time of the crusades in the eleventh century, he said, there was an absence of strong nations in Europe. Christianity filled the need that people had for a sense of national identity (1:87–88/ 67).

Early Christian schools, to the extent that they mixed Christian doctrine with classical learning, which conflicted with Christian morality, thus contained a contradiction between the sacred and the profane, according to Durkheim. As a result of this contradiction, Christian schools took on an increasingly secular character (1:32–33/25). Beginning around the twelfth century, educational institutions struggled with the Church to free themselves from its domination (1:97ff/75ff). During the Renaissance, the ethics of the Humanists, whose thought reflected that of the ancient authors they studied, placed little emphasis on duty (2:55/216). Jesuit schools were founded beginning in the sixteenth century to combat the increasingly Humanistic, secular leanings of the university system (2:69ff/227ff). Although they, too, emphasized the classics, they taught the classics in a way that they hoped would minimize the influence of pagan ideas. They did this by teaching the classics in a way that was completely ahistorical, deemphasizing what was in them that was particular to their time and emphasizing the ways the characters in classical literature were like people of all times and places. Classical heroes were used to represent various virtues the Jesuits wanted to impart (2:98–99/250–251).

In addition to comparing Christianity with pagan and Hindu thought, Durkheim compared Catholicism with Protestantism. According to Durkheim, Protestants are more concerned with temporal interests than Catholics. That is, Protestants see education as directed not just at making good Christians but at making good citizens as well. Children must be equipped to satisfy the secular needs of society, to serve a practical function, and to follow a profession (2:142–143/284–285). The rise of Protestantism affected what was taught in Catholic schools as well. In early Christian schools, oddly enough, there was little or no religious instruction among the basic subjects for the baccalaureate. It seems that the clergy, as well as the students, were largely ignorant of religion and theology. All that seems to have been required of ordained priests was that they know how to say mass. Instruction in church doctrine or on the significance of religious ceremonies became important only during the Counter-Reformation (1:179/140).

One last aspect of L'Évolution pédagogique that is relevant to a discussion of Durkheim as a teacher of religion concerns his account of the medieval dispute over the ontological status of universals. This account actually links his early lycée philosophy lectures with his sociology of religion in The Elementary Form in a way that suggests that his sociological theories grew at least in part out of his reflection on the debate between the realists and the nominalists.

Around the time of Peter Abelard (1079–1144), philosophers and theologians argued over whether universals or general kinds of things were mere constructions of the human mind or whether they actually existed outside of us in some way. The reason this debate excited such passions is that it touched the most fundamental beliefs of Christianity. It was not so much the truth of Christian doctrine that was at stake as its meaningfulness. Fundamental dogmas of Christianity become unintelligible on the nominalist philosophy. For the nominalist, only individual substances exist and the genus is nothing but a collection of such individual substances to which we give a name. On this philosophy, the three persons of the Trinity become three distinct substances, and Christianity thus becomes a polytheistic religion. Alternatively, we could insist that these three persons are only different aspects of one and the same substance, but this would only be to wind up with a unitarianism that is no less contrary to church teachings. Similarly, how would a nominalist explain the mysteries of the Eucharist? If a piece of bread is just an individual substance, how does one explain how this substance is made to disappear and be replaced by a different one, all the while retaining the outward appearance of bread? Nor would a nominalist be able to explain the concept of original sin. If human beings are individual substances with nothing in common but a name, then how could the sin of the first human being be something other than his own strictly personal sin? How could this sin be communicated to other human beings? (1:93–95/71–73).

Given these problems with nominalism, realism thus seems to be implied by Catholic orthodoxy:

> Thus, for example, for realism, everything is formed from two elements; on the one hand, the genetic principle, which is the same for all the individuals of the genus, which is the soul of these individuals, which is invisible, impalpable, and purely spiritual; then there is the sensible envelope, through which this principle is individualized, and which allows for it to present different forms in different places in space. (1:94/72)[33]

On the realist principle, we can explain how in the Eucharist, the genetic and spiritual principle in the bread can be replaced by another. However, even if realism makes certain articles of faith intelligible, it creates problems of its own. If the genus exists, it is the true reality, and the individual is but a sensible appearance. The individual disappears in the genus, and one thus ends up with a pantheist conception of the universe (1:94/72).

Interestingly enough, if in the passage just quoted one were to substitute "totemism" for "realism," "totemic" for "genetic," and "totem" for "genus," one would obtain a fairly adequate summary of Durkheim's theory of totemism in *The Elementary Forms*. Of course, one could argue that the whole point of Durkheim's sociology of religion is precisely to show that our modern or contemporary religious ideas have their origin in totemism. Indeed, Durkheim has been accused of making Australian totemists sound too much like Catholics. Another way Durkheim's account of the medieval debate over universals is significant for his sociology involves the way Abelard tried to resolve this dispute, at least according to Durkheim. As he had explained in his early philosophy lectures given at the Lycée de Sens, Abelard had developed a philosophy called "conceptualism" that provided a middle way between realism and nominalism. According to conceptualism, universals or general ideas are neither mere words nor independently existing substances but exist "subjectively" or "substantially" as "concepts" in the minds of each individual who knows the meaning of the corresponding term (Durkheim 1884, 207–208). These "concepts" are then shared mental entities that very much resemble Durkheim's own "collective representations." One must seriously consider the surprising possibility that this central explanatory notion in Durkheim's sociology was suggested to him by his reading of a medieval philosopher. In *L'Évolution pédagogique*, Durkheim extolled Abelard's virtues, praising him as the most important intellectual of the Middle Ages (1:91/69–70).[34]

Durkheim's Lecture at the École des Hautes Études

In this contribution to Croiset's course on the nontheological teaching of morality, Durkheim set out to prove the thesis that, practically and historically, God is Society, and that society, conceived in this way, can furnish all the support to morality that one expects from revealed religion.[35] The thesis that God is society goes back to his sociology course on the physics of morals and law, and the idea that society can be substituted for God as the foundation of morality was defended already in his lectures on moral education. What appears to be new in this lecture is a sense that the idea of moral duty was not just something invented by Christianity, as he claimed in *L'Évolution pédagogique*, but something that is to be explained by the very social origins of religion.

Durkheim argued for the thesis that God is identical with society by pointing out that the attributes we assign to God are the attributes of society. These attributes are those of a superior force, in the image of which we are created and to whom we owe our language, the very condition for thought and knowledge. This superior force is one that unites us, that determines what is good and bad, and that infinitely surpasses us and survives generation after generation. In addition, one can explain religious rites on this supposition that God is society. When we feel weak and ask for strength, it is the feeling of unity with the collectivity that gives us strength. Sacrificial rites support and strengthen the reciprocal relation between the individual and God or society, where each depends on the other (255–256).

For what Durkheim called "barbarous" peoples, each ethnic group had its own god, struggling with the gods of other ethnic groups. In more civilized times, the enlargement of society has led to a monotheism in which all men are brothers. Hence, he claimed, the positivist cult of humanity has realized a profound truth: it is not that God has disappeared into humanity, but rather that humanity has discovered God in itself (256). Lévy-Bruhl thus said to Lalande that although Durkheim may have been a stranger to the folks at the positivist church headquartered at Comte's former home on the Rue Monsieur-le-Prince, that Durkheim was nevertheless the true successor of Comte (257 n. 1).

Durkheim concluded from his identification of God with society that there is therefore a rational basis for the connection between religion and morals, and we cannot secularize morality without changing the character of religion at the same time. However, once morality is secularized, no other changes in morality should be made. That is, it should still be grounded in a sense of duty.

Supported by a reality greater than the individual, that is, by society, "duty remains what it was for Kant" (256–257). Duty cannot be reduced to other things or balanced against other interests. It is categorical and must be obeyed for its own sake. An act done for some material advantage may conform to what duty requires, but it is not for that reason moral. Duty demands pain and sacrifice and forces the individual to conquer and surpass himself or herself. To deny all this is to deny morality itself. To recognize it is to recognize the need for an external foundation for morality, which is confirmed by the history of religion and morality (257).

One might think that what Durkheim said about duty in this lecture was already implicit in his lectures on moral education, where he said that a spirit of discipline was one of the essential elements of morality. After all, discipline also requires individual sacrifice. However, one may also sacrifice one's own interests in favor of the greater good, and to do so would not be to act out of a sense of duty. As Durkheim explained, a duty is a categorical imperative and not a means to an end. Of course, this only raises the philosophical question as to how society, or theology for that matter, can provide a foundation for moral duty. Be that as it may, it was important for Durkheim to recognize that the concept of moral duty was not a peculiar invention of Christianity but is something that can be found in other religions and cultures as well.[36]

Durkheim's Course on the Origin of Religion

In the academic year 1906–7, Durkheim presented a public course at the Sorbonne with the title "La religion—les origines." The purpose of this course, Durkheim said, was to study the simplest and most primitive religious system we know (5:528/65).[37] In this course we find many of the arguments that Durkheim would use later in The Elementary Forms. It begins with a definition of religious phenomena. This is followed by Durkheim's argument that totemism is the oldest religion, along with his defense of the claim that totemism is in fact a religion. We then find an exposition of his theory of the social origins of totemism and his thesis that the totemic forces are nothing but collective or social forces. This is followed by a brief discussion of some other religious ideas that can be found in totemism, including the soul, spirits, and positive and negative rites. The most important difference between this course and The Elementary Forms seems to be that the latter contains a sociological theory of the categories that is barely implied in the former. The course discusses only the social causes and origins of the ideas of force and causality, whereas The Elementary Forms includes space, time, genus, and other categories and discusses their social functions as well. That is, The Elementary Forms combines themes from his sociology of religion course with themes from the primitive classification essay of 1903 written with Mauss (1903a). Another important difference is that The Elementary Forms pays a lot more attention to detail about primitive religions than the 1906–7 course. For instance, more different kinds of religious rites are discussed in *The Elementary Forms*. Nevertheless, the course can be regarded as a working draft of the book.

Durkheim's discussion of the definition of religious phenomena in this course resembles that of both his 1899 article "On the Definition of Religious Phenomena" (1899) and *The Elementary Forms*. When undertaking the study of some subject or other, he said, one must begin with a clear definition of it so as not to confuse it with something else. This must be only a preliminary definition that defines things from an external, observable point of view, as we cannot get at the essence of a thing until the end of our study. Durkheim spelled out two rules for such preliminary definitions. First, we ought not to be misled by preconceived ideas. Second, the definition should be based on the common characteristics that all known religions share. As in his published works just mentioned, he rejected Spencer's and Max Müller's definitions of religion in terms of the supernatural, arguing that the conception of natural law and thus the distinction between natural and supernatural is only of recent origin. Similarly, he rejected definitions in terms of gods or spiritual beings because these definitions do not include religions such as Jainism and Buddhism. In addition, he pointed out, even in deistic religions, many of the prohibitions make no reference to God. For Durkheim, the distinguishing characteristic of religion is the distinction between the sacred and the profane (5:528–531/65–69).

The definition of religion at which Durkheim finally arrived is: "a system of beliefs and practices relative to sacred things—beliefs and practices common to a determined collectivity" (5:533/70). The collectivity or church is what distinguishes religion from magic (5:532/70). Thus the definition he gave in this course is actually closer to that of *The Elementary Forms* than to the one he gave in the 1899 article on the definition of religious phenomena. As he explained in a footnote to *The Elementary Forms*, in the earlier 1899 article, he had defined religious beliefs solely in terms of their obligatory character. But he now realized that this obligatory character arises from the fact that they belong to the group that imposes them on its members.[38] This realization appears to have occurred to him already by the time of this course on the origin of religion.

Durkheim then arrived at the conclusion that totemism is the oldest form of religion in the same way that he arrived at his definition of religion, that is, by first laying out the alternatives and then providing reasons to reject them. Once again, his procedure in this course resembles that of *The Elementary Forms*. Specifically, he laid out the arguments of book one, chapters two and three, where he criticized Edwin Burnett Tylor and Herbert Spencer's animist theory, according to which religion begins with the cult of spiritual beings, and Müller's naturist theory, according to which the cult of material things is the most ancient. His account of totemism as the oldest religion then resembles that given in book two of *The Elementary Forms*.

In his argument against the animist theory of the origin of religion, Durkheim examined three theses maintained by this theory and then rejected them. First, he considered how people came to have the notion of a soul. According to Tylor, it derives from attempts to explain dreams. Because one can dream that one traveled somewhere without one's body leaving the spot, one comes to think that one is composed of two beings, body and soul. Durkheim, however, argued that many of our dreams, such as dreams of the past, could not be explained in the same way. Second, he took up the issue as to how the idea of a soul acquired a sacred character. According to Tylor, for the animist the soul acquires its sacred character on death, which is conceived as an indefinitely long sleep. But Durkheim did not see why death should impart a sacred character on the soul. In addition, this theory would then imply that the earliest religion was the cult of ancestors, which ethnographic studies do not support. Third, Durkheim criticized Tylor's account of how this cult of souls was extended to natural things. According to Tylor, the primitive does not clearly distinguish the animate from the inanimate, but rather conceives of things in nature as analogous to himself, with souls, by which he explains the phenomena of nature. Durkheim then questioned why only certain things in nature would have been considered divine. He also made Spencer's point that Tylor's account assumes that primitives are like children. In addition, on this theory, the gods would have the same characteristics as human souls. But they do not, as they are not as intimately attached to things as we are to our bodies. Finally, on the animist theory, gods would have been created in our image. But pagan gods have animal elements, and they do not have the *conscience* or the duties of men, either (5:533–537/71–75 and notes).

Durkheim then turned to criticize Müller's naturist theory of the origin of religion. According to Müller, the first gods are personifications of natural forces. Through the use of language, which is impregnated with the concept of human action, we began to conceive of these natural forces as analogous to ourselves. Durkheim objected that this theory, as much as the animist theory, makes religion rest on an error or an illusion. Both theories make the mistake of trying to derive the notion of the sacred from ordinary experience. Religion must be grounded in reality (5:537–539/76–77).

For Durkheim, totemism is the oldest religion, because it is linked to the organization of society by tribes and clans, which is the simplest social organization we have ever observed and perhaps the simplest we are able to conceive (7:102/88). Totemism contains the germs of all the religious notions that will develop over the course of history, including the distinction between the sacred and the profane and the notions of religious forces, souls, spirits, and gods. It also includes both negative and positive rites, that is, prohibitions, sacrifices, offerings, and rites of communion (7:92/78; 7:95/81).

Since Durkheim's account of totemism as a religion in this course embraces many of the points and arguments that are familiar from book 2 of *The Elementary Forms*, I will give only the briefest summary here, emphasizing the differences between his course and this book. In the totemic religion, each clan in the tribe has its own totem, which serves as the emblem of that clan. Totemic images and the totemic species themselves are sacred things that are not supposed to come into contact with the profane except under special circumstances, for example in religious rites. The classification of things into sacred and profane extends to all things in the universe. Every species of thing is attached to some clan or other. These other kinds of things also have a sacred character and are surrounded with prohibitions. They serve as secondary totems or totems of subgroups within the clan (7:93ff/79ff). In book 2, chapter 3, of *The Elementary Forms*, Durkheim also introduced the notion of a phratry and went on to argue that our system of classification by genus and species has its origin in the totemists' classification of things by phratry and clan. However, he did not make this argument in this course on the origin of religion.

Durkheim defended his claim that totemism is the oldest religion against James Frazer's argument that totemism is not a religion at all but only a form of magic. In reply to Frazer, Durkheim argued that totemism is a collection of beliefs and practices common to a group of people and hence a religion. The cult of each clan forms a part of a whole. Each clan shares the beliefs of the others, and they participate in the same rites together. Totemism may then be defined as the religion made up by the union of the cults of all the clans of the same tribe (7:99–100/86). On the other hand, Frazer's attempt to distinguish religion from magic in terms of psychical beings versus rites directed at material benefits will not work, since each of these elements are found in both (7:102/88).

Since totemism is the oldest religion for Durkheim, the question of the origin of religion then becomes one of the origin of totemism. He first took up the question as to whether individual or collective totems came first, examining Frazer's theory in *The Golden Bough* that totemism began with individual totems. Durkheim found Frazer's explanation that totemism began with the individual hiding his or her soul in an animal or plant to keep it safe to be question begging, for where did the primitive get the idea of a soul in the first place? He then gave five more reasons against the hypothesis that collective totems grew out of individual ones. First, a person will let another eat his clan totem but not his personal one. Second, Frazer's hypothesis does not explain why no two clans in the same tribe have the same totem. Third, the individual totem, unlike the clan totem, is not hereditary. Fourth, if the individual totem were earlier, individual totems would be more widespread in more primitive societies and less so in more advanced ones. But Durkheim found the opposite to be the case. Finally, individual presupposes collective totemism in that the individual must choose his or her personal totem from things associated with his or her clan (7:102–104/89–91).

Hence, Durkheim concluded, to explain the origin of totemism, one must explain the origin of collective totemism. He reasoned that the sacred character of totemic beings cannot derive from their own nature, given all the different sorts of things that have been used for this purpose, but must come from their participation in some principle that the senses do not perceive. It is this principle that is the true object of worship; that is, the primitive worships not the plant or animal but an anonymous and impersonal force in each of these things. He cited as examples of this force the Sioux's notion of *wakan* or *wakanda*, the Dakota's *orenda*, the Algonquin's *manitou*, and the Melanesian *mana*. The totem is simply the observable representation of this force (7:104–105/91–92). With this introduction of the notion of a totemic principle, Durkheim thus appears to have first made the analogy mentioned earlier between totemism and the medieval realist position on universals, an analogy that is also implied in *The Elementary Forms*. But already in this course he explained that this notion of an impersonal force contains the germ of the idea of a divinity. Mythology transforms these forces into gods. He also argued here that this represents the earliest notion of force or cause and that this notion is of religious origin (7:106/93 and n. 32). According to Durkheim, religion thus gives us the first form of explanation, that is, of linking diverse things through a link that is not perceived in things but added by the human mind, and is therefore the predecessor of philosophy and science (7:114/102). These claims about causality and explanation appear to be the only hint of the sociology of knowledge that he defended in *The Elementary Forms*. In this course, he considered only the concepts of force and cause, not space, time, or genus. In addition, he did not make the argument here that he did in *The Elementary Forms* that the totemist hypothesis explains the origin of these concepts of cause and force better than the animist and naturist hypotheses do.

Since the true object of worship in the totemic religion, according to Durkheim, is the totemic principle or force, the next question for him to consider is then the origin of this notion of an impersonal force. He did not present the detailed, philosophical arguments against deriving this idea from individual experience that he gave in the introduction to *The Elementary Forms* but simply said that it does not have its origin in the sense impressions caused by the things through which the primitive represents these forces. Because the sacred character resides above all in the totemic images, rather than the totemic species themselves, he reasoned, one is thus led to think that the religious character of the totem derives from that of which it is a symbol. However, the totemic images represent two things, the god and the clan. Durkheim then argued that if god and the clan are represented in the same way, they must be the same thing. Hence the totemic divinity is nothing but the clan or the society itself sublimated and hypostasized. Society has everything necessary to awaken religious feelings in us: both the divinity and society impose rules of action on the individual and are forces that raise us up above ourselves and give us strength. The primitive does not realize that the intense feelings he or she experiences when the tribe gathers for religious rites derive from the energy of the collectivity, so he or she attributes these forces to the totem. However, people are not deceived in thinking that they are in the presence of a superior moral force that is external to them and from which comes all that is best in them. They may misrepresent this reality but they are not deceived about the fact of its existence. Hence, unlike the naturist and animist hypotheses, Durkheim's totemist hypothesis does not derive religion from illusion; that is, his theory does not try to derive it from individual experience of physical or psychological facts that have nothing sacred about them (7:106–111/93–99).

Durkheim argued that his totemistic hypothesis is superior to Tylor's animist hypothesis in another way as well. The totemist hypothesis is better able to account for the Australian's notion of the soul than is the animist hypothesis, in spite of the fact that the notion of the soul is the key explanatory concept in the animist hypothesis. According to Durkheim, for the totemist, the souls of the dead are reincarnated in new births. There are only a finite number of souls for each clan. These souls are the founders of the clan. They are super-human beings, nearly gods, of a sacred or religious character. They are of a mixed nature, that is, they have some human characteristics and some of the characteristics of the totemic plant or animal. Durkheim argued that the primitive's idea of a soul derives from neither an attempt to explain dreams nor a concern with otherworldly sanctions or an afterlife. Instead, this is the only way for the primitive to explain new births. Life is not possible without a soul, and where else would each person get one? The primitive has no concept of a higher being who is an inexhaustible source of new life (12:620–625/103–108).

Tylor's animist hypothesis cannot explain how it is that people think there is something sacred as well as profane in each of us. For Durkheim, this duality of human nature is not an illusion. He explained that there are two kinds of mental representations in each of us: those that derive from our own organism and moral beliefs and practices. The second come from society. Hence there is an objective basis for the belief in the soul, that is, the duality that really exists in each of us (12:623–624/107).

According to Durkheim, the idea of a soul then gives rise to that of a spirit as the souls of ancestors are thought to divide into two, one that inhabits some place or object and is a spirit and the other that gets reincarnated. The spirit becomes a tutelary or guardian genie or demon. These spirits evolve into divinities not only for the clan but for the whole tribe. The spirit that inhabits some particular rock or tree then becomes the spirit of that category of things. This belief then gives rise to tribal rites that suggest the idea of a tribal divinity. Some regard the idea of a tribal deity as a European import, but Durkheim found this hypothesis unnecessary, as he considered these ideas to be the "logical" result of totemism (12:625–627/109–111).

Durkheim then ended his course on the origin of religion with an account of religious rites. As in *The Elementary Forms*, he distinguished negative from positive rites. The object of negative rites is to maintain the separation between the sacred and the profane. They consist of ritual prohibitions, interdictions, or taboos against various sorts of contact between or mixing of the sacred and profane. These sorts of interdictions continue to exist in religions today, such as the prohibition against working on the sabbath. Durkheim explained these prohibitions in terms of the contagiousness of religious forces. These forces are powerful, and it is dangerous to come into contact with them. In addition, the sacred cannot pass into the profane without profaning itself. This contagion in turn is explained in terms of Durkheim's theory that religious forces are hypostasized social forces: they are not inherent in the things themselves but penetrate them from without (12:628–633/112–117).

The goal of positive rites, on the other hand, is to put the faithful in relation with the sacred thing so that it can render him or her the services he or she expects. Durkheim briefly described the Intichiuma rite reported by Baldwin Spencer and Francis James Gillen, in which the idea is to assure the reproduction of totemic species. This rite involves the chief eating the sacred animal and distributing its parts to the members of the clan. These rites are periodic, because the sacred forces get used up or wear out and must be replenished. The individual revives this force in himself or herself by consuming the sacred animal. Durkheim thus saw in these rites the origin of the communion rite. He also offered an interpretation of sacrificial rites grounded in the work of Robertson Smith, in which these rites are considered to be both offerings and a form of communion. These rites are not to be thought of merely as presents or offerings to the gods, except in the case of expiatory rites. The idea that sacrifices are attempts to gain favor with the gods can explain neither their periodicity nor their obligatory character. They should rather be thought of as a feast in which the faithful join in with the gods, reserving the most sacred parts of the animal for the gods, in order to create a durable relationship between the people and their god. Durkheim mentioned that Robertson Smith thought it absurd to regard sacrifice as an offering or tribute, since that would make the gods depend on people and people on the gods at the same time. Hence Robertson Smith thought that sacrifice began as a feast to establish a bond with the gods. People forgot that and came to regard the parts reserved for the gods as an offering. Durkheim said that he used to find Robertson Smith's argument plausible but now had come to believe that the primitive does in fact think both that people depend on the gods and the gods on people. The divine forces get used up, and the gods will die if people do not periodically carry out the appropriate rites. For Durkheim, it is easy to see how gods and people need each other once we realize that the divinity is nothing but society itself (12:634–637/118–121).

The Elementary Forms of course goes on to discuss other sorts of positive rites, most notably the mimetic rites with their relationship to the concept of causality. These discussions are not present in this course. Durkheim concluded this course by saying that it is not necessary to the existence of individuals that they represent society to themselves in the hypostasized form of gods or believe in the material efficacy of rites over material things. However, the moral and social services rendered by the cult are indispensable to the continued existence of society (12:637/122).

The Lectures on Pragmatism

Durkheim's course on pragmatism strikes a contemporary philosopher trained in the Anglo-American tradition as rather odd, since it starts off with such assertions as that the pragmatists are "preoccupied" with religion, that religion is the "principal point of departure" for pragmatism, and that James is the "true father" of pragmatism (1955, 36–37/1983, 7).[39] Surely the founder of pragmatism is Charles Sanders Peirce, who is more highly regarded as a philosopher of science than of religion. Durkheim was not ignorant of Peirce, however. In fact, he credited Peirce with having invented both the term "pragmatism" and the pragmatic method for making our ideas clear, and he cited several of Peirce's articles.[40] The reason Durkheim identified pragmatism with James's philosophy of religion has to do with the fact that James was receiving a lot more attention in the French philosophical community at this time. A French translation of James's *Pragmatism* with a preface by Henri Bergson was published in 1911 (41 n. 7/9 and 116 n. 16). Even earlier, Lalande had begun the article on French philosophy mentioned earlier with a discussion of pragmatism and did not bring up Durkheim's thought until the second section, where he summarized Durkheim's lecture on the nontheological teaching of ethics. For Lalande, pragmatism in France was best represented in France by Maurice Blondel but also included Henri Poincaré, Gaston Milhaud, and René Berthelot.[41] In his introduction to the 1983 translation of Durkheim's lectures on pragmatism, John Allcock provides a detailed account of James's influence on French philosophy through his personal relationships with Charles Renouvier, Emile Boutroux, and Bergson.

Durkheim, on the other hand, criticized James for trying to claim Bergson and Poincaré for the pragmatists and said that pragmatism was more appropriately associated with the Catholic modernist philosopher Edouard Le Roy, who he claimed based his apologetics on principles borrowed from pragmatism (41/9). Durkheim regarded Jamesian pragmatism as a philosophy that supported French philosophies that were in opposition to his own secularizing, social scientific approach. In his opening lecture, he found pragmatism to be an attack on reason and French culture, which for Durkheim was rationalist. Durkheim found Jamesian pragmatism to be a threat because pragmatism, due to its preoccupation with religion, was making truth relative to the individual, while Durkheim of course wanted to emphasize the social character of thought and religion. According to Durkheim, Jamesian pragmatism was the only theory of truth available at that time. Indeed, one of the reasons that Durkheim was not interested in Peirce was that he did not present a theory of truth (27–28/1; 35–36/6–7).[42]

Durkheim's twelfth lecture, which is largely concerned with James's *Varieties of Religious Experience*, explicitly criticized James for his exclusive concern with personal, inner religious experience and his neglect of the social aspects of religion, that is, with "institutions, churches, [and] sacred practices" (130/60). Furthermore, according to Durkheim, in addressing questions of the truth of religion, James disdained the arguments for the existence of God and other such theological issues as unnecessary and serving no purpose and placed greater value on mystical intuitions. For James, the science of religion is to be based on psychological fact, and the value of religion was best learned through a study of the lives of the saints. The study of such things as mystical states, conversion, and prayer will reveal to us that the basis of religious life is the experience of some force that is greater than us and that we experience only through its effects on us (131–134/61–63). As Durkheim explained in the first lecture, for James the gods or supernatural beings are in nature, they are real forces that we can experience only indirectly through their effects. We come to discover them gradually, just as we have come to discover physical forces that existed before we discovered them (32/4). However, James linked these forces to the subconscious or unconscious. He said that these forces need not be a single god, but may be just a larger, more god-like self, of which the present self is but a mutilated expression. The universe may be a collection of such spirits with no unity to it. We draw strength from such spirits, and the experience of drawing strength from these spirits is religion. Durkheim, however, argued that there are in fact religions in which the inner mystical experiences James described do not even occur and that the psychological facts from which James argued for the truth of religion could alternatively be evidence of the disintegration of the personality (131/61; 135–136/63–64).

James's pluralistic universe of spiritual forces bears a strong resemblance to the spiritualist metaphysics defended in Durkheim's early lycée philosophy lectures. Perhaps what made James's philosophy so well received in France was the presence of this spiritualist philosophy that was already conducive to it. Alternatively, James's philosophy may have reflected his reading of the French. Durkheim was so opposed to James precisely because James took this spiritualist philosophy in a direction that explained the experience of religious forces in terms of the individual subconscious, while Durkheim of course wished to explain the same experiences in terms of social forces. Durkheim reiterated the claims he had made the previous year in *The Elementary Forms* that religious forces are collective in origin and that religion and mythology express social realities and their effects on individuals (177/87). Hence he felt the need to defeat Jamesian pragmatism.

Conclusion

In this chapter I have shown how Durkheim developed his ideas about religion through preparing detailed lectures for the various courses he taught. His thought reflects a remarkable continuity over a thirty-year period, with his sociology of religion drawing on concepts from his early teaching of the philosophy of religion. At the same time, he resisted certain other directions of thought that came from the same metaphysical roots. His career can be interpreted as an attempt to rebuild philosophy on a new sociological foundation in order to replace the eclectic spiritualism he inherited from Cousin and his followers. Instead of grounding philosophy in the introspective study of our individual spiritual power, it is to be based on an empirical study of the effects that the collective spiritual power has on us. This makes it possible to replace God with Society as the living moral law. However, not only ethics but also epistemology and logic were to be placed on a sociological foundation, and the sociology of religion was to replace metaphysics, especially that part that dealt with God and the soul. Durkheim's sociology of knowledge may not have been reflected all that well in his teaching. However, we can find him working out his sociological accounts of the ideas of God and the soul and the basis for his sociological ethics through the courses he gave in both Bordeaux and Paris.

NOTES

1. See Durkheim 1901; 1976, 380, 386–387.

2. Lalande's notes for Durkheim's philosophy course were discovered in 1995 by Neil Gross, then a graduate student in sociology at the University of Wisconsin conducting research at the Sorbonne. See Gross 1996.

3. Besnard 1993, 121; see Lukes 1973, 618.

4. Besnard 1993 121.

5. Besnard 1993 120.

6. See Pickering and Walford 1998, 7–8.

7. See Durkheim 1938, 1:3; 1977a, xiii.

8. For specific details on Cousin's career, see Brooks 1998, 36ff.

9. Brooks (1998, appendix) provides translations of the official philosophy syllabi of nineteenth-century France, including the syllabus of 1880.

10. Lukes 1973, 297; see Brooks 1996, 379–407; Janet 1885, 483–484.

11. Unless otherwise indicated, all references in this section are to the page numbers in André Lalande's original manuscript notes. These notes have been transcribed and placed online and are available, without page numbers, at: www.relst.uiuc .edu/durkheim/Texts/1884a/00.html. A detailed English summary of these lectures, written by Robert Alun Jones, is available online at: www.relst.uiuc.edu/durkheim/ texts/1884a/tr.abst.html.

12. See Lukes 1973, 64. Lalande's claim that Durkheim wrote the outline on the

board at the end of each class, which Lukes quotes here, seems inconsistent with the appearance of his actual notes, in which Lalande provides the outline at the beginning of each day's notes. The most likely explanation is that Lalande simply left the first page blank and saved it for the end of class. The actual text of each day's notes always begins on a fresh page, even when the outline does not fill the entire page. The outline never fills more than one page; Lalande wrote the more detailed outlines in a smaller hand to make them fit on one page.

13. See Brooks 1998, 59, 157.

14. See Durkheim 1912, 493 n. 1; 1995, 349 n. 55.

15. See Durkheim 1909, 756.

16. See Lalande 1906, 257.

17. See Lukes 1973, 95, 66ff.

18. See Lukes 1973, 238.

19. Durkheim also gave a course with the title "Physiology of Law and Morals" as early as 1890–91, but according to Lukes this course appears to have been restricted to that part of the topic that deals with the family (1973, 617).

20. See the list of Durkheim's courses that Lukes provides (1973, 618). Durkheim also referred to a discussion of Greek and Roman cities in a course given the previous year (1950, 71/1957, 58), but I do not know which course he had in mind.

21. See Lukes 1973, 617–618.

22. See Besnard 1993, 125.

23. See Besnard 1993, 126–127.

24. Unless otherwise indicated, all subsequent references in this section will be to the page numbers of first the original French edition of 1950 and then the English translation of 1957.

25. I offer my own translation from the French original, which may differ from the corresponding passage in the English translation. I tend to favor a more literal translation that is closer to Durkheim's actual thought over those translations that sacrifice literalness for readability.

26. Again, unless otherwise indicated, all subsequent references in this section will be to the page numbers of first the original French edition of 1925 and then the English translation of 1961. In addition, I will be offering my own translations from the French.

27. The 1961 translation attempts to disguise Durkheim's metaphysics by translating *peuplent* as "fill" instead of "people."

28. According to Lukes (1973, 620), this course was called "*L'enseignement de la morale à l'école.*"

29. See Lalande 1906, 254.

30. All subsequent references in this section, unless otherwise indicated, will be to first the volume and page numbers of the original two-volume 1938 French edition, followed by the page numbers to the 1977 English translation.

31. Similarly, he said again in a later lecture that Christianity is an "idealist" religion, meaning that God seeks dominion over the mind and spirit, not the body. Christian virtue consists not in outward acts but in inner spiritual states (2:139/282).

32. Indeed, Durkheim's own concern with moral education indicates that he, too, conceives education as having the goal of shaping character.

33. Peter Collins translates *génésique* as "generic" instead of "genetic."

34. Abelard's works had become accessible and familiar to nineteenth-century French scholars, including Durkheim, through the efforts of Cousin, who had edited and published the *Ouvrages inédits d'Abélard* in 1836 and Abelard's two-volume *Opéra* in 1848–59.

35. Lalande 1906, 255. The pages of Lalande (1906) that concern Durkheim's lecture have been translated into French and published in Durkheim 1975b, 2:10–12. All subsequent references in this section are to Lalande 1906. I shall refer to the page numbers in the original English version.

36. See Sen 2000: 480–482.

37. The first number in parentheses is the issue and page number from the original publication of Fontana's summary of this course in the *Revue de philosophie* of 1907. This summary appeared in issues numbers 5, 7, and 12 of vol. 7 of this journal. The second number is the page number in Karady's more recent reprinting of this series of articles in Durkheim 1975b, vol. 2.

38. *Elementary Forms*, 1912, 65–66 n. 1/1995, 44 n. 68.

39. Subsequent references in this section, unless otherwise indicated, will be to first the page numbers in the 1955 French edition and then to the page numbers in the 1983 English translation.

40. See 33–34/5; 44/11. Unfortunately, Durkheim's notes for the lecture on the pragmatic method, lecture 11, were not preserved.

41. Lalande 1906, 241–250.

42. Durkheim may have been overstating his case. In his review of pragmatist thought in France, Lalande attributed a philosophical position to Poincaré and Milhaud that recognized the social character of knowledge and objectivity and perceived a Durkheimian influence on at least Milhaud (1906, 250).

REFERENCES

Allcock, John B. 1983. Editorial introduction to the English translation. In Durkheim 1983.

Besnard, Philippe. 1993. "De la datation des cours pédagogiques de Durkheim à la recherche du thème dominant de son oeuvre." In *Durkheim, sociologue de l'éducation*, edited by François Cardi and Joelle Plantier. Paris: L'Harmattan.

Brooks, John I., III. 1996. "The Definition of Sociology and the Sociology of Definition: Durkheim's *Rules of Sociological Method* and High School Philosophy in France." *Journal of the History of the Behavioral Sciences* 32 (4): 379–407.

———. 1998. *The Eclectic Legacy*. Newark, Del.: University of Delaware Press.

Clark, Terry N. 1972. "Emile Durkheim and the French University." In *The Establishment of Empirical Sociology*, edited by Anthony Oberschall. New York: Harper and Row.

Durkheim, Emile. 1884. *Cours de philosophie fait au Lycée de Sens*. Bibliothèque de la Sorbonne, manuscript no. 2351. Also available from the University of Wisconsin–Madison, Microforms Center, film no. 9307, and online at: www.relst.uiuc.edu/durkheim/Texts/1884a/00.html.

———. 1893. *De la division du travail social: Étude sur l'organisation des sociétés supérieures*. Paris: Alcan. Translated in Durkheim 1984.

————. 1895. *Les Règles de la méthode sociologique*. Paris: Alcan. Translated Durkheim 1982.

————. 1897. *Le Suicide: Étude de sociologie*. Paris: Alcan. Translated in Durkheim 1951.

————. 1898. "La Prohibition de l'inceste et ses origines." *L'Année sociologique* 1: 1–70. Reprinted in Durkheim 1969. Translated in Durkheim 1963a.

————. 1899. "De la définition des phénomènes religieux." *L'Année sociologique* 2: 1–28. Reprinted in Durkheim 1969. Translated in Durkheim 1975a.

————. 1901. "Rôle des universités dans l'éducation sociale du pays." In *Congrès international de l'éducation sociale*. Paris: Alcan. Translated in Durkheim 1976.

————. 1902a. *De la division du travail social*. 2nd ed. Paris: Alcan. Translated in Durkheim 1984.

————. 1902b. "Sur le totemisme." *L'Année sociologique* 5: 82–121. Reprinted in Durkheim 1969. Translated in Durkheim 1985.

————. 1903a. "De quelques formes primitives de classification: contribution à l'étude des représentations collectives." With Marcel Mauss. *L'Année sociologique* 6: 1–72. Reprinted in Durkheim 1969. Translated in Durkheim 1963b.

————. 1903b. "Pédagogie et sociologie." *Revue de métaphysique et de morale* 11: 37–54. Reproduced in Durkheim 1922. Translated in Durkheim 1956.

————. 1906a. "L'Évolution et le rôle de l'enseignment secondaire en France." *Revue bleue*, s. 5, 5: 70–77. Reprinted in Durkheim 1922. Translated in Durkheim 1956.

————. 1906b. "Summary by A. Lalande of a lecture by Durkheim on religion and morality, delivered at the École des Hautes Études in the winter of 1905–6." *Philosophical Review* 15: 255–257. See Lalande 1906. The pages concerning Durkheim's lecture are translated into French and published in Durkheim 1975b.

————. 1907a. "Cours d'Émile Durkheim à la Sorbonne." *Revue de philosophie* 7, 5: 528–539; 7: 92–114; and 12: 620–638. Summary by Fontana of 1906–7 lecture course "La Religion—Les origines." Reprinted in Durkheim 1975b.

————. 1907b. "Lettres au Directeur de la *Revue néo-scolastique*." *Revue néo-scolastique* 14: 606–607, 612–614. Translated in Durkheim 1982.

————. 1909. "Sociologie religieuse et théorie de la connaissance." *Revue de métaphysique et de morale* 17: 733–758, all of which, except pp. 754–758, was incorporated into the introduction to Durkheim 1912. These missing pages are reprinted in Durkheim 1975band translated in Durkheim 1982.

————. 1912. *Les Formes élémentaires de la vie religieuse*. Paris: Alcan. Translated in Durkheim 1995.

————. 1922. *Éducation et sociologie*. Paris: Alcan. Translated in Durkheim 1956.

————. 1925. *L'Éducation morale*. Paris: Alcan. Translated in Durkheim 1961.

————. 1938. *L'Évolution pédagogique en France*. Paris: Alcan. Translated in Durkheim 1977.

————. 1950. *Leçons de sociologie: physique des moeurs et du droit*. With a foreword by H. N. Kubali and introduction by G. Davy. Paris: Presses Universitaires de France. Translated in Durkheim 1957.

————. 1951. *Suicide: A Study in Sociology*. Translation of Durkheim 1897 by J. A. Spaulding and G. Simpson. New York: Free Press.

————. 1955. *Pragmatisme et Sociologie*. Paris: Vrin. Translated in Durkheim 1983.

———. 1956. *Education and Sociology.* Translation of Durkheim 1922 by Sherwood D. Fox. Glencoe, Ill.: Free Press of Glencoe.

———. 1957. *Professional Ethics and Civic Morals.* Translation of Durkheim 1950 by Cornelia Brookfield. London: Routledge and Kegan Paul.

———. 1961. *Moral Education: A Study in the Theory and Application of the Sociology of Education.* Translation of Durkheim 1925 by Everett K. Wilson and Herman Schnurer. New York: Free Press of Glencoe.

———. 1963a. *Incest: The Nature and Origin of the Taboo.* Translation of Durkheim 1898 with an introduction by Edward Sagarin. New York: Lyle Stuart.

———. 1963b. *Primitive Classification.* With Marcel Mauss. Translation of Durkheim 1903a by Rodney Needham. Chicago: University of Chicago Press.

———. 1969. *Journal sociologique.* Edited by Jean Duvignaud. Paris: PUF.

———. 1975a. *Durkheim on Religion.* Edited by W. S. F. Pickering and translated by J. Redding and W. S. F. Pickering. London: Routledge and Kegan Paul.

———. 1975b. *Textes.* Edited by Victor Karady. Paris: Éditions de Minuit. These three volumes provide the original pagination of the articles included.

———. 1976. "The Role of Universities in the Social Education of the Country." *Minerva* 14, 3: 380–388. Translation of Durkheim 1901.

———. 1977. *The Evolution of Educational Thought: Lectures on the Formation and Development of Secondary Education in France.* Translation of Durkheim 1938 by Peter Collins. London: Routledge and Kegan Paul.

———. 1982. *The Rules of Sociological Method and Selected Texts on Sociology and Its Method.* Translation of Durkheim 1895 and other essays by W. D. Halls. New York: Free Press.

———. 1983. *Pragmatism and Sociology.* Translation of Durkheim 1955 by J. C. Whitehouse. Cambridge: Cambridge University Press.

———. 1984. *The Division of Labor in Society.* Translation of Durkheim 1893/1902a by W. D. Halls. New York: Free Press.

———. 1985. On Totemism. *History of Sociology* 5, 2: 79–121. Translation of Durkheim 1902b with an introduction.

———. 1995. *The Elementary Forms of Religious Life.* Translation of Durkheim 1912 by Karen Fields. New York: Free Press.

Gross, Neil. 1996. "A Note on the Sociological Eye and the Discovery of a New Durkheim Text." *Journal of the History of the Behavioral Sciences* 32, 4: 408–423.

Janet, Paul. 1885. *Victor Cousin et son oeuvre.* Paris: Calmann Lévy Éditeur.

Lalande, André. 1906. "Philosophy in France (1905)." *Philosophical Review* 15: 241–266.

Lukes, Steven. 1973. *Emile Durkheim: His Life and Work.* New York: Penguin Books.

Pickering, William S. F., and Geoffrey Walford. 1998. Introduction to *Durkheim and Modern Education.* London: Routledge.

Sen, Amartya. 2000. Consequential Evaluation and Practical Reason. *Journal of Philosophy* 97, 9: 477–502.

PART III

Courses

8

The Socratic Durkheim

Teaching Durkheim on Moral Obligation

Stephen P. Turner and Carlos Bertha

"Are you attempting to tell me my duties, Sir?"
  "No, but I'm having a lot of fun trying to guess what they are."
          —Raymond Chandler, *The Big Sleep*

The concept of duty, as Max Weber once said of the notion of a calling, "prowls about in our lives like the ghosts of dead religious beliefs."[1] The term "duty," which looms so large in Kant and also in nineteenth-century ethics and social and political thought, was once obviously true as a description of commonplace moral situations and intelligible without academic instruction; today it is arcane and puzzling. When we teach the meaning of texts about duty and obligation, we are typically forced to explain them in terms of concepts that still survive as part of daily life, such as promises, which lack the original force and significance of "duty." As a consequence, learning ethics as an academic subject is very often a matter of mastering this archaic language and "applying" it where it no longer naturally fits, and puzzling over its failure to fit.

Yet these concepts are so pervasively bound up with our philosophical understanding of ordinary normative concepts that we can neither ignore them nor do without them. And what holds for teaching ethics holds also for political and social thought. To understand such notions as "political obligation," for example, requires that one understand the notion of obligation in the first place, and consequently many of the same problems of pedagogy that arise for ethics arise for social philosophy, political philosophy, and legal philosophy. So teaching ethics or political theory in a way that makes sense of the notion of obligation is correspondingly more difficult than it would have been either at the time of Kant or a century ago.

Using *The Elementary Forms* in Class

In this chapter we will discuss some pedagogical uses of Durkheim that serve to make sense of obligation by enabling students to see how these and related moral concepts are based on, and express, actual moral feelings and bear on actual moral experience. We collaborated in the teaching of a course that was directed at a multidisciplinary audience, including students interested in political philosophy, sociological theory, and political theory. The course itself was defined as a mass section, and for most of the time it was taught was presented through the internal television course delivery system of the university, which transmitted the course to branch campuses. Total enrollments were typically over one hundred. The course was team taught, and there were sections on four major nineteenth- and early twentieth-century thinkers: Marx, Weber, Durkheim, and a fourth figure, usually a pragmatist; different individuals were included as the fourth thinker at various times in which the course was offered. This discussion will relate exclusively to a four-week section of the course devoted to Durkheim, which focused on readings from Pickering's *Sociology of Religion*. The course readings also included substantial material from selections in Durkheim's *Elementary Forms of Religious Life*. A second class, to be discussed later, is a class in military ethics, originally taught primarily to Reserve Officer Training Corps students as a philosophy class.

The first of these classes consisted of lectures and discussion, but a major feature of the class was a take-home exam, which was designed to compel students to reflect on their own moral experiences in Durkheimian terms. The key feature of this exercise was that it enabled students to identify, through the use of Durkheimian strategies, both ritual structures and social forms that embodied and signified obligations for them, and to see how these forms (and the enactment of the rituals they required) produced feelings of obligation.

The approach was "Socratic" in the sense that it made no attempt to instruct students about their obligations, or to derive them from ethical maxims about obligations that they might have rationally acquiesced to, or to treat obligation in any respect as the product or consequence of a theory. Like Chandler's celebrated detective Philip Marlowe, we asked what our duties are. But our questioning was disciplined by basic Durkheimian reasoning, together with a consideration of the kinds of facts the Durkheimian account of obligation points to. The method could only succeed if students already in some way felt obligations of the kind we considered and also could be made to recognize moral feelings as the product of ritualized social interaction and participation in something "higher" than and distinct from the individual will.

Needless to say, this sharply contrasts with much of current ethical teaching. The recent revival of interest in Kantian approaches in ethics has often been only very distantly linked to substantive senses of obligation. When pressed, a present-day Kantian in ethics, such as Thomas Nagel and Christine Korsgaard, will characteristically provide a highly generic and often very thin example that they claim can be unequivocally established through the resources of reason itself. The focus is on what can unequivocally be said to be rational. An obligation not to torture other people, for example, is a characteristic example of these obligations. Whether this is a convincing strategy in ethics is a metaphilosophical question that can be left to others. But it is evident that whatever agreement about philosophical methods might tie together Kantian ethical thinkers, there is a substantial problem about content that arises from these arguments, and this problem is well known to anyone who teaches Kant's ethics as a source of usable insight into actual ethical questions, as distinct from a formal exercise in ethical theory. People typically do not regard these ethical dictates of reason as relevant to them, and, specifically, they do not recognize them as motivating. There is a large gap between the sorts of things that do powerfully motivate people, such as family bonds, and the status of such bonds in ethical theory. Family feeling, indeed, is barely intelligible to ethics. It appears to be a matter of irrationality and therefore a source of conflict with the "ethical."

Historical Background

Difficulties with Kant's ethics akin to these contemporary pedagogical problems were of course well known to thinkers of the nineteenth century, and they focused on two particular problems with the Kantian analysis of obligation. First, the fact that Kant fails to provide a plausible motivation for acting in accordance with these obligations, was the point that concerned such figures as the legal philosopher Rudolph Ihering, who commented: "You might as well hope to move a loaded wagon from its place by means of a lecture on the theory of motion as the human will by means of the categorical imperative."[2] The second problem, equally serious, was the inadequacy of any universalistic account of obligation to make sense of the diversity of actual obligations in terms of which actual moral agents operated. It was evident in the nineteenth century that different cultures cultivated different senses of obligation, that different professions cultivated different kinds of obligations, and so forth.

Durkheim was of course well aware of these discussions and in particular in his earliest writings commented on attempts to account for cultural diversity like those of Wundt, which provide a substantive moral psychology that does so, and the writings of various figures on the general topic of moral psychology, including Ihering.[3] Durkheim was also aware, especially through Spencer but probably also through Victor Cousin,[4] of the peculiar legacy of the dispute between intuitionism and utilitarianism of the middle part of the nineteenth century. The course provided a useful pretext for introducing this historical background. The arguments in this dispute are summarized in the first part of W. E. H. Lecky's *History of European Morals,* which defends intuitionism. The key to this defense is the notion of moral feeling, and the claim that intuitionism rests on an induction

> quite as severe as any that can be employed by their opponents. They examine, analyze, and classify their existing moral feelings, ascertain in what respects their feelings agree with or differ from others, trace them through their various phases, and only assign them to a special faculty when they think they have shown them to be . . . generically different from all others.[5]

The intuitionists' claim, which is similar to Durkheim's own famous emphasis on externality, was that if moralists approach the problem inductively, they will arrive at the core fact on which intuitionism rests: first by "perceiving in ourselves a will, and a crowd of intellectual and emotional phenomenon that seem wholly different from the properties of matter,"[6] and, second, from this perceived difference, inferring the existence of a power of perceiving the differences, and, third, by naming this power. From reasoning of this sort Bishop Butler took the next, explanatory step, arguing that "the sense of obligation that is involved in" moral judgments "separates them from all other sentiments" and therefore requires a separate perceptual apparatus, "a special faculty of supreme authority called conscience."[7] The reasoning, in short, was this: we perceive the difference between obligatory feeling and other feelings, and thus have an autonomous power, or faculty, that enables us to do this, which we may call conscience.

Spencer respected this statement of the problem, particularly the basic idea that, as Lecky says,

> a theory of morals must explain not only what constitutes a duty, but also how we obtain the notion of there being such a thing as duty. It must tell us not merely what is the course of conduct we ought to pursue, but also what is the meaning of this word "ought," and from what source we derive the idea it expresses.[8]

But Spencer came to different conclusions from Lecky. Spencer grasped that the fundamental problem with the intuitionist account of moral feeling was a problem that paralleled Kant's problem, namely, that moral feeling, to the extent that it is grounded in something—either intuition given by God or reason that is universal—can only with great difficulty, if at all, be reconciled with the diversity of moral feeling between cultures. Conscience is culturally diverse, and many societies operate in terms of shame. Spencer's solution to the problem of diversity in *The Data of Ethics* was to accept the phenomenology of intuitionism, its sense that the sources of moral feeling were immediate and not rationalized or the product of calculation, but to account for diversity by arguing that intuitions, though they existed internally and were experienced as internal, were the product of society and evolved through social evolution. Thus Spencer claimed to resolve the dispute between the utilitarians and the intuitionists,[9] and Durkheim's views are in some respects a close critique, largely in the same terms (such as differentiation and representation), of this resolution.

For Spencer, "unquestionably the essential trait in the moral consciousness is the control of some feeling or feelings by some other feeling or feelings." Sufficiently developed minds do not do this consciously, and cannot access the conflicts of feeling by introspection. But when social evolution makes life complex, people have numerous experiences and can generalize inductively about them, making the benefit of self-restraint familiar, indeed producing "a sufficient massing of individual inductions into a public and traditional induction impressed on each generation as it grows up."[10] Moral ideas involve self-restraint, but are the last to differentiate from other forms of self-restraint, and involve consciousness of the intrinsically evil results of an act, say of murder, which are embodied in such things as representations of the suffering of the victim. The concept of duty originates as other abstract ideas do, that is, by way of a recognition of a common component of certain kinds of moral feelings, and thus is arrived at through a kind of induction, a superinduction on the inductions that produced the self-restraining feelings in the first place.[11] Spencer even predicts the disappearance of the feeling of obligation in the future, at the point that complete adaptation to the social state occurs, and action occurs harmoniously.[12]

Current Forms of These Issues: Philosophy of Law

It may be observed that the problem of feelings of obligation and the relations to real obligations persist in Anglo-American ethics into the twentieth century, for example in H. L. Hart's discussion of the distinctions between feelings of obligation and actual obligations, and because this has become a standard argument for the irrelevance of moral feeling in ethics, it provides a useful entry to the problems of concern to Durkheim, as well as the peculiarities of Hart's and the analytic tradition's response to these problems. In *The Concept of Law*, Hart's example is a stickup: a man holding a gun demands that a victim hand over the money.[13] Certainly the victim does not have a *real obligation* to give him the money, yet it is easy for us to imagine why he *feels obliged* to do so. We may feel obliged, for instance, to donate to charity, say at a public fundraiser, but we do not have an outright obligation to give to the poor or the infirm. On the other hand, we may not feel particularly obliged to drive below the speed limit on a practically deserted highway, but the speed limit signs remind us that we do, in fact, have a legal obligation to drive under a certain speed. Finally, one may feel obliged to remove one's hat on entering a church, and although there is no written law that so directs, one does have an obligation to remove such headgear.

In the first case, the person handing over the money feels obliged because he perceives that his life is in danger; that is, that his failure to give in to the robber's demands could result in serious harm. In the second case, although no harm would be forthcoming should we elect not to give to charity, we feel shame when we are pressured in public to give "even if it's just a little bit." When we speed, we are breaking a law, and should we get a ticket, local statutes *make it* our obligation to pay the fine. Not paying the fine may result in stiffer penalties and maybe even time in jail. But we may consider all this a small matter and therefore simply may not feel that strongly about obeying posted speed limits. In the last example, though there may not be an organized system of enforcing compliance with a rule like removing headgear in a church, a man who enters a church wearing a hat might be reminded by a few bystanders to remove it. His refusal to comply may be cause for contempt, stopping short of physical sanctions; he may even be asked to leave. The punch line is that feelings are not the mark of actual obligation, and the means of determining our obligations must be found elsewhere.

The problem with this distinction between feeling and obligation becomes apparent when one considers the problem of why law is accepted as law, that is to say, in sociological terms, the problem of legitimacy, or, in the philosophy of law, the problem of recognition. Hart follows a tradition in legal positivism that seeks to depsychologize this problem so that the legal system appears not to rest on something as dubious and variable as the feelings of the ruled. And he had good reasons for doing so, notably those he found in Axel Hägerström's arguments against the "will theory" of consent, in which he noted that most of the law is not known to those who are under it, much less the subject of their willing.[14] But the bare idea of recognition, aside from its psychological dubiousness, has another problem. It too is a feeling, even if it is a feeling apparently unlike "obligation," and it cannot easily be made purely cognitive or rational. Yet the "feeling" of legal obligation, and the fact that it conflicts with other feelings, can be given a standard Durkheimian explanation—the feeling of obligatoriness of the law is rooted in a set of rituals that differs from those of familial obligations or personal preferences. So there may be conflicts between feelings of obligation. These conflicts do not disqualify feelings as a mark of the obligatory, but the reverse: the fact that they are experienced as conflicting feelings shows that the law has something to do with feeling, and the fact that one cannot give a plausible account of the obligation to obey the law in terms of such (psychological) notions as will and recognition means that one must look elsewhere. Feelings that arise in connection with the law, such as a feeling of guilt for violating the law, may point to a more plausible basis for legal obligation.

Exercises in Identifying Obligations

Professional philosophy, of course, took another path. In the concluding chapter of *The Methods of Ethics,* Sidgwick argues that the principle that is known intuitively is none other than the utilitarian principle itself.

> We have found that the common antithesis between Intuitionists and Utilitarians must be entirely disregarded: since such abstract moral principles as we can admit to be really self-evident are not only incompatible with a Utilitarian system, but even seem required to furnish a rational basis for such a system. Thus we have seen that the essence of Justice or Equity (in so far as it is clear and certain), is that different individuals are not to be treated differently, except on grounds of universal application; and that such grounds, again, are supplied by the principle of Universal Benevolence, that sets before each man the happiness of all others as an object of pursuit no less worthy than his own; while other time-honored virtues seem to be fitly explained as special manifestations of impartial benevolence under various circumstances of human life, or else as habits and dispositions indispensable to the maintenance of prudent or beneficent behavior under the seductive force of various nonrational impulses.[15]

This had the effect of leaving immediate moral experience aside, and also of leaving the topic of the diversity of morals to sociology and the seductive force of various nonrational, and nonrational *because* nonuniversal, impulses. When Durkheim inherited these issues, particularly the conflict between intuitionism and utilitarianism, he approached them in a way that respected some of them, particularly with the Kantian idea that obligations were the central moral phenomena; that they were experienced both immediately within the individual, that is, intuitively as external but also as real facts; that they varied between societies and in some sense evolve. In addition, by distinguishing between obligations that were universal within a particular society and obligations that were characteristic of particular social groupings, such as professions, Durkheim opened up the possibility of actually accounting for the content of the distinctive moral life of individuals.

The problem in teaching is to exoticize the experiences that students have had, to make them available for analysis. In a sense, self-exoticizing for the purposes of questioning is at the core of the Socratic method. A Durkheim-aided version of this questioning begins with seeing ordinary or at least familiar activities as rituals, and then allowing us to see how these rituals are the sources of feelings of obligation. In one version of our course, this was done by thinking through the notion of special *objects*, such as sacred objects and their nonreligious analogues, illustrating Durkheim's point about the intermingling of the physical with the spiritual and collective,[16] and this proved to be especially effective. Durkheim says that

> because collective sentiments cannot become conscious of themselves without being attached to external objects, these moral forces have assumed some of the characteristics of things in order to become established. In this way they have acquired a kind of physical nature which has enabled them to intermingle with the life of the material world and through them an explanation of what is happening in it has been thought possible.[17]

Two exercises were based on this text:

> 1. Think about your religious experience. Discuss it in terms of the rituals involved. Identify them. Tell me what the rituals do. How is the spiritual and collective stuff intermingled with the material and mundane stuff? What are the effects of participating in the rituals? How do they attach you to some people and separate you from others?

This produced interesting results, such as a paper by an Asian American student who described the household gods in the foyer of her family house and the rituals of respect for them. But the approach of beginning with the material objects also works nicely in terms of ordinary household objects that have a special significance, for example, for family reasons, such as Great-grandma's china service, as embodiments of, and ritual celebrations of familial obligation, expressed as ritual obligation toward an object, or involving an object. To get at examples of this sort, the following assignment was given.

> 2. Think about a nonreligious ritual in the same way. Ask the same questions as in 1.

The example of military medals, to be discussed shortly, is an example of an object in which the intermingling occurs. Needless to say, such questions require a good deal of elaboration in class, especially through examples.

In other versions of the class, the focus was on collective events, and these too produced interesting responses. Among the questions were the following.

> 3. Think about public rituals in a Durkheimian way. Describe and analyze your own personal feeling and experiences of these rituals—this can be anything from a wedding, to a hockey game, to a court

case. The important thing is that it is one in which you have shared feelings.

4. Durkheim describes the formative moments in which collective sentiment is strong, collective ideas are somewhat fluid, and something new emerges out of a collective gathering. Think about recent examples of this, such as the Million Man March or the AIDS quilt presented in Washington. Describe what happened in a Durkheimian way. How important was the "collective" feeling that was generated? How did it change the participants? Did these heightened moral feelings diminish when people returned home?

One of these exercises asked the student to consider some episode in his or her own life that indicated the presence of some sort of higher moral reality, and with this starting point the exercise required students to think about the external social forms that sustained this experience of externality. A typical example would be a wedding ceremony or a court appearance in which in passing into some special ritual state an atmosphere of heightened moral feeling was produced by particular rituals with a particular audience, such as public swearing of an oath or public promise-making in the eyes of God and the presence of the kin and friends of the betrothed. The second approach was to examine changes in moral feelings and to identify these changes, which the student typically experiences as internal, with the group identities that sustained and encouraged these changes. These were all examples of beginning with moral feelings and analyzing them in terms of the ritual structures that sustained them.

The more accessible approach, however, was to go the other way around and to begin with a ritual and to see what sorts of things the ritual does, what statuses are changed by the ritual, and consequently what kinds of connections between particular groups of people are produced by or enacted in the ritual act, what moral intuitions might be thought to derive from the ritual practice in the feelings of the individual, and what sorts of moral beliefs follow from a moral experience structured in terms of these rituals and the intuitions they produce.

One point perhaps should be added. As with any performance, Socratic questioning along Durkheimian lines has its risks, and the yield is sometimes poor. But in many cases students themselves were able to produce quite vivid and interesting examples that were interesting in themselves and a pleasure to read. It is a pity that the class that used these exercises did not allow them to be shared and developed in class; a smaller class would have allowed for the exercises to be shared, discussed, and analyzed by the group. This would have left the participants with a more vivid experience. But many students made genuinely Socratic discoveries about their own obligations from this exercise.

The problem of making this kind of exercise work is in large part a matter of preparation, and the preparation had to include examples from contemporary life that students could use as a guide to their own thinking. *The Elementary Forms* itself provides a great deal of usable guidance, but something more is needed. In what follows we illustrate this with two case studies we have used to make the relevance of *The Elementary Forms* (and other Durkheimian and Maussian texts) clear.

Examples and Models 1: Abortion

In the class itself, contemporary examples of the dual structure of ritual and moral feeling were considered; we will briefly elaborate one example here. The example is discussed in a somewhat different connection elsewhere.[18] One of the obvious moral disagreements of the day concerns abortion policy, and students can be counted on to have opinions on this subject and to suppose that these opinions are opinions about moral principle. Indeed the whole vocabulary of the discussion, in terms of rights, leads a student to suppose that abortion is a fundamental case of an issue that an approach to ethics that appeals to the rationality of principles ought to eliminate. But even more striking about the issue of abortion is the sense, which students in classroom discussions characteristically attempt to suppress, that the true principles do not correspond perfectly to their own principles or feelings.

Typically this takes the form of a student who strongly believes in the right to choose and the right of women to control their bodies but who would personally be unable to have an abortion. And the same goes for students who in principle regard abortion as murder but who accept either the reality of the moral difficulty involved in, for example, bringing a genetically flawed child into the world or the humanity of insisting that a pregnancy that is the product of rape be carried to its term. A small amount of questioning or even an examination of proposed laws that restrict abortion but provide for exceptions in various cases will be enough to elicit some sense of the conflicting feelings of virtually every student who is in the class.

When students attempt to formulate the principles involved and their basis, it quickly becomes evident that the formulations do not capture the intuition, and that moral psychology, that is, the intensity of the feeling in relation to actual experiences, also is a poor match for the arcane and ad hoc distinctions that students and lawyers are forced to employ in the face of these issues. Abortion is particularly good at bringing out these discrepancies because the distinctions are so dramatically consequential and so apparently arbitrary. How can any line of a verbal sort distinguish between fetuses that are allowed to live and those that will die?

More important, however, is the fact that most people, and especially women, have extensive experience with the feelings, and more interestingly, the rituals associated with pregnancy, birth, and the recognition of social existence of a child, as well as the distinctive statuses that are attached to motherhood, the protection of babies, our responsibilities to them, and so forth. Here such practical issues as "Should a pregnant woman drink wine?" can be used to exemplify the actual obligations as real people experience them. The ritual of announcing a pregnancy, informing people in the order of their connection and importance to the mother and to the child, represents a good ritual form with which to begin. Announcements of pregnancy are ritual events in primitive cultures as well as contemporary culture. The announcement represents, indeed produces, a status change: the mother-to-be is treated substantially differently from the person who has not made this announcement. Students can easily be made to see the diversity, the intricacy, and the social and moral significance of the act of annunciation, and can also be shown that the significance for the individual is both produced through socialization and sustained by rituals of congratulation and the endless rituals of ceremonial preparation for the birth itself, from Aunt Jane knitting baby booties to the exchange of furniture, and so forth and so on. In particular, the ritual of the baby shower, with its marvelous potlatch-style exchange and ceremonial and its clear significance in altering and recognizing the alteration of the status of a woman in the eyes of other women, is a rich source of stories, personal experience, and so forth.

These rituals are of course in part about the mother. But clearly the procedures and the sense of obligation and the moral feelings that are triggered by the normal process of announcing pregnancy and having the unborn child recognized socially as an object of responsible action, and common concern, clearly makes sense only if the rituals signify the existence of a human being. So strong is this feeling that a pregnant woman ordering a glass of wine in a restaurant is likely to be accosted and insulted by other patrons. So these examples show very nicely the pervasiveness and centrality of the ritual support for the intuitive feeling that a fetus, at least a sufficiently advanced one, is morally no different from a child. And this enables us to understand the discrepancy with which the class discussion begins: between articulated principle and the by now well-established reality of the moral structures of obligation external to the individual that are the source of the intuition that the fetus is the child.

To say this of course was not to take sides on the abortion debate so much as to show why there is a discrepancy between these "real" senses of obligation and principles and also to show why the feelings of obligation are so resistant to being overturned by principled arguments. This general strategy can be extended to ever more interesting cases, notably those cases that students have become fashionably cynical about.

Examples and Models 2: Military Medals

One such example was elaborated in the dissertation of one of us[19] and was used in a course on military ethics. The subject matter is military medals, a characteristic example of a sacred object. If we begin with the idea that medals and ceremonies of this kind are rituals about obligations, and medals are objects in which a kind of intermingling occurs, one can raise a variety of interesting questions. The peculiar thing about medals is this: on the one hand, they appear to be, and are characterized within the military as, a management tool. On the other hand, some medals, such as the Congressional Medal of Honor, do not seem to make sense as management tools.

The regulation that governs the award of such medals (in the United States army) is quite clear: an awards program is in place in order to "motivate soldiers to high levels of performance."[20] This motivation is presumably accounted for by the feeling of awe that is inspired in the awardees' *fellow* soldiers. If these awestruck soldiers want a medal too, they will do whatever the honored soldier did to get his medal. The interesting question here is how and why military medals relate to the management objective of morale that they are designed to produce.

Medal-giving has the characteristic form of a Maussian gift exchange, in which one side of the exchange acknowledges the receipt of a gift (the soldier's sacrifice) by responding with a gift that is not the exact return of the same but a gift of a different type (the medal). In the case of service ribbons and medals in the lower end of the spectrum, such as the Army Service Ribbon, the State Active Duty Ribbon, and the Reserves Overseas Training Ribbon, the exchange is automatic; that is to say, soldiers who fulfill a given set of criteria are *due* these awards. When we come to other awards that are of higher precedence (that is, all decorations), however, the exchange is no longer mandatory, giving it a voluntary character. Yet even at this level, decorations given for service or achievement, such as the Air Force Achievement Medal and the Meritorious Service Medal, remain highly predictable in nature. A Meritorious Service Medal on the lapel of a lieutenant colonel, for example, almost invariably means that he or she has had a successful battalion command.

Decorations given exclusively for heroism, such as the Medal of Honor, are even more dramatically voluntary, and have much more problematic relation to management objectives. Even if the ceremony causes a sense of awe in the minds of the honoree's fellow soldiers, this feeling could hardly be responsible for increased acts of heroism in the battlefield. Moreover, rewards for valor are not necessarily, and are even not often, rewards for "following orders" but rather are rewards for unusual actions. Falling on a grenade to save a squad, for instance, can sometimes be the *wrong* move (from small unit operational standpoint), yet these sacrifices often warrant a high decoration.

When we turn to such questions as who is emotionally involved in and who feels obligation in relation to the action and the rewarding of the medal, we notice another anomaly.

The debt is one imposed on the intended beneficiaries by the exemplary soldiers and by the outstanding actions of the hero. It is a kind of gift that is recognized as imposing an obligation to do something in response to the gift on the part of the intended beneficiaries. The military in this case supports morale by enabling the colleagues of the hero to discharge their obligation. A little reflection shows that the nature of this obligation points directly to the basic realities of mutual obligation of soldiers in conditions of combat and therefore to the hidden order of mutual dependence and obligation under which men at arms operate.

A class about military ethics, which attracts a preponderance of students either with a military background or with intentions of joining the military (ROTC students and the like), obviously ought to spend a great deal of time evaluating different notions of duty, including (as it did in this case) what Kant and Mill had to say about it. At first students are puzzled: given the amount of emphasis the military profession puts on the absolute necessity to do certain things, such as follow orders, they figure that the military must be a Kantian-like entity. On the other hand, they must balance this notion with the fact that the military decision-making process is quite overtly a utilitarian process, listing a few possible courses of action and always striving to choose the one that leads to the highest overall military (or political) advantage. Be that as it may, students normally do not fully grasp why they ought to be motivated by either of these imperatives, especially if they put themselves, if only for a moment, in the shoes of a soldier in a foxhole, with bullets whizzing by and grenades falling next to him.

In order to help resolve this paradox, a Durkheimian move is made that is similar to the one discussed in connection with the abortion example. Students are asked to think of military *rituals* (which are abundant enough), and are encouraged to identify what feelings these rituals help to invoke, and how such rituals change the status of the soldiers involved in them. Invariably, some students pick a graduation from an academy or training course, or, more often still, award ceremonies, citing that these bring about feelings of awe, a sense that they owe the recognized soldiers a degree of gratification (soldiers whose status changes by virtue of the recognition), and even (perhaps deep down) a mild feeling of jealousy. Students typically identify with these feelings as motivators for the entire group of soldiers involved in the ceremony, that is, award-ees and spectators alike, to stay in and continue to be a part of their unit. In other words, these experiences, in noncombat roles or in peacetime, can often account for at least some of the feelings of obligation that unite soldiers in the most difficult of times.

It is not that hard to convince the average student that neither Kantian thinking nor utilitarian calculations are behind the obligations soldiers feel in battle. A far more convincing explanations is proffered by Samuel Stouffer, among many others, who suggested that the real motivator in battle is the realization that soldiers' lives depend on their buddies being alive, so there is an instant camaraderie that binds these men in battle.[21] Rituals such as award ceremonies serve to enhance these relationships and therefore strengthen these feelings of obligations between the soldiers who participate in them. Durkheim seems to provide a more viable framework with which to address the origin, importance, and effectiveness of this account of military duty.

NOTES

Carlos Bertha's contributions to this essay should not be taken as official U.S. government policy.

1. Max Weber, *The Protestant Ethic and the Spirit of Capitalism*, trans. Talcott Parsons (New York: Scribner's, 1958), 182.

2. Rudolf von Ihering, *Law as a Means to an End*, trans. Isaac Husik (New York: Kelley, 1913; reprint, South Hackensack, N.J.: Rothman,1968), 39.

3. Durkheim, *Ethics and the Sociology of Morals*, trans. Robert T. Hall (Buffalo, N.Y.: Prometheus Books, 1993).

4. See William Lecky, *History of European Morals from Augustus to Charlemagne*, 3rd ed. rev., vol. 1 (New York: Appleton, 1925), 74–75.

5. Ibid., 74.

6. Ibid., 75.

7. Ibid., 76.

8. Ibid., 5.

9. Herbert Spencer, *The Data of Ethics* (New York: Appleton, 1879), 147.

10. Ibid., 135

11. Ibid., 179.

12. Ibid., 153.

13. H. L. A. Hart, *The Concept of Law* (London: Oxford University Press, 1961), 79–83.

14. Axel Hägerström, *Inquiries into the Nature of Law and Morals*, trans. C. D. Broad and ed. Karl Olivecrona (Uppsala: Almqvist and Wiksells, 1953), 20–28.

15. Henry Sidgwick, *The Methods of Ethics* (London: Macmillan, 1930), 496–497.

16. Durkheim, *Durkheim on Religion*, ed. W. S. F. Pickering (Atlanta, Ga.: Scholars Press, 1994), 148.

17. Durkheim, *Durkheim on Religion*, 148.

18. Stephen Turner, "Kohlberg's Critique of Durkheim's Moral Education," in *Durkheim and Modern Education*, edited by W. S. F. Pickering and Geoffrey Walford (London: Routledge, 1998).

19. Carlos Bertha, "Honor and Honors: An Ethical Study of Military Duty and Its Relationship to the Practice of Awarding Medals," Ph.D. diss. (University of South Florida, Tampa, 2000).

20. Department of the Army, *Military Awards, Army Regulation 600-8-22* (Washington, D.C.: U.S. Government Printing Office, 1998), 1.

21. Samuel Stouffer, et. al., *The American Soldier: Combat and Its Aftermath*, vol. 2 (Manhattan, Kans.: Sunflower University Press, 1977; originally published Princeton: Princeton University Press, 1949).

REFERENCES

Bertha, Carlos. 2000. *Honor and Honors: An Ethical Study of Military Duty and its Relationship to the Practice of Awarding Medals*. Ph.D. diss., University of South Florida, Tampa.

Chandler, Raymond. 1966. *The Big Sleep* New York: Knopf.

Department of the Army. 1998. *Military Awards, Army Regulation 600-8-22*. Washington, D.C.: U.S. Government Printing Office.

Durkheim, Emile. 1995. *The Elementary Forms of Religious Life*. Translated by Karen E. Fields. New York: Free Press.

———. 1994. *Durkheim on Religion*. Edited by W. S. F. Pickering. Atlanta, Ga.: Scholars Press.

———. 1993. *Ethics and the Sociology of Morals*. Translated by Robert T. Hall. Buffalo, N.Y.: Prometheus Books.

Hägerström, Axel. 1953 *Inquiries into the Nature of Law and Morals*. Edited by Karl Olivecrona and translated by C. D. Broad. Uppsala: Almqvist and Wiksells.

Hart, H. L. A. 1961. *The Concept of Law*. London: Oxford University Press.

Ihering, Rudolf von. 1913 (1968). *Law as a Means to an End*. Translated by Isaac Husik. New York: A. M. Kelley; reprint, South Hackensack, N.J.: Rothman.

Lecky, William. 1925. *History of European Morals from Augustus to Charlemagne*. 3rd ed. rev. Vol. 1. New York: Appleton.

Pickering, W. S. F. 1984. *Durkheim's Sociology of Religion: Themes and Theories*. London: Routledge and Kegan Paul.

Sidgwick, Henry. 1930. *The Methods of Ethics*. London: Macmillan.

Spencer, Herbert. 1879. *The Data of Ethics*. New York: Appleton.

Stouffer, Samuel A., et. al. 1977 [1949]. *The American Soldier: Combat and Its Aftermath*. Vol. 2. Manhattan, Kans.: Sunflower University Press; originally published Princeton: Princeton University Press.

Turner, Stephen. 1998. "Kohlberg's Critique of Durkheim's Moral Education." In *Durkheim and Modern Education*, edited by W. S. F. Pickering and Geoffrey Walford. London: Routledge.

Weber, Max. 1958. *The Protestant Ethic and the Spirit of Capitalism*. Translated by Talcott Parsons. New York: Scribner's.

9

Confronting the Canon in the Classroom

Approaches to Teaching the Significance of Women,
Sex, and Gender in the Work of Emile Durkheim

Jean Elisabeth Pedersen

There is another thing. The division of labor between the sexes is
capable of being more, and capable of being less. It can relate only
to the sexual organs and some secondary traits that depend on
them, or, on the contrary, can extend to all organic and social functions.

—Emile Durkheim, *The Division of Labor*
in Society (1893)

What teachers do with Durkheim depends, of course, on where they
are, who else is in their classrooms, and what kinds of classes they
are trying to teach. Although I heard about Durkheim for the first
time from friends in a methods seminar in sociology, for example, I
studied his work for the first time myself in a seminar on French
intellectual history. My friends, preparing for their field exams in sociology, wanted to know how Durkheim's theories might serve as
the basis for their future sociological research. Working toward my
own doctoral orals in European history, I learned, instead, to identify
Durkheim's inheritance from figures such as Auguste Comte and
Fustel de Coulanges, to analyze his arguments with Gabriel Tarde,
and to reconstruct his rise to prominence in *fin-de-siècle* French academic life.[1]

My interest in the place of gender in Durkheim's work began on the day I started reading *The Division of Labor in Society*. When I came to the passage that compared the division of labor in society to the "sexual division of labor" in "conjugal society," I knew I had to know more about his contemporaries' positions on marriage and the family to understand his own.[2] Durkheim seemed to have meant his references to marriage to be self-explanatory: the special category of "conjugal solidarity," an easy example to introduce the more important category of "organic solidarity." Even as I followed his intentionally provocative argument that the primary results of the division of labor were moral rather than economic, though, I remained puzzled by his confident assertions: "It is certain that . . . sexual labor is more and more divided [in modern times]" or "Today, among cultivated people, the woman leads a completely different existence from that of the man."[3] Rereading Durkheim's work almost twenty years later, I am struck by the contemporary ring of Durkheim's assertion that the categories of sexual difference are not necessarily only biological, "relate[d] only to the secondary organs and some secondary traits that depend on them," but also potentially "organic and social" as well. Nevertheless, even as I appreciate that insight, which I have taken as the epigraph for this essay, I also remain ambivalent about Durkheim's work and its influence because I know that Durkheim looked forward to increasingly civilized societies in which sexual difference meant "more," while I imagine that I would be even happier in some future society where it meant "less."[4]

As I have made the transition from student to professor, I have developed my own approach to Durkheim's work in conversation with colleagues who have approached it from an extraordinary range of fields: not only history and sociology but also religion, philosophy, anthropology, literary criticism, political theory, and cultural studies.[5] The last time I taught his work in class, for example, I was the guest lecturer in a political science seminar that had also attracted students in American history and English literature.[6] We read the *Division of Labor* in combination with Durkheim's essay on "Individualism and the Intellectuals" and grappled with the question of how a writer who seemed so focused on the needs of society in the first piece could come to such a radical defense of the individual in the second. We also argued over whether Durkheim's "individual" could ever be an individual woman, or whether his attitudes toward gender suggested that he would reserve the public roles of social scientist and social critic for men alone. We left the room in some disagreement about whether the political implications of Durkheim's ideas would be radical or conservative.[7]

Although I have not yet had occasion to teach *The Elementary Forms of the Religious Life*, it remains my favorite of all of Durkheim's books. It is a pleasure, then, to think about what I would do with Durkheim's work on religion if I were planning to take it into the classroom. The several sections of this essay explore several possibilities that I have already found particularly fruitful in my previous work on Durkheim's own ideas and the ideas of a wide variety of other turn-of-the-century French men and women who also argued over the real and ideal relationships between the two sexes. The first section offers an analysis of the ways gender appears in three of Durkheim's major works, *The Division of Labor in Society, Suicide,* and *The Elementary Forms of the Religious Life.* The second section explores the relationships between Durkheim's sociological conclusions and his political positions, especially his arguments over two issues that raised particularly pressing questions about men, women, and the relationships between them: divorce and sex education. A final, speculative section suggests ways one might study the *Elementary Forms* in conjunction with recent work in the philosophy of science, sociology of knowledge, and history of the social sciences, including the feminist scholarship in these areas.

The social theorist Donald Levine has pointed out that "although there is wide variation regarding which past figures get selected as originative figures, it is difficult to imagine any history of the sociological tradition that does not devote some attention to the work of Emile Durkheim."[8] Durkheim's work has been important, not only for sociologists and social theorists, but for anthropologists, scholars in religious studies, and many other academic specialists as well. While such canonical status makes him a particularly important subject for feminist study, it should also make feminist findings important for any scholar who is interested in his work. Indeed, looking at the significance of gender in that work raises a series of questions that are central to inquiry in literature, history, philosophy, science, and social science: the relationship between an author's canonical major works and his less popular minor works, the relationship between social theory and public policy, the relationship between science and social science, and the complex relationships among social science, social criticism, and social activism.

Feminist scholars have wrestled with such canon questions from many different directions, even when they have been working in a single field.[9] As I think about the many ways of approaching the social scientific canon, I have found particular help in the work of Elisabeth Schüssler Fiorenza, a feminist theologian who has focused her attention on approaches to that foundational canon, the books of the Old and New Testament. Schüssler Fiorenza, who is particularly interested in the ways feminist interpretations of biblical texts might improve the status of women in contemporary Judeo-Christian communities, has recently identified ten different ways of contesting the biblical canon.[10] Scholars who share a parallel concern for the position of women as the authors or subjects of social scientific studies might also find some interest in the multiplicity of critical approaches she offers. Although I have not used Schüssler Fiorenza's categories to divide my own essay, her suggestions about how to study the Bible often resonate with my own questions about how to study Durkheim's work, the implications of his words about women in their relationship to men, and the enduring effects of his canonical position in the past and present practices of a wide variety of academic disciplines.

My own experiences teaching Durkheim or introducing feminist theory have always occurred in those seminar settings where the dominant pedagogical approach is reading and discussion. Each section hereafter takes a similar approach, beginning with an overview of the existing work on Durkheim in a particular area, continuing with my own analysis of its relevance to the *Elementary Forms*, and including a series of possible discussion questions for classroom use. Durkheim's work raises new questions in my mind whenever I return to it. In the sections that follow, I offer not only the discussion questions I have used in the past but also those that I have stored up to try in the future. I hope they will enliven other classrooms as well.

Women, Sex, and Gender in Durkheim's Major Works

Although Durkheim himself connected his work in the *Elementary Forms* to his earlier work by citing himself in a series of strategically significant footnotes, subsequent scholars have never agreed about how to assess the relationship between his last book and all the books and articles that came before it.[11] As a historian drawing distinctions among different disciplines and national traditions, for example, I learned to think about the difference between Durkheim the sociologist, who influenced Talcott Parsons in the United States, and Durkheim the anthropologist, who influenced Radcliffe-Brown in the United Kingdom. In the field of philosophy, David Bloor has suggested that the *Elementary Forms* offers a new argument for the social construction of all scientific knowledge, while Warren Schmaus has insisted in return that Durkheim's last book is better read as the logical culmination of a lifelong professional interest in founding a positive science of society instead.[12]

Looking at the importance of gender in Durkheim's major works raises similar questions about how to assess the relative significance of continuity and discontinuity in his intellectual development from his first book to his last. Despite the fact that Durkheim's writings at first appear to be remarkable for what the sociologist Jennifer Lehmann has characterized as a "conspicuous absence of women," his central sociological arguments in the *Division of Labor*, *Suicide*, and the *Elementary Forms* all turn out to rely on arguments about the changing social relationships between men and women.[13] For example, in the *Division of Labor*, as I mentioned earlier, he introduced his argument that the division of labor was the source of social solidarity by examining the "history of marital relations" to prove that the sexual division of labor was "the source of conjugal solidarity."[14] Similarly, in *Suicide*, he discussed not only "religious society" and "political society" but also "domestic society." In his section on egoistic suicide, for example, he compared the suicides of a chief's followers after their leader's death with the suicide of a wife after her husband's death. More extensively, in his section on anomic suicide, he analyzed not only the "economic anomie" caused by "economic crises," "economic disasters," or "chronic" economic uncertainty but also the "domestic anomie" caused by the "family catastrophe" of widowhood or the even "more chronic" catastrophe of divorce.[15] Finally, in the *Elementary Forms*, where he described a series of Australian tribal societies in which men and women usually led strikingly separate lives, he located the roots of religious feeling in the "collective effervescence" that accompanied the *corroboree*, a vast social gathering that unleashed so much excitement that men broke the normal rules of social life and sexual behavior by sharing their women in common among themselves.

The social theorist Mike Gane, who has characterized Durkheim's approach to gender as "a puzzle and a problem," has pointed out a decisive shift in Durkheim's work from the "initial theory" of the *Division of Labor* and *Suicide*, which argued that the sexual division of labor only became increasingly apparent and important with the development of modern civilization, and the "completely new" theory of the "Prohibition of Incest" and the *Elementary Forms*, which argued that a crucial dichotomous distinction between men and women had already existed from the beginning in the primitive societies of Australia.[16] In the *Division of Labor*, Durkheim had relied on anthropologists' evidence to argue that primitive men and women, who exhibited a greater similarity in "general build and appearance" than civilized men and women, also exhibited a greater similarity in their social organization, a similarity that was particularly apparent when women participated in "political life" or went "off to war with the men, stimulating them to fight, and even participating very actively in the fighting[,] . . . fighting side by side with them."[17] By contrast, in the *Elementary Forms*, he relied on a different selection of ethnographic evidence to describe the many ways in which Australian and Native American societies persistently distinguished between men and women in the practice of rituals that separated masculine and sacred from feminine and profane.

While this dramatic change in Durkheim's description of early sex roles and relationships would seem to support those who argue for the discontinuity between Durkheim's earlier and later work, feminist scholars' separate assessments of each individual work seem to point instead to an important continuity when they consistently argue that Durkheim's sociological theories failed to adequately acknowledge or explain women's social experiences. For example, R. A. Sydie, who provided one of the earliest feminist analyses of many of Durkheim's books and articles, argued that the key word "society," which appears so often in Durkheim's work "is, in fact, a code word for the interests and needs of men as opposed to those of women."[18] Similarly, Victoria Jay Erickson, who focuses on Durkheim's contributions to the social theory of religion, has argued that Durkheim's description of the gendered dichotomy between sacred men and profane women "[makes it] possible to hypothesize that what produced 'religion' was not a collective experience, but a masculine one, and to argue that what Durkheim 'saw' when he looked at religion was activity produced primarily to satisfy the needs of men."[19] Most recently, Nancy Jay has responded to the *Elementary Forms* by asking: "If the capacity for conceptual thought is acquired only through a [ritual] process that excludes women, how does it come about that women can think?" She concludes: "If you hold fast to Durkheim's analysis, there is no way to answer this question."[20]

While I think there might be ways to answer Jay's question in Durkheim's terms by pointing out that women could have experienced the crucial contrast between sacred and profane as powerfully from the outside as men did from the inside, I would never want anyone to underestimate the often profoundly exclusionary significance of gender in Durkheim's work. While it is intriguing to wonder, with Gane, why Durkheim's descriptions of primitive society changed so dramatically from the beginning to the end of his scholarly career, it is also important to remember that his descriptions of civilized society did not necessarily undergo a similar transformation. While the *Elementary Forms*, unlike Durkheim's earlier work, says nothing about relationships between modern men and women, it is hard to imagine that his new insistence on the importance of sexual difference in the past would have done anything but confirm his earlier insistence on the importance of sexual difference in the present and for the future.

My own approach to Durkheim in the classroom would differ depending on whether I were teaching the *Elementary Forms* after reading several of his other works, or whether I were focusing on the *Elementary Forms* alone. Even in the latter case, though, I would want my students to think about what Durkheim had already said about gender in his earlier work while they were discussing the significance of gender in his last book. If I had the time in the syllabus, I would ask them to read at least the relevant sections from the *Division of Labor*, especially Durkheim's discussion of marriage in chapter 1 of book 1, and from *Suicide*, especially his analysis of the impact of marriage and divorce on male and female suicide rates in chapters 3 and 5 of book 2 and his resulting policy considerations in chapter 3 of book 3. If I had to focus immediately on the *Elementary Forms*, I would substitute for the students' own reading an introductory lecture on the significance of gender in his earlier work. Either way, with that background in mind, we could turn to the discussion of the *Elementary Forms* itself with a greater awareness and understanding of the significance of gender in Durkheim's developing ideas.

In the *Division of Labor*, Durkheim had predicted that as societies became more and more civilized, the sexual division of labor would become more and more important. In his own time, he observed that women were in charge of "affective" functions, while men were in charge of "intellectual" ones. Although he acknowledged that women "in certain social classes" were starting to share men's interest in "art and literature," he did not see this as a sign that the two sexes were coming together. Instead, he imagined a future in which men would move away from the feminized field of "art and letters" to "devote" themselves "more especially to science," which would become the new masculine field instead.[21] He concluded *Suicide* with a similar prediction that the women of the future, who would become progressively "more different" from men, would concentrate on "aesthetic functions" while men would become "more and more absorbed by functions of utility." Even when he promised in a footnote that "woman would not be excluded from certain functions and relegated to others," he still imagined that the "free choice[s]" that women made based on their "aptitudes" would be "uniform."[22]

If we had time for discussion at this point, I would ask students what they thought of Durkheim's predictions. Did they agree that the world was becoming more and more sex-segregated? If so, did they think this was a positive or a negative development? My own students tend to think that the world is changing in exactly the opposite direction, which usually provokes me to ask them if they can still think of any ways men and women walk in different worlds. Teaching in the humanities department of a music school, for example, I can usually get provocative responses if I ask my students to try and explain the relative rarity of female conductors or male piccolo players. Even in a world where everyone but me, the teacher, is often coming to class in blue jeans, I have also gotten interesting results by asking my students to talk about the difference between men's and women's formal concert attire as a way of starting a conversation on the gender differences in their everyday clothing and hairstyles.

Durkheim argued that the sexual division of labor was a necessity for modern marriage. In his view, the complementary differences between men and women were what generated the "passion" that first drove them together and then maintained their interest in lifelong monogamous marriages.[23] Even students who seek an egalitarian society might not necessarily question the romantic quality of Durkheim's brief descriptions of the men and women who meet and complete each other in this way. To get discussion going, I might ask them whether his model could deal with same-sex attraction, and, if so, what it would suggest about gay or lesbian relationships. I would also want to ask them whether they would agree that the study of marriage is an appropriate microcosm for the study of society and, if so, to what extent and in what situations. Whether or not they agreed with Durkheim's predictions for the families of the future, I would also ask them what they thought of his preferences for those families, especially his persistent intellectual adherence to the necessity and the desirability of the sexual division of labor.

Jennifer Lehmann, the author of the first major book on "Durkheim and women," has argued that Durkheim never envisioned a world in which men and women might share a legitimate interest in the same occupations or activities.[24] While Lehmann herself did not discuss Durkheim's positions in the *Elementary Forms*, my own reading of that final text seems to confirm the conclusions she came to based on his earlier work. Indeed, unless one were

to assume that Durkheim had changed his mind about women's special interest in arts and letters, one could argue that the whole of the *Elementary Forms*
stands as an explanation of the emergence of the very world of scientific inquiry
that Durkheim had earlier identified as the privileged realm of men and men
alone. One of his most provocative conclusions is the assertion that modern
scientific thought was descended from primitive religious thought. It seems
unlikely, though, that he had come to think that women generally could or
should be scientists.

Working to approach the book with my students, I would start by asking
them to identify places in the text where Durkheim reported distinctions between men and women. For example, when Durkheim discussed the ways in
which Australian tribes treated their sacred instrument, the churinga, he noted,
"the women and the uninitiated cannot approach it." Similarly, totemic draw-
ings were so sacred that "women and children may not see them." In other
tribes, he related, "it frequently happens that certain animals are designated
as the food of women; for this reason, they believe that they partake of a feminine nature and that they are consequently profane." Or again, "We know that
as blood is a sacred thing, women must not see it flow."[25]

After we had a good list of examples to work with, I would ask my students
what difference Durkheim's descriptions of these dichotomous societies made
to their assessment of his conclusions. In particular, I would ask: Did they
think he was describing the religious life of both sexes or the religious life of
men alone? Before they decided too quickly that Durkheim was simply talking
about men only, I would want them to think about other possibilities as well.
What other distinctions besides gender seemed to be important in the world
Durkheim described? What about, for example, those cases where the tribes
associated "women and the uninitiated" or "women and children"? How did
these references to mixed groups of boys, girls, and women confirm or challenge the image of the primitive tribe as a place where men and women led
separate lives? Were factors such as age, marital status, or clan affiliation as
important as gender in assessing an individual's social and religious situation,
or was gender truly the single foundational category of classification for Durkheim and the tribes he studied?

In the process of such a discussion, I hope that my students would begin
to notice not only what Durkheim put in but also what he left out. For example,
they might observe that the *Elementary Forms*, which offers several discussions
about the processes by which boys became men in Australian and Native American tribal societies, says nothing about how girls became women in the same
societies. Did young women's rituals exist? If not, why not? If so, why didn't
Durkheim discuss them? Did he know about them? Durkheim relied on other
men's work rather than going into the field himself, but what would any male
anthropologist have been able to find out about the worlds of women in sex-

segregated societies? Were there any female ethnographers, who might have had more access to the lives of Australian or Native American women? In a seminar, any of these questions might also inspire several student research papers. Asking whether Durkheim's silence on such topics was intentional or unintentional would provide a way of looking not only at the significance of gender in his work but also at the significance of gender in the world in which he wrote.

Finally, after asking my students to think about the significance of different constructions of gender, the various social systems that divided men and women, I would ask them to think about the significance of different practices of sex, the one social practice that seemed to bring them together. In the *Division of Labor*, Durkheim had opened his analysis of the sexual division of labor in marriage by asserting: "It is because men and women differ from one another that they seek out one another with such passion. . . . In fact, men and women in isolation from each other are only different parts of the same concrete whole that they reconstitute by uniting with each other."[26] One of Durkheim's most striking analyses in the *Elementary Forms* also opens with a description of intense sexual communion between men and women, the corroboree. Where his description in the *Division of Labor* stressed the importance of passion as the foundation of modern monogamous marriage, though, the *Elementary Forms* shows another face of sex altogether in his description of such a ritual clan gathering:

> People are so far outside of the ordinary conditions of life, and so conscious of the fact, that they feel a need to set themselves above and beyond ordinary morality. The sexes come together in violation of the rule governing sexual relations. Men exchange wives. Indeed sometimes incestuous unions, in normal times judged loathsome and harshly condemned, are contracted in the open and with impunity. If it is added that the ceremonies are generally held at night, in the midst of shadows pierced here and there by firelight, we can easily imagine the effect that scenes like these are likely to have on the minds of all those who take part.[27]

Accepting Durkheim's invitation to "imagine the effect . . . on the minds of all those who take part" in such a ritual, I would ask students to think about whether they expected such effects to be the same in the minds of all the participants. What might the "men" be thinking and feeling? What about the "wives"? Where might students imagine children or single adults of either sex in this scenario? And what about the participants in the occasional "incestuous unions"? What might their ordinary kin relationships be? Would these be crossgenerational couplings, like the father–daughter incest we most often hear about today? Or would they be members of the same generation who were forbidden to engage in sex because they were also members of the same clan? Either way, how might the two participants in one of these improper pairs respond similarly or differently to the experience of such illicit sex?

Durkheim, who characterized his vivid description of the corroboree as an "unavoidably sketchy tableau," fleshed it out with scenes he borrowed from the ethnographic work of Spencer and Gillen. In the first such example, he described a ceremony that united two phratries of the Warramunga, the Uluuru and the Kingilli:

> Around ten or eleven o'clock [at night], Uluuru and Kingilli arrived
> on the scene, sat on the mound, and began to sing. All were in a
> state of obvious excitement. . . . A short time later in the evening,
> the Uluuru brought their wives and handed them over to the Kin-
> gilli, who had sexual relations with them. The recently initiated
> young men were brought in, and the ceremony was explained to
> them, after which there was uninterrupted singing until three in the
> morning.[28]

A close reading of this passage, which suggests that the "recently initiated young men" arrived on the scene too late to participate in the older men's sexual sharing of their women, suggests that gender was not the only important distinction among the Warramunga. Again, then, how would students characterize the social significance of initiation, either in this passage or in Durkheim's other descriptions of male initiation rites?

What might tribal life look like if we had more extensive accounts of women's varied practices and experiences as well as men's? Durkheim argued that the seeds of "the religious idea" lay in the dramatic difference between the "colorlessness" of regular tribal life and the "hyperexcitement" of clan gatherings such as the corroboree.[29] If we expanded our understanding of tribal behavior beyond the study of men's initiation rituals and the corroboree, I would ask my students, would we have to modify Durkheim's explanations of religious impulses as well? If so, how? And, if not, what would it say about religious practices to believe that they had their roots in the scenes of violently excited and socially unorthodox sexual behavior that Durkheim describes?

This last question might also relate to a series of more contemporary questions. For example, one might ask students if they still experienced the dichotomy between sacred and profane as a foundational fact of religious experience. If so, how and why? If not, what distinctions seemed to have become important instead? Would it be possible to redefine Durkheim's dichotomous distinction between sacred and profane in ways that did not depend on similar social or symbolic distinctions between men and women, male and female, or masculine and feminine? What might such a new definition look like?

Social Science and Public Policy: Durkheim on Divorce and Sex Education

Although Durkheim may be best remembered for his canonical works of social science, he was also a frequent participant in arguments over French public policy. As a historian, I remain particularly interested in situating Durkheim and his work in the historical context of the *fin de siècle* and *belle époque*. Whether one is primarily interested in the development of Durkheim's own ideas or in the subsequent public debate over the persistently controversial questions he addressed, the study of his articles, editorials, book reviews, and other interventions can provide a fascinating supplement, or even alternative, to the study of his canonical works.

Although Durkheim insisted on a key methodological distinction between theoretical "social science," which sought general rules of behavior, and practical "political art," which sought immediate solutions to specific social problems, he also insisted that all those "writers and scholars" who constituted the "intellectual elite" of France should exercise civic responsibility by advising their contemporaries through "books, seminars, and popular education."[30] Durkheim took his own advice when he wrote and spoke on a wide variety of topics, including public education, professional associations, the separation of church and state, the Dreyfus affair, and World War I.[31]

Durkheim's attitudes toward women, sex, and gender are particularly apparent in his public interventions on two additional topics: divorce and sex education. Unfortunately for those who must teach Durkheim in English, many of the pieces where he expressed his ideas on issues such as these have never been presented in a complete English translation. Furthermore, the works of the divorce reformers and would-be sex educators with whom Durkheim originally argued are largely out of print, even in French. The following sections explore ways of getting around this problem through the use of recent work in French history. Books and articles can set the historical context, for example, while document collections of materials by and about women can give students a vivid sense of how Durkheim's contemporaries wrote about the issues that he addressed.[32] In this way, one can sense the significance of Durkheim's *fin-de-siècle* French political opinions even in an English-speaking college classroom.

Durkheim, Divorce, and Fin-de-Siècle Feminism

Most of the work on Durkheim's sexual politics has focused on the positions about marriage and divorce that he elaborated not only in the *Division of Labor* and *Suicide*, but also in a column on divorce by mutual consent in the *Revue bleue* in 1906, in his contributions to a seminar on "marriage and divorce" at the Union for Truth in 1909, and in his response to a presentation on sex education at the French Society for Philosophy in 1911.[33] Two of my favorite introductions to the broader study of marriage and divorce in France are Theresa McBride's essay on "divorce and the republican family" or, for those whose syllabus allows them to assign a longer reading, Edward Berenson's book on the 1914 trial of Madame Caillaux, a woman who murdered a powerful newspaper editor for publishing one of the private letters she had received from her second husband when he was still her adulterous lover.[34] Lawyers and journalists made much of the fact that Henriette and Joseph Caillaux had both divorced their first spouses to marry each other instead, and Berenson uses the coverage of the trial as a fascinating window into French attitudes toward sex and gender in the period from 1890 to 1914.[35]

I like to accompany even the most vivid secondary history with a selection of primary documents. In this case, selections might include: sections of the French Civil Code on marriage, French feminist attacks on that code by activists such as Léon Richer and Maria Deraismes, Jeanne Schmahl's assessment of the French women's movement in 1896, and, from the debates over divorce in particular, the statement made in 1880 by Pope Leo XIII on the sanctity of marriage, the radical deputy Alfred Naquet's justification for divorce in 1881, and the feminist lawyer Maria Martin's further demands for divorce by mutual consent in 1907. These materials, along with excellent historical introductions and hundreds of other original sources for the study of women, the family, and feminist reform in western Europe and the United States, are all available in Susan Groag Bell and Karen Offen's two-volume set on "women, the family, and freedom."[36]

To explore Durkheim's own positions on marriage and divorce, one can begin by examining the *Division of Labor* and *Suicide* themselves. Although the first chapter of the first book, which he published in 1893, says nothing about divorce, it helps both to explain his investment in the importance of marriage and to illustrate what he thought the ideal marriage would be like. His anxieties over the social impact of divorce are readily apparent in the chapters on egoistic and anomic suicide that he included in *Suicide*, which appeared in 1897, thirteen years after the passage of the Naquet Law had reaffirmed the dual principles of secular marriage and legal divorce in France for the first time since the defeat of Napoleon and the restoration of the Bourbon monarchy in 1815.

Durkheim's comparative statistical research on the relationships between divorce and suicide had showed him a "problem [that was] especially disturbing": in countries where divorce was legal, male suicide rates went up while female suicide rates went down. In other words, the members of the two sexes had opposing interests in the constitution of the couple: men, "the product of society," needed the regulation of marriage, while women, still "to a far greater extent the product of nature," needed the freedom of divorce. Durkheim hoped that the conflict would disappear once women found their own ways of participating in social activity. Where men were already active in "functions of utility," he hoped that women would become more active in "aesthetic functions." In the meantime, he warned social reformers, "the champions today of equal rights for woman with those of man," not to get ahead of themselves by trying to create legal equality before cultural conditions were ripe for it: "the work of centuries cannot be instantly abolished . . . juridical equality cannot be legitimate so long as psychological inequality is so flagrant."[37]

Durkheim wrote *Suicide* to exemplify the power of his sociological methods, but I would also be interested in asking students what they thought of the implications of his political recommendations. For example, would students agree that legal reforms were premature if basic social and psychological changes had not already occurred first? To what extent might laws themselves act as catalysts for social change instead? If one chose not to address social problems with legal solutions, what other options might one have at one's disposal?

The Naquet Law had been a compromise law that rejected any form of no-fault divorce in favor of divorce for a limited list of causes: adultery, cruelty, or a serious criminal conviction. Feminists, socialists, and radical republicans had been pushing for its expansion at least since 1896, when one Madame Coutant, the president of the Syndicate of Laundresses and Washerwomen, demanded the legalization of divorce by mutual consent at the International Feminist Congress in Paris.[38] By 1900, the novelists Paul and Victor Margueritte had begun an explosive public campaign for divorce by mutual consent and divorce at the persistent request of one partner alone, demands that had also featured prominently in the discussions of the hundreds of men and women who had again converged on Paris from around the world for the International Congress on the Condition and Rights of Women in Paris earlier in the year.[39] In 1904, the French government passed the first significant extension of the Naquet Law by allowing a guilty partner who had been divorced for adultery to marry his or her adulterous lover.

In 1906, Durkheim himself moved from the elaboration of a new social science to the advocacy of a new public policy when he attacked contemporary demands for divorce by mutual consent in an article for the *Revue bleue*, a weekly journal that covered literature and politics. Writing nine years after his initial work in *Suicide*, Durkheim reexamined his statistics and reinterpreted his results in what the French sociologist Pierre Besnard has characterized as "a brutal reversal" of his earlier position.[40] Although Durkheim still found that divorce raised male suicide rates, he now argued that it had no significant effect on female suicide rates at all. Reassured that men's and women's interests in marriage were not as different as he had originally feared, he warned contemporary "men of letters, men of law, and men of state" against the dangers of expanding the Naquet Law to allow easier divorce.[41] Besnard has argued

that Durkheim's arguments here are symptomatic of an "incompatibility between Durkheimian sociology and women."[42]

Besnard's analysis exists only in French, but Durkheim's own article is
available in English for students to read.[43] I might encourage those with a
mathematical bent to see if they could duplicate Besnard's work by studying
Durkheim's statistics themselves. Once they had presented their results to the
class, we could talk about the extent to which Durkheim's position seemed to
have changed. How did his work appear different when he presented it in the
Revue bleue, a journal that presumably commanded a broader audience than
the readership of *Suicide*? To what extent did his social science seem appropriate as a guide for future public policy? Would students agree with his policy,
or would they be more sympathetic to the opponents whose views they had
studied in the secondary historical literature and primary source documents
on the issue?

Faculty who read French themselves would have the option of continuing
their discussion of Durkheim's opinions on divorce even further by lecturing
their students on his intervention at a March 1909 seminar on marriage and
divorce at the Union for Truth, a group whose original founders had described
their monthly "open conversations" as discussions for people who wanted to
think about contemporary issues without confining themselves to the point of
view of a single "journal, . . . party, . . . church, . . . or block."[44] This particular
meeting was the fifth in a series of six sessions on feminism that had begun
in November 1908, just a few months after the French parliament modified
the Naquet Law a second time by allowing any spouse who had obtained a
simple separation to convert it into a divorce after a three-year waiting period.
Besides Durkheim, the diverse participants in the meeting on marriage and
divorce included novelists, journalists, philosophers, law professors, and practicing lawyers from the French appellate courts.[45]

The transcript of these discussions offers a rare chance to follow Durkheim's face-to-face arguments with some of the men and women who were
also interested in what the moderator, Paul Desjardins, characterized as "the
contemporary crisis of marriage." Durkheim's last intervention, which began
with his abrupt interruption of a liberal judge who had just accused him of
opposing divorce altogether, was a clarification of his own position:

> I admit [the necessity of limited] divorce . . . I believe that abso-
> lute[ly] permanent marriage is impossible . . . What I want is that
> the magistrate who is faced with a particular case does not simply
> take account of the desires expressed by the parties involved, but
> thinks more about the great social interests which are engaged in
> any question of this kind and for which he is responsible.[46]

I would ask students whether they accepted Durkheim's argument that
the state was taking an ever-stronger hand in the definition of marriage, or

whether they agreed with the feminist Louise Compain and the liberal lawyer Jules Dietz that recent laws had actually weakened marriage by allowing divorce and offering rights to illegitimate children.[47] I would also wonder whether they supported Durkheim's argument that divorce was dangerous for any couple, or whether they would agree with Jules Dietz and Jeanne Chambon that one could make meaningful distinctions between couples with and without children. Finally, I would ask them what they thought of Durkheim's recommendations for the limited form of divorce he accepted. What, if anything, would they see as one of the "great social interest[s]" that should prevent a couple from ending a marriage?

As far as I know, Durkheim's last published word on marriage and divorce appeared in the transcript of his participation in a debate on sex education at the French Society for Philosophy in 1911. Here he spoke less about the social implications of marriage and divorce, which he had derived from his work on the division of labor and suicide, and more about the emotional and psychological implications of these practices, which he understood in terms of his comparative ethnographic work on incest and religion. Seeking to explain "the moral embarrassment" observers might feel when they were present at an encounter between the two members of a divorced couple, he noted:

> We are aware that there is something abnormal in two individuals treating each other like strangers whereas, in fact, neither holds any mystery for the other. This is not, of course, to deny the evidence that divorce is an indispensable necessity. But there is no altering the fact that there is something disconcerting in certain of its effects that one should be able to recognize.[48]

Teaching this text, I would be curious to know whether students shared Durkheim's sense of the social awkwardness of the scene he described. What had or had not changed in the ninety years since he wrote? If they accepted that such meetings could have the impact he described, how would they discuss the relationship between divorce as a public policy and divorce as a personal reality? How, if at all, would their own understanding of the individual or cultural consequences of divorce affect their position on the legal provisions for obtaining a divorce? Would they change the law if they could? How and why?

Social Science and Sex Education

Durkheim's positions on sex education have received less attention than his positions on divorce, but in some ways I find them even more interesting.[49] His 1911 debate with Dr. Jacques-Amédée Doléris at the French Society for Philosophy opened up a whole series of fascinating questions about the extent to which sex is a simple biological behavior or a complex cultural practice.

Discussing the highlights of the argument might work particularly well as a followup to the discussion of Durkheim's earlier work on the incest taboo, which also rejected biological explanations, or as a preparation for the discussion of Durkheim's later work on the *Elementary Forms*, which also claimed to illuminate contemporary practices by returning to their primitive expressions.

While I know of no single source for a general treatment of early twentieth-century French debates over sex education, faculty might prepare an introductory lecture on the topic by consulting current work on the history of prostitution, attitudes toward venereal disease, and debates over the use of birth control and abortion.[50] Those who wish to assign a range of primary sources on turn-of-the-century French attitudes toward sex and sexuality might consider some of the following: almost any novel by Emile Zola; the more politically explicit novels and plays of authors such as Eugène Brieux, Lucie Delarue-Mardrus, and Marcelle Tinayre; or the revolutionary speeches of birth control activists such as Nelly Roussel and Madeleine Pelletier.[51]

Jacques-Amédée Doléris, who started the discussion at the French Society for Philosophy, was a prominent doctor with a background in obstetrics who ultimately achieved the presidency of the prestigious French Academy of Medicine. In his presentation on sex education and sexual hygiene, he argued that medical doctors had a responsibility to combat traditional ignorance, religious superstition, and parental silence by teaching children about the mechanics of reproduction and the perils of venereal disease in explicit scientific terms. He proposed a curriculum that began with botany, moved through animal biology, and ended with human biology and embryology.[52]

Emile Durkheim, the first person in the audience to respond, caused a new controversy of his own when he objected that sexual acts might seem mysterious for good reasons that science should not seek to explain away. Although Durkheim agreed with Doléris that sex education was necessary, that preventive hygiene should be taught, and even that girls as well as boys should learn about the physical details of reproductive sex, he also argued that sex was much more than just another "biological function" like "digestion and circulation." Instead, its social character, "the contradictory, mysterious, and exceptional character which public opinion acknowledges it to have," must also be an "integral part" of its definition. Instead of seeing the modern reticence to talk about sex as the remains of some primitive superstition, he argued that the very fact that so many societies approached the study of sex with trepidation was the proof that there must be real reasons for their reluctance to discuss it: "when a collective sentiment is affirmed with persistence through the total length of history, one can be assured that it is founded in the facts."[53]

Doléris responded to this attack with an attack of his own. In what may have been a veiled reference to Durkheim's Jewish background, the doctor accused his critic of confusing personal prejudice with professional expertise: "I believe that M. Durkheim . . . is still under the influence of a particular setting and education and that that influence invincibly prevents him from considering the sexual act as it is, simple and fundamental."[54] Durkheim, in turn, responded by stressing his impeccable professional credentials:

> It is not at all as a man that I have spoken of the necessarily myste-rious character of the sexual act; but . . . exclusively as a sociologist. I am conscious that I do not owe to education the sentiment that I have tried to analyze summarily. The obscure, mysterious, and re-doubtable character of the sexual act has been revealed to me by his-torical and ethnographic research, and I even know the very mo-ment when I was struck by the extreme generality of the fact and all its implications.[55]

He closed by repeating the distinction between the "exterior gestures" of sex, which the physiologist could understand, and the more important "sentiments, ideas, and institutions that give these acts their uniquely human character."[56]

Whether or not my students were also reading Durkheim's earlier eth-nographic work on the incest taboo, or his later work on the *Elementary Forms*, I might start by drawing their attention to the similarities of Durkheim's ap-proaches in the three works. I would ask them what they thought of his asser-tion that the best way to understand a social phenomenon in a single place was to study its appearance in a wide variety of earlier times and other places. Did they think this approach was equally appropriate for such seemingly dis-parate topics as incest, legitimate sex, and modern religion?

I would also want to know what students thought of Durkheim's insistence on the distinction between the simple biological gestures of sex and its complex human significance. Whether or not they accepted this separation, would they, then, share his uneasiness about the potential perils of any purely scientific sex education? What kinds of curricula might they design to teach people of different ages and social situations about sex? What particular purposes might such different curricula serve?

Especially if my students were going on to read the *Elementary Forms*, I would ask them to focus on Durkheim's description of the sex act itself: a "singular" act, an act that could be "troubling and disconcerting," an act that could be simultaneously "immoral" and "moralizing," a "complex" and "am-biguous" act that could leave one's conscience or consciousness "hesitant, trou-bled, perplexed, [and] divided against itself."[57] How would Durkheim's descrip-tion of civilized sexual behavior here shed new light on his description of the power that he would later attribute to primitive sexual behavior in the corrob-oree? What might this suggest about Durkheim's position on continuity and change between past and present? What might it add to our own understanding of that question?

Finally, I would ask my students what they thought of Doléris's charge that Durkheim's positions were personal rather than professional. To what extent did Durkheim's assertions about sex seem consistent or inconsistent with his other work? If they seemed consistent, would this mean that they were professional opinions, as he asserted, or might it mean that all his academic work was also colored by his personal situation? How might one draw meaningful distinctions between personal positions and professional practices? To what extent would students see these distinctions as desirable or undesirable, and why?

Feminist Theory and Durkheimian Social Realism

One final way in which I would love to bring questions of sex, gender, and feminism to bear on the teaching of Emile Durkheim's work would be the design of a course that would combine the study of his original contribution to epistemology in the *Elementary Forms* with more recent studies in the sociology of knowledge and the history and philosophy of science and social science, including the recent feminist work in these fields. While Durkheim himself opposed feminist protest, I have often thought that some aspects of his so-called social realism seem surprisingly compatible with what more recent scholars might call "social constructionism." In the course I imagine, I would have a chance to test this hypothesis and its implications with a group of willing students, checking to see if we might find ways to turn Durkheim's work to our purposes in spite of his own relatively conservative sexual politics.

Starting with a reading of the *Elementary Forms* itself, I would ask students to consider the competing interpretations of David Bloor and Warren Schmaus, who disagree over the extent to which Durkheim's work should count as an argument for the social construction of all scientific knowledge.[58] Continuing with Robert Alun Jones's recent study of Durkheim's social realism in the works preceding the *Elementary Forms*, I would ask how Jones's interpretation of Durkheim's previous work might shed light, first on Durkheim's intentions in his later work, then on the Bloor/Schmaus controversy.[59] Because Jones frames his own work with reference to Thomas Kuhn and Richard Rorty, some reading or lecture and discussion of the controversy around these figures would undoubtedly be helpful here.[60]

While none of these scholars pay particular attention to feminist work, I have often thought that their questions about the social construction of knowledge have certain similarities to feminist critiques of scientific and social scientific claims. I would continue, then, with Sandra Harding's classic survey of feminist approaches to "the science question."[61] How would students compare it either to the work of the scholars above or to Helen Longino's exploration of "science as social knowledge" and other work on feminist epistemology?[62] Faculty in different fields could end the seminar with appropriate work on the epistemological foundations, methodological assumptions, and historical formations of their own disciplines. A historian myself, I would probably end this imaginary seminar by considering the implications for history, reading the roundtables and reviews around a series of books I would also want to assign: Peter Novick's work on the "objectivity question" in the historical profession; Joyce Appleby, Lynn Hunt, and Margaret Jacobs's work on "telling the truth about history"; Joan Scott's essays on "gender and the politics of history"; and Bonnie Smith's work on the gendered history of "men, women, and historical practice."[63]

This last is the most speculative of the course outlines I have proposed in this essay. As readers take the opportunity to put this, or any of the other pedagogical suggestions I have outlined, into effect in their classrooms, I hope they will let me know what happens, and I look forward to hearing the results.

NOTES

1. I thank Jan Goldstein for teaching the University of Chicago seminar in French intellectual history that introduced me to Durkheim.

2. I was reading the 1933 George Simpson translation. The newer 1984 W. D. Halls translation now renders Simpson's "conjugal society," Durkheim's original "so-ciété conjugale," as "marital relationships." See Emile Durkheim, *The Division of Labor in Society*, trans. George Simpson (New York: Free Press, 1933), 56; *De la division du travail social* (Paris: Presses universitaires de France, 1930) 19; *The Division of Labor in Society*, trans. W. D. Halls (New York: Free Press, 1984) 17.

3. Durkheim, *Division of Labor* [1933], 60. I'm using Simpson's older translation here to be true to my own original reading experience.

4. Durkheim, *Division of Labor* [1984], 18. Here I've switched to citations from the more modern Halls translation that I use, with Durkheim's French original, as the basis of my current scholarship.

5. I particularly thank the participants in the University of Chicago Workshop in the History of the Human Sciences, the Research Seminar of the Susan B. Anthony Institute for Gender and Women's Studies at the University of Rochester, and the NEH Summer Institute on the Idea of a Social Science for helping me work through the implications of Durkheim's ideas.

6. I thank Annabelle Lever for the invitation to teach this University of Rochester political science seminar.

7. We were in good company in this debate. Durkheim himself avoided political labels, leaving it for subsequent scholars to try to pin him down. For one good overview of the issues involved, see Steve Fenton, *Durkheim and Modern Sociology* (Cambridge: Cambridge University Press, 1984). On Durkheim as a conservative, see Alvin Gouldner, *The Coming Crisis of Western Sociology* (New York: Equinox, 1970); as a liberal, see Steven Seidman, *Liberalism and the Origins of European Social Theory* (Berkeley: University of California Press, 1983); as a radical, see Frank Pearce, *The Radical Durkheim* (London: Unwin Hyman, 1989). None of these assessments take gender into account. For a range of assessments that focus on Durkheim's sexual politics,

then, see R. A. Sydie, *Natural Women, Cultured Men: A Feminist Perspective on Sociolog-ical Theory* (New York: New York University Press, 1987); Terry Kandal, *The Woman Question in Classical Sociological Theory* (Miami: Florida International University Press, 1988); Mike Gane, *Harmless Lovers? Gender, Theory, and Personal Relationships* (London: Routledge, 1993); Jennifer Lehmann, *Durkheim and Women* (Lincoln: University of Nebraska Press, 1994); Jean Elisabeth Pedersen, " 'Something Mysterious': Sex Education, Victorian Morality, and Durkheim's Comparative Sociology," *Journal of the History of the Behavioral Sciences* 34, 2 (1998): 135–151; and "Sexual Politics in Comte and Durkheim: Feminism, History, and the French Sociological Tradition," *Signs* 27, 1 (2001): 229–263.

8. Donald N. Levine, *Visions of the Sociological Tradition* (Chicago: University of Chicago Press, 1995), 87.

9. For reviews of many different feminist approaches to the single field of history, for example, see Joan Wallach Scott, *Gender and the Politics of History*, rev. ed. (New York: Columbia University Press, 1999), and Ann-Louise Shapiro, ed., *Feminists ReVision History* (New Brunswick, N.J.: Rutgers University Press, 1994).

10. See Schüssler Fiorenza, "Charting the Field of Feminist Biblical Interpretation," in *But She Said: Feminist Practices of Biblical Interpretation* (Boston: Beacon Press, 1992), 20–50.

11. For example, when Durkheim outlined his method in book 1, chapter 1, he referred readers to his *Rules of the Sociological Method* (*Elementary Forms*, 22; see also 233). Similarly, when he came to discuss the social organization of Australian tribes in book 1, chapter 4, the first chapter on totemism, he cited his own *Division of Labor in Society* as a source (*Elementary Forms*, 93; see also 226, 275, 412). As he expanded on the significance of totemism in the opening chapters of book 2, he added references to his articles on the prohibition of incest, the matrimonial organization of Australian tribes, and primitive classification (*Elementary Forms*, 107, 109, 142, 145, 168; see also 319). The concluding section of his chapter on the soul referred to the *Division of Labor* and *Suicide* (*Elementary Forms*, 270, 275), and the concluding chapter of the entire work cited not only his article for the *Année sociologique* on primitive classification but also his contribution to the *Revue de morale et de métaphysique* on individual and collective representation (*Elementary Forms*, 426, 443). Even when Durkheim admitted that his new 1912 definition of religion was different from his earlier 1899 "definition of religious phenomena," he still insisted that the two definitions "overlap[ped]" and that the new "modifications" made no difference to the "fundamental . . . conceptualization of the facts" (*Elementary Forms*, 21, 44, 203). One excellent collection of Durkheim's work on religion in the *Elementary Forms* and elsewhere is *Durkheim on Religion: A Selection of Readings with Bibliographies*, ed. W. S. F. Pickering (London: Routledge and Kegan Paul, 1975).

12. David Bloor, "Durkheim and Mauss Revisited: Classification and the Sociology of Knowledge," *Studies in History and Philosophy of Science* 13 (1982): 267–297, and Warren Schmaus, *Durkheim's Philosophy of Science and the Sociology of Knowledge: Creating an Intellectual Niche* (Chicago: University of Chicago Press, 1994).

13. Lehmann, *Durkheim and Women*, 32.

14. Durkheim, *Division of Labor* [1984], 17–18.

15. Emile Durkheim, *Suicide*, trans. John A. Spaulding and George Simpson (New York: Free Press, 1951), 8, 208, 219, 222, 240–259.

16. Gane, *Harmless Lovers?* 1, 30, 39.

17. Durkheim, *Division of Labor* [1984], 19.

18. Sydie, *Natural Women, Cultured Men*, 46.

19. Victoria Jay Erickson, *Where Silence Speaks: Feminism, Social Theory, and Religion* (Minneapolis: Fortress Press, 1993), 10.

20. Nancy Jay, *Throughout Your Generations Forever: Sacrifice, Religion, and Paternity* (Chicago: University of Chicago Press, 1992), 136.

21. Durkheim, *Division of Labor* [1984], 20–21.

22. Durkheim, *Suicide*, 385.

23. Durkheim, *Division of Labor* [1984], 17.

24. Lehmann, *Durkheim and Women*, 32–73.

25. Emile Durkheim, *The Elementary Forms of Religious Life*, trans. Karen E. Fields (New York: Free Press, 1995), 430. Fields argues that classic works deserve to be read and reread with "pleasure and excitement"; her sensitive literary translation of Durkheim's text makes this dream a reality for the *Elementary Forms* (xxiii).

26. Durkheim, *Division of Labor* [1984], 17–18.

27. Durkheim, *Elementary Forms*, 218.

28. Durkheim, *Elementary Forms*, 219.

29. Durkheim, *Elementary Forms*, 221.

30. For progressive elaborations of this principle, see Durkheim, "The Principles of 1789 and Sociology" (1890), "Sociology in France in the Nineteenth Century" (1900), and "The Intellectual Elite and Democracy" (1904), all translated by Mark Traugott, in *Emile Durkheim on Morality and Society*, ed. Robert Bellah (Chicago: University of Chicago Press, 1973).

31. See the indispensable biography by Steven Lukes, *Emile Durkheim: His Life and Work, A Historical and Critical Study* (Stanford: Stanford University Press, 1986), esp. 109–136, 320–360, 530–559.

32. In addition to the works cited hereafter, the most extensive bibliographies of work by and about French feminists are available in Karen Offen, *European Feminisms, 1700–1950: A Political History* (Stanford: Stanford University Press, 2000).

33. In addition to the works cited in note 7, see Lukes, *Durkheim*, 530–534, and Philippe Besnard, "Durkheim et les femmes, ou *Le Suicide* inachevée," *Revue française de sociologie* 14, 28 (1973): 27–61.

34. Theresa McBride, "Divorce and the Republican Family," in *Gender and the Politics of Social Reform in France, 1870–1914*, edited by Elinor A. Accampo, Rachel G. Fuchs, and Mary Lynn Stewart (Baltimore: Johns Hopkins University Press, 1990); Edward Berenson, *The Trial of Madame Caillaux* (Berkeley: University of California Press, 1992). The core of Berenson's argument about divorce is available in a shorter article format, "The Politics of Divorce in France of the Belle Epoque: The Case of Joseph and Henriette Caillaux," *American Historical Review* 93, 1 (1988): 31–55. My own work on divorce analyzes the public response to popular plays about divorce, paternity suits, abortion and birth control as a way of gauging the cultural resonance of these controversial topics. See Jean Elisabeth Pedersen, *Legislating the French Family:*

Feminism, Theater, and Republican Politics, 1870–1920 (New Brunswick, N.J.: Rutgers University Press, 2003).

35. Berenson's analysis of the trial discusses not only marriage and divorce but also a range of other fascinating *fin-de-siècle* topics including the rise of the independent woman and the republican interest in the duel. See Berenson, *Trial of Madame Caillaux.*

36. See, particularly, the parts entitled "Woman as Wife in the Wake of the French Revolution," "Attacks on the Civil Code in France," "The Women's Movement Organizes," and "Civil Divorce and the Catholic Church," in *Women, the Family, and Freedom: The Debate in Documents,* edited by Susan Groag Bell and Karen M. Offen (Stanford: Stanford University Press, 1983), 1:37–41, 448–455, 2:97–106, 181–190. Another rich collection of documents on the French feminism of Durkheim's day is Jennifer Waelti-Walters and Steven Hause, eds., *Feminisms of the Belle Epoque: A Historical and Literary Anthology* (Lincoln: University of Nebraska Press, 1994). See particularly Countess Pierre Lecontre's pamphlet on "the state of the feminist question in France," which provides a chronology of "recent changes in the French legislation regarding women" from 1850 to 1905, a list of legal proposals that were still pending in 1907, and the complete programs of some of the major feminist groups of the period (Waelti-Walters and Hause, *Feminisms of the Belle Epoque,* 42–57).

37. Durkheim, *Suicide,* 384–386.

38. Clotilde Dissard, "Opinions féministes à propos du Congrès féministe de Paris en 1896," *Revue internationale de sociologie* 4, 7(1896): 539.

39. *Congrès international de la condition et des droits des femmes . . . Questions économiques, morales, et sociales; Education; Législation, droit privé, droit publique* (Paris: Imprimerie des arts et manufactures, 1901), 302–305.

40. Besnard, "Durkheim et les femmes," 58.

41. Durkheim, "Le divorce par consentement mutuel," *La revue bleue,* 5th series, 5, 18 (1906): 549.

42. Besnard, "Durkheim et les femmes," 28.

43. French and English reprints are available in Emile Durkheim, *Textes,* ed. Victor Karady (Paris: Editions de minuit, 1975), 2:181–194; and *Emile Durkheim on Institutional Analysis,* ed. Mark Traugott (Chicago: University of Chicago Press, 1978), 240–252.

44. Union pour l'action morale, "Avant-Propos," *Libres entretiens,* 1st series, 1 (1904): 1. The Union for Truth succeeded the Union for Moral Action as the organizer of these monthly conversations in the interval between the first series and the second. Although the group changed names, it kept the same coordinator, address, general ideals, and, most likely, core membership and attendance at the ongoing annual series of what it continued to call "libres entretiens." For the new group's rules and regulations, see Union pour la vérité, "Statuts," *Libres entretiens,* 2nd series, 1, supplement (1905): 1–8; and "Conventions libres," *Libres entretiens,* 2nd series, 1, supplement (1905): 9–18. For comments on the relationship between the two groups, see Paul Desjardins's introduction to their second series, Union pour la vérité, "Esprit de ces entretiens," *Libres entretiens,* 2nd series, 1, supplement (1905): 3–5.

45. Union pour l'action morale, "Mariage et divorce," *Libres entretiens,* cinquième série, 242–303. Viktor Karady has recently reprinted a substantial section of this de-

bate in Durkheim, *Textes*, 2:206–215. On Durkheim's interactions with the women who went there, see Pedersen, "Sexual Politics in Comte and Durkheim."

46. Union pour la vérité, "Mariage et divorce," 245–246, 293.

47. For pertinent readings on divorce, see the sources in notes 33–35. On single motherhood, illegitimacy, and paternity suits, see Rachel Ginnis Fuchs, *Poor and Pregnant in Paris: Strategies for Survival in the Nineteenth Century* (New Brunswick, N.J.: Rutgers University Press, 1992); Fuchs, "Seduction, Paternity, and the Law in Fin de Siècle France," *Journal of Modern History* 72 (December 2000): 944–989; and Pedersen, *Legislating the French Family*.

48. Société française de philosophie, "L'éducation sexuelle," *Bulletin de la Société française de philosophie* 11 (February 28, 1911): 47. Highlights of this debate have recently been reprinted in French in Durkheim, *Textes*, 2:241–251; and in English in *Durkheim: Essays on Morals and Education*, ed. W. S. F. Pickering (London: Routledge and Kegan Paul, 1979), 140–148.

49. See Lukes, *Durkheim*; Durkheim, *Durkheim: Essays*; Larry Portis, "Sexe, moralité, et ordre social dans l'oeuvre d'Emile Durkheim," *L'homme et la société* 99–100 (1991): 67–77; and Pedersen, " 'Something Mysterious.' "

50. For one survey of the literature, see Pedersen, " 'Something Mysterious,' " 137–139.

51. For a variety of excerpts from literary and political sources, see, for example, "Depopulation and Motherhood in France" and "Sex Education for Girls?" in Bell and Offen, *Women, the Family, and Freedom*, 2:129–136, 172–180, and "Prostitution and the Double Standard" and "Issues of Maternity" in Waelti-Walters and Hause, *Feminisms of the Belle Epoque*, 165–188, 215–262.

52. Société française de philosophie, "L'éducation sexuelle," 29–33.

53. Société française de philosophie, "L'éducation sexuelle," 33–35.

54. Société française de philosophie, "L'éducation sexuelle," 36–37.

55. Société française de philosophie, "L'éducation sexuelle," 37–38.

56. Société française de philosophie, "L'éducation sexuelle," 38.

57. Société française de philosophie, "L'éducation sexuelle," 34–35.

58. Bloor, "Durkheim and Mauss Revisited"; Schmaus, *Durkheim's Philosophy of Science*.

59. Robert Alun Jones, *The Development of Durkheim's Social Realism* (Cambridge: Cambridge University Press, 1999).

60. For useful bibliographies on a wide variety of relevant topics in the philosophy of social science, see Alexander Rosenberg, *Philosophy of Social Science*, 2nd ed. (Boulder, Colo.: Westview Press, 1995).

61. Sandra G. Harding, *The Science Question in Feminism* (Ithaca, N.Y.: Cornell University Press, 1986).

62. Helen E. Longino, *Science as Social Knowledge: Values and Objectivity in Scientific Inquiry* (Princeton, N.J.: Princeton University Press, 1990); Susan Haack, ed., "Feminist Epistemology: For and Against," special issue of *Monist* 77, 4 (1994): 403–553; and Alison Wylie, "Doing Philosophy as a Feminist: Longino on the Search for a Feminist Epistemology," *Philosophical Topics* 23, 2 (1995): 345–358.

63. Peter Novick, *That Noble Dream: The "Objectivity Question" and the American Historical Profession* (Cambridge: Cambridge University Press, 1988); Joyce Appleby,

Lynn Hunt, and Margaret Jacobs, *Telling the Truth about History* (New York: Norton, 1994); Scott, *Gender and the Politics of History;* Bonnie Smith, *The Gender of History: Men, Women, and Historical Practice* (Cambridge, Mass.: Harvard University Press, 1998).

REFERENCES

Appleby, Joyce, Lynn Hunt, and Margaret Jacobs. 1994. *Telling the Truth about History.* New York: Norton.

Bell, Susan Groag, and Karen M. Offen, eds. 1983. *Women, the Family, and Freedom: The Debate in Documents.* Stanford: Stanford University Press.

Berenson, Edward. "The Politics of Divorce in France of the Belle Epoque: The Case of Joseph and Henriette Caillaux." *American Historical Review* 93, 1 (1988): 31–55.

———. 1992. *The Trial of Madame Caillaux.* Berkeley: University of California Press.

Besnard, Philippe. 1973. "Durkheim et les femmes, ou *Le Suicide* inachevée." *Revue française de sociologie* 14, 28: 27–61.

Bloor, David. 1982. "Durkheim and Mauss Revisited: Classification and the Sociology of Knowledge." *Studies in History and Philosophy of Science* 13: 267–297.

Durkheim, Emile. 1909. Contributions to "Mariage et divorce." *Libres entretiens,* 5th series, 5: 258–259, 261–262, 266–268, 270, 273, 277–282.

———. 1930. *De la division du travail social.* Paris: Presses universitaires de France.

———. 1933. *The Division of Labor in Society.* Translated by George Simpson. New York: Free Press.

———. 1984. *The Division of Labor in Society.* Translated by W. D. Halls. New York: Free Press.

———. 1906. "Le divorce par consentement mutuel." *La revue bleue,* 5th series, 5, 18: 549–554.

———. 1979. *Durkheim: Essays on Morals and Education.* Edited by W. S. F. Pickering. London: Routledge and Kegan Paul.

———. 1975. *Durkheim on Religion: A Selection of Readings with Bibliographies.* Edited by W. S. F. Pickering. London: Routledge and Kegan Paul.

———. 1995. *The Elementary Forms of Religious Life.* Translated by Karen E. Fields. New York: Free Press.

———. 1978. *Emile Durkheim on Institutional Analysis.* Edited by Mark Traugott. Chicago: University of Chicago Press.

———. 1973. *Emile Durkheim on Morality and Society.* Edited by Robert Bellah. Chicago: University of Chicago Press.

———. 1982. *The Rules of the Sociological Method.* Edited by Steven Lukes. New York: Free Press.

———. 1951. *Suicide.* Translated by John A. Spaulding and George Simpson. New York: Free Press.

———. 1975. *Textes.* Edited by Victor Karady. Paris: Editions de minuit.

Erickson, Victoria Jay. 1993. *Where Silence Speaks: Feminism, Social Theory, and Religion.* Minneapolis: Fortress Press.

Fenton, Steve. 1984. *Durkheim and Modern Sociology.* Cambridge: Cambridge University Press.

Fuchs, Rachel Ginnis. 1992. *Poor and Pregnant in Paris: Strategies for Survival in the Nineteenth Century.* New Brunswick. N.J.: Rutgers University Press.

————. 2000. "Seduction, Paternity, and the Law in Fin de Siècle France," *Journal of Modern History* 72 (December): 944–989.

Gane, Mike. 1993. *Harmless Lovers? Gender, Theory, and Personal Relationships.* London: Routledge.

Gouldner, Alvin. 1970. *The Coming Crisis of Western Sociology.* New York: Equinox.

Haack, Susan, ed. 1994. "Feminist Epistemology: For and Against." Special issue of *Monist* 77, 4: 403–553.

Harding, Sandra G. 1986. *The Science Question in Feminism.* Ithaca, N.Y.: Cornell University Press.

Hause, Steven, and Jennifer Waelti-Walters, eds. 1994. *Feminisms of the Belle Epoque: A Historical and Literary Anthology.* Lincoln: University of Nebraska Press.

Jay, Nancy. 1992. *Throughout Your Generations Forever: Sacrifice, Religion, and Paternity.* Chicago: University of Chicago Press.

Jones, Robert Alun. 1999. *The Development of Durkheim's Social Realism.* Cambridge: Cambridge University Press.

Kandal, Terry. 1988. *The Woman Question in Classical Sociological Theory.* Miami: Florida International University Press.

Lehmann, Jennifer. 1994. *Durkheim and Women.* Lincoln: University of Nebraska Press.

Levine, Donald N. 1995. *Visions of the Sociological Tradition.* Chicago: University of Chicago Press.

Longino, Helen E. 1990. *Science as Social Knowledge: Values and Objectivity in Scientific Inquiry.* Princeton: Princeton University Press.

Lukes, Steven. 1986. *Emile Durkheim: His Life and Work, A Historical and Critical Study.* Stanford: Stanford University Press.

McBride, Theresa. 1990. "Divorce and the Republican Family." In *Gender and the Politics of Social Reform in France, 1870–1914,* edited by Elinor A. Accampo, Rachel G. Fuchs, and Mary Lynn Stewart. Baltimore: Johns Hopkins University Press.

Novick, Peter. 1988. *That Noble Dream: The "Objectivity Question" and the American Historical Profession.* Cambridge: Cambridge University Press.

Offen, Karen. 2000. *European Feminisms, 1700–1950: A Political History.* Stanford: Stanford University Press.

Pearce, Frank. 1989. *The Radical Durkheim.* London: Unwin Hyman, 1989.

Pedersen, Jean Elisabeth. 2003. *Legislating the French Family: Feminism, Theater, and Republican Politics, 1870–1920.* New Brunswick, N.J.: Rutgers University Press.

————. 2001. "Sexual Politics in Comte and Durkheim: Feminism, History, and the French Sociological Tradition." *Signs* 27, 1: 229–263.

————. 1998. " 'Something Mysterious': Sex Education, Victorian Morality, and Durkheim's Comparative Sociology." *Journal of the History of the Behavioral Sciences* 34, 2: 135–151.

Portis, Larry. 1991. "Sexe, moralité, et ordre social dans l'oeuvre d'Emile Durkheim." *L'homme et la société* 99–100: 67–77.

Rosenberg, Alexander. 1995. *Philosophy of Social Science.* 2nd ed. Boulder, Colo.: Westview Press.

Schmaus, Warren. 1994. *Durkheim's Philosophy of Science and the Sociology of Knowledge: Creating an Intellectual Niche.* Chicago: University of Chicago Press.

Schüssler Fiorenza, Elisabeth. 1992. *But She Said: Feminist Practices of Biblical Interpretation.* Boston: Beacon Press.

Scott, Joan Wallach. 1999. *Gender and the Politics of History.* rev. ed. New York: Columbia University Press.

Seidman, Steven. 1983. *Liberalism and the Origins of European Social Theory.* Berkeley: University of California Press.

Shapiro, Ann-Louise, ed. 1994. *Feminists ReVision History.* New Brunswick, N.J.: Rutgers University Press.

Smith, Bonnie. 1998. *The Gender of History: Men, Women, and Historical Practice.* Cambridge, Mass.: Harvard University Press.

Société française de philosophie. 1911. "L'éducation sexuelle." *Bulletin de la Société française de philosophie* 11 (February 28): 29–52 (Durkheim's contributions on 33–36, 37–38, 44–47).

Sydie, R. A. 1987. *Natural Women, Cultured Men: A Feminist Perspective on Sociological Theory.* New York: New York University Press.

Union pour l'action morale. 1904. "Avant-Propos." *Libres entretiens,* 1st series, 1: 1–15.

Union pour la vérité. 1905. "Conventions libres." *Libres entretiens,* 2nd series, 1, supplement: 9–18.

———. 1905. "Esprit de ces entretiens." *Libres entretiens,* 2nd series, 1, supplement: 3–5.

———. 1909. "Mariage et divorce." *Libres entretiens,* 5th series, 5: 242–303.

———. 1905. "Statuts." *Libres entretiens,* 2nd series, 1, supplement: 1–8.

Wylie, Alison. 1995. "Doing Philosophy as a Feminist: Longino on the Search for a Feminist Epistemology." *Philosophical Topics* 23, 2: 345–358.

10

Durkheim's Theory of Misrecognition

In Praise of Arrogant Social Theory

Jacques Berlinerblau

We believe it a fruitful idea that social life must be explained not by
the conception of it formed by those who participate in it, but by the
profound causes which escape their consciousness.

> —Durkheim, "Marxism and Sociology, Review of
> Antonio Labriola, 'Essais sur la conception materi-
> aliste de l'histoire' " (translated by W. D. Halls)

We can certainly perceive the great events that unfold in the full
light of public awareness; but the internal operations of the machine,
the silent functioning of the internal organs, in a word all that
makes up the very substance and continuity of collective life—all
this is beyond our purview, all this escapes us. Undoubtedly, we
hear the muffled sounds of the life surrounding us; and we understand very well that there is, all around us, an enormous and complex reality. But we have no direct awareness of it, any more than of
the physical forces informing our physical environment. Only the effects get through to us.

> —Durkheim, *Moral Education: A Study in the Theory
> and Application of the Sociology of Education* (trans-
> lated by Everett Wilson and Herman Schnurer)

I find myself somewhat concerned about the "life chances," if you
will, of Durkheimian theory within the American university. At odds
with countless academic and cultural trends, Durkheim's ideas are
encircled by strange pincers: their implications are often odious to
many of my colleagues *and* those who sit in their classrooms.

As for undergraduates, it has been my experience that Durkheim is the bearer of a message they tend to find disagreeable at best and incomprehensible at worst. It is conveyed in what Robert Bellah referred to as an "unrelieved tone of high moral seriousness," and it must strike students reared on the literary copy of the day, be it advertisements, magazines, or contemporary fiction, as an invitation to parody.[1] His writing style—sometimes grandiloquent, often elegantly precise, and always unyieldingly intense in its quest for answers—offers few incentives to young textual consumers.

Leaving aside the stylistic and technical challenges of his *oeuvre*, it is Durkheim's challenge to prevailing conceptions of the conscious, knowing self that most vexes students. As Jennifer Lehmann phrased it, "Durkheim maintains that the individual is an inferior subject of knowledge; and that individual empiricism is an inferior form of knowledge."[2] This is a theorist, after all, who tells us again and again—and in ever more ingenious ways—that much of what we believe to be true about ourselves, others, the divine, whatever it might be, is, in all likelihood, not really true. In this regard, Durkheim demands from students—from all of us—a sort of intellectual surrender, a willingness to concede that our conscious selves have *misrecognized* that reality that he and his colleagues uncovered in the course of their diligent researches.[3] In place of this "illusory," *misattributed* conception of the world, we are enjoined to ponder the role played by veiled, hypercomplex social forces that are partly autonomous and partly generated (albeit unknowingly) by associating agents across history. Most college students never even imagined that such "collective representations" exist; getting them to imagine their influence on their own thought and action is the "heavy lifting" of Durkheimian pedagogy.[4]

"It is a natural tendency," Durkheim once wrote, "to regard what is first in the order of knowledge as first in the order of reality."[5] What an apt description of the manner in which our young charges approach the world! They are afflicted with a sort of ontological literalism, beyond anything even Durkheim could have imagined. The reality that confronts their perceptions is assumed to be real, no questions asked. It is certainly not a coincidence that the popular culture they consume is so symbolically impoverished. If one can bear sitting through an American sitcom or film, one comes to the conclusion that there is almost no symbolic level to be found in the product. The actions and words of the characters mean whatever it is that they are supposed to mean. No signs are intentionally "given off"—and, not surprisingly, none are received. Only the ubiquitous double-entendre of a prurient nature disturbs the symbolic silence of popular television, movies, and music. A suspicious hermeneutist such as Durkheim, with his attribution of causality to virtually imperceptible collective phenomena, does not have many sympathizers among this audience.

Nor is his assessment of individual agency likely to go over swimmingly with today's youth. Members of this generation believe that they are agents by birth. It follows that change, be it personal or social, is merely a question of cultivating or unleashing certain genetic proclivities. Raised on a corporate/consumerist culture, they are repeatedly told that they are capable of anything, that they have "the power," that their actions (that is, purchases) are capable of making the world a different place. Having hummed this treacly national anthem of the self from childhood forward, they can only be flummoxed by the Durkheimian notion that, in terms of effecting change, the individual is worth a penny or so, "one among innumerable units."[6] Little prepares the student, secular or otherwise, for the type of sober, learned resignation to the awesome determinative majesty of *society* demanded by Durkheimian ethics.[7] Being the "organ of an organism" and finding beauty in "conscientiously performing [one's] role as an organ" are not aspirations currently shared by many in this country.[8]

Cultural limitations aside, the American undergraduate is, generally speaking, an affable sort; not necessarily dogmatic or incorrigible. Open-minded to a fault, our students are willing to grant contrarian wisdom its rightful hearing—if only because the culture they consume ascribes legitimacy to dissent as mode of personal expression. And let it be duly noted that Durkheim's thought does not lack for contrarian content. These dimensions of his work were delineated in Stjepan Meštrović's *Emile Durkheim and the Reformation of Sociology* (1988)—a delightfully original, and somewhat quirky, work of scholarship that did much to inject vitality into an area of inquiry that had grown somewhat dull. This study marked the first of many attempts to undo nearly a century of what Susan Stedman Jones has recently called "vulgar Durkheimianism."[9] What has emerged in the aftermath of Meštrović's study is a new Durkheim—one whose works need to be seriously reassessed. No longer the square positivist to Marx's groovy revolutionary, no longer the tedious champion of social order, integration, and values that his Anglo-American interpreters often made him out to be, this Durkheim appears as something of a French-style theoretical hipster. As much a philosopher as a sociologist, this Durkheim invokes the unconscious, the irrational, the ineluctable damage done to the individual by the advance of civilization, the cryptic logic of the collective representation.[10] Effective Durkheimian pedagogy on the undergraduate level, I shall maintain, calls attention to that which is singular—and oftentimes profoundly strange and disturbing—about his thought.

Pitching Durkheim to graduate students and scholars, however, is a much harder sell. The reasons for this are complex, but suffice it to say that much—though not necessarily all—of what Durkheim has to say clashes with current intellectual, ideological, and pedagogical trends, especially those emanating from the university's radical or progressive wing.[11] One wonders what the editor of *L'année sociologique* would make of those countless scholars who believe that it is their duty to raise consciousness, to empower students to repair a broken or unjust world. Might he "privilege the subjectivity" of those to whom he lectured? Would he have referred to himself as a "facilitator"? Would he insist, as do more than a few, that all knowledge claims are reducible to the positioned interests of the scholar who makes them? So many statutes of the Durkheimian intellectual and moral code are violated by these ideas that one hardly knows where to begin. These transgressions will become apparent in the forthcoming analysis.[12]

A certain chill, a "take-the-pain" ethos, marks Durkheim's understanding of intellectual responsibility, and this too is at odds with the "positive thinking" pedagogy of the age, if not the current economic realities of our profession. In this regard, note 13 to chapter 3 of *The Rules of Sociological Method* has always struck me as a defining moment in his understanding of the scholar's ethical code. After having discussed the beneficial and normative aspects of criminal activity, Durkheim feels obliged to assuage his readers' concerns. In this astonishing aside he concedes that crime, naturally, is abhorrent. His work, it goes without saying, is not an apologia for criminality. But then, carried by the momentum of his own peculiar convictions, he insists that such unpleasant deductions invariably arise from the endeavor to "study moral facts objectively and to speak of them in language that is not commonly used."[13]

In other words, *the objectivity of the sociologist forces him or her to say objectionable things.* "Peace is in itself no more desirable than war," he once declared, and this sentiment accords well with a person who believes that "for science, good and evil do not exist."[14] Science, in fact, is not concerned with morals— it simply states laws.[15] In so doing, it invariably—though by no means intentionally—offends common sentiments. If "positionality," "empowerment," "self-esteem," and "consciousness raising" are watchwords on some quadrants of the college campus, then Durkheim's thought is not of especial use to progressive university politics. And if the approval of students on "course evaluations" is important to an adjunct or junior faculty member's own "life chances," then one teaches this unseasonal theorist at one's own risk.

In the remainder of this chapter, I would like to offer a brief exegesis of Durkheim's theory of misrecognition, a component of his work that has received little sustained attention. Although he never explicitly employed the term misrecognition, the designation accurately describes a basic idea which courses throughout all of his major works and many of his minor ones. The analysis of this concept is germane to this inquiry in the following bipartite respect. First, this theme lies at the intersection of nearly everything that irks students and scholars about Durkheimian theory. Second, enfolded within the notion of misrecognition are a variety of pedagogical orientations which may be of use to those who lecture on theory.

I do not wish to argue that an understanding of misrecognition will solve the literal theoretical puzzle that is Durkheim's legacy. While the presence in his writings of this intriguing theme is undeniable, it actually underscores dilemmas within the overall context of his thought. Much in the same way that Durkheim could champion a steely scholarly objectivity, all the while maintaining the aforementioned moral seriousness, his accumulated remarks on misrecognition are at points quite contradictory. Last, I wish to suggest that misrecognition theory, be it in its Durkheimian incarnation or some other, makes a useful orientation, albeit a widely ignored one, for religious studies.[16]

Misrecognition of Antecedents

For purposes of analysis I will distinguish between two types of misrecognition that in reality form a theoretical unity. "Misrecognition of antecedents" will be defined, generically, as *a state in which an agent fails to accurately recognize the true reasons, motivations, influences, and so on, that underlie his or her thoughts, feelings, and actions, as well as those of others*. The antecedent that is misrecognized in Durkheimian theory is almost always the same: the agent fails to identify the overwhelming causal torque of society, social forces, collective ideas, collective representations, and so on.[17] So widespread is this problem that it might be described as the inherent flaw, the cognitive curse, that afflicts the consciousness of each member of the species. Lehmann notes that "Durkheim . . . regards the failure to 'recognize' social determinism itself as an illusion, the grand human illusion."[18] It is only the modern thinker, aided by science—more exactly, Durkheimian science—who is poised to break free from the recurring loop of apprehension/misapprehension that characterizes humanity's every engagement with the given reality to be recognized.

Perhaps the single best known example of misrecognition in Durkheim's work, if not in the whole history of sociological thought, can be found in his analysis of religion. Returning to a theme he had explored many times before, Durkheim declares in *The Elementary Forms of Religious Life*: "But merely because there exists a 'religious experience' . . . it by no means follows that the reality which grounds it should conform objectively with the idea the believers have of it."[19] Put differently, *homo religiosus* does not properly identify the true object of his or her worship. She or he never really does comprehend that "the Gods are no other than collective forces personified and hypostasized in material form. Ultimately, it is the society that is worshiped by the believers."[20] In *The Elementary Forms* Durkheim advances one explanation—there will be others—of what causes agents to misrecognize that which they are venerating. Here the error is triggered by the sheer complexity of the collective forces that confront them:

> The mythological interpretations would doubtless not have been born if man could easily see that those influences on him come from society. But the ordinary observer cannot see where the influence of society comes from. It moves along channels that are too obscure and circuitous, and uses psychic mechanisms that are too

complex, to be easily traced to the source. So long as scientific analysis has not yet taught him, man is well aware that he is acted on but not by whom.[21]

The notion of misrecognition is not confined to the analysis of religion. Rather, it serves as something of a roving epistemological surmise in Durkheim's writings. We should not be surprised, then, to seem him apply it to the particular question of historical methodology in his 1897 review of Antonio Labriola's "Essais sur la conception materialiste de l'histoire." Durkheim endorses Labriola's (and Marx and Engels's) contention that historians err when they predicate their analysis on what agents believe to be true. "These subjective explanations," he continues, "are worthless, for men never do perceive the true motives which cause them to act."[22] Later in the same article it is noted: "The course of our representations is determined by causes concealed from their subject."[23] What is of interest in this passage, as I will show, is the inclusion of the term "representation"—a mediating structure between the subject's consciousness and that reality that she or he is trying to understand.

In *Suicide* it is maintained that the reasons a person gives for having attempted to take his or her or life are not one and the same with the actual reasons which led him or her to this particular act: "Intent is too intimate a thing to be more than approximately interpreted by another. It even escapes self-observation. How often we mistake the true reasons for our acts! We constantly explain acts due to petty feelings or blind routine by generous passions or lofty considerations."[24] Needless to say, those who attempt to take their lives are incapable of seeing the real sociological antecedents of their actions. They fail to recognize that their behavior is influenced by "collective inclinations," "a social condition," "collective force," and the "suicidogenetic causes" that emanate from the social body.[25]

In *Montesquieu and Rousseau: Forerunners of Sociology*, Durkheim challenges the common illusion of seeing the lawgiver as bringing about the law by an act of will. This "widespread superstition" fails to recognize that laws "derive from custom, that is, from life itself, by a process of almost imperceptible development unrelated to the concerted intentions of legislators."[26] Better to assume that "laws are produced by efficient causes of which men may often be unaware. . . . Social phenomena are not, as a rule, the product of calculated action. Laws are not devices that the lawgiver thinks up."[27]

There is also a theme of intellectual misrecognition or, better yet, the *intellectual's* misrecognition in Durkheim's writings. For scholars too, *in their analysis of determining variables,* fail to identify the correct ones (that is, those pertaining to the social). Even a casual reader of Durkheim notices the countless disagreements he had with contemporaries and precursors. Steven Lukes has called attention to the "polemical" nature of Durkheim's form of argumentation, as well as the typical strategies he used to eliminate claims that differed from his own.[28] Jorge Larrain points to the rather broad scope of the challenge issued to other scientists: "Durkheim believes that sociology up to his own time has merely dealt with preconceptions and not with things."[29] The pages of Durkheim's writing are strewn with the husks and remains of ransacked theories and theorists. Even the reasoned deliberations of scientific men do not necessarily lead to accurate recognition.

Misrecognition of Consequences

This leads us to what shall be called misrecognition of consequences, or (generically again) *the inability of the agent to either accurately predict or understand what the actual consequences of his or her actions will be.* This initiative is explicitly indebted to Wilhelm Wundt's notion of "the law of the heterogeneity of ends," which Durkheim discussed in his 1887 article "La Science positive de la morale en Allemagne."[30] Durkheim writes: "How often do we act without knowing the goal we intend! . . . the notion that all of our actions have conscious goals is highly contestable."[31] "Voluntary actions," he continues, "produce consequences that surpass the motives that caused them. When we become conscious of consequences that we did not foresee, they become the object of new actions and give rise to new motives. These in turn produce effects which extend beyond them and so on indefinitely."[32]

I would venture that echoes of Wundt's law may find a broader structural corollary in Durkheim's repeated insistence that social evolution cannot be consciously directed by the will or planning of agents.[33] In his 1888 "Course in Sociology: Opening Lecture" he spoke of social institutions that "serve ends which no one foresaw."[34] On the very first page of *The Division of Labor* it is insisted that the evolution of commerce occurs "spontaneously and unthinkingly."[35] In an earlier study he averred that "it is nearly always impossible for social change to be created with methodical reflection."[36] In a moment, however, I will present a seemingly contradictory strain in Durkheim's thought.

Consequential misrecognition is also identifiable in the analysis of punishment advanced in *The Division of Labor*. There it was remarked that the actual role punishment plays: "is not one commonly perceived. It does not serve, or serves very incidentally, to correct the guilty person or to scare off possible imitators." "Its real function," he affirms, "is to maintain inviolate the cohesion of society by sustaining the common consciousness in all of its vigour."[37] It is interesting to note how perceptions are here sharply contrasted to "real functions." Those who either participate in the act of punishment or contemplate its uses fail to recognize that it is "above all intended to have its effect on honest people."[38]

Extrapolating a bit from these examples, I would like to note that the theme of misrecognition is implicit in Durkheim's central—and for some reason often ignored—explanation of social change. Whereas countless commentators have accused him of ignoring this issue, he consistently held that change is stimulated via the coming together of bodies situated in time and space. Or, as Jones phrases it, "association is the determining condition of social phenomena."[39] Durkheim proposed in his 1909 "Sociology and the Social Sciences" to refer to the analytical level through which such changes might be studied as "social morphology."[40] This is, in part, defined as "the study of population: its volume, its density, and its disposition on the earth."[41] Fluctuations in the morphological base, via what he called "moral" and "physical" density, trigger new possibilities for the social.[42] In *The Division of Labor* he writes about the result of these interactions as follows: "the more numerous they are and the more closely they exert their action on one another, the more strongly and rapidly do they react together. Thus, as a result, the more intense social life becomes. It is this intensification that constitutes civilization."[43] Later he opines: "But as societies grow larger and above all more densely populated, a psychological life of a new kind makes its appearance . . . a host of things that remained outside the individual consciousness because did not affect the collectivity become the object of representations."[44]

It must be emphasized that Durkheim vacillates in terms of the nomenclature he uses when describing the dividends of this association. In the previous quotation, collective representations are created by interaction. But in other instances association creates "social facts,"[45] "civilization,"[46] "the progress of the division of labor,"[47] "collective phenomenon,"[48] and so on. We may leave aside questions of nomenclature for another forum. For now, I simply wish to delineate the following. The agents who associate *have no intention of precipitating social change, nor are they aware that social change will be an outcome of their individual interactions.* It emerges from this that associating humans are the stimulants of crucial changes in their own social world that they never intended, willed, or were even aware of. Social change, then, is caused by human activity, but not purposeful, social activity in the name of social change.

If my analysis is correct, then it may be plausible to conclude that the notion of misrecognition is present in some of Durkheim's most basic surmises about sociology—it is tantamount to an unstated rule of his sociological method. I close this section by citing a remark that reunites the organic unity of misrecognition of antecedents and of consequences in Durkheim's thought: "Quite often—perhaps most of the time—we are ignorant not only of the distant goals of our behavior, but also of the real motives which govern it."[49]

Why Misrecognition?

I am now prepared to pose an important, and fairly obvious, question; why do agents misrecognize? It is here where we run into a variety of sometimes useful, sometimes perplexing ambiguities in Durkheimian thought. One possible answer is raised in the remarkable preface to the second edition of *The Rules of Sociological Method*:

> It is disagreeable for man to have to renounce the unlimited power over the social order that for so long he ascribed to himself. *Moreover, it appears to him that, if collective forms really exist, he is necessarily condemned to be subjected to them without being able to modify them. This is what inclines him to deny their existence.* Repeated experiences have in vain attempted to teach him that this all-powerfulness, the illusion of which he so willingly entertains, has always been for him a cause of weakness; that his dominion over things only really began when he recognized that they had a nature of their own, and when he resigned himself to learning from them what they are. Banished from all other sciences, this deplorable prejudice stubbornly survives in sociology. Hence there is nothing more urgent than to seek to free our science from it: this is the main purpose of our efforts.[50]

Here Durkheim insinuates that there is a flash of recognition, a moment in which the agent fleetingly glimpses the social in all of its thought-defying immensity. Out of guile, or fear, she or he retreats to the psychological safety of a narcissistic conception.

This quotation, incidentally, also points to the notion of *misattribution* in Durkheimian theory. Agents not only fail to recognize the true stimulants of their thought and action; they then attribute them to erroneous causal factors. It is important to realize that for Durkheim some types of misattribution are worse, that is, more erroneous, than others. As with Auguste Comte, he repeatedly railed against those explanations that arrogate causal efficacy to the self. "We are the victims of the illusion," he asserts, "which leads us to believe we have ourselves produced what has been imposed on us externally."[51] Durkheim voices exasperation at what he calls the "anthropocentric postulate," which "blocks the path to science."[52] Notice that the attribution of causality to religious forces is for Durkheim an empirically incorrect surmise, albeit one resting on a much firmer foundation than narcissistic explanations. Far from blocking the path to science, religious belief is a precursor to its development.

But back to the original query: Why misrecognition? In contrast to answers examined earlier, Durkheim elsewhere argues that misrecognition (and consequently misattribution) are linked to the inherent limitations of human consciousness. This is a theme Durkheim probed with particular enthusiasm. He spoke of "the feeble scope of human intelligence."[53] "Conscience," he reminds us, "is a poor judge of what occurs in the depths of one's being, because it does not penetrate that far."[54] Durkheim views symbols as the means by which the conscious subject can recognize a "moral power." It "is only with the aid of religious symbols," he suggests, "that most have ever managed to conceive of it with any clarity at all."[55] Perhaps, then, we might need to envision a dialectic between a deficient individual consciousness and socially generated phenomena in all of their immeasurable complexity. Herein lies a recipe for the human cognitive plight: couple a limited, faulty consciousness with a hypercomplex, veiled reality, and nearly every member of the species misrecognizes and misattributes.

Yet there are still other possibilities to be explored. In recent years commentators have devoted increasing scrutiny to the importance of representations in Durkheim's philosophy. Steven Lukes comments that "much of Durkheim's later work can be seen as the systematic study of collective *représentations.*"[56] W. S. F. Pickering, the editor of the volume *Durkheim and Representations*, notes that this line of inquiry was "essential to Durkheim's sociological thought."[57] "We cannot live," Durkheim maintained, "without representing to ourselves the world around us and the objects of every sort which fill it."[58] In *Moral Education* he alleged that "everything in the physical world is represented in our consciousness by an idea."[59] "The world itself" is elsewhere said to be "but a system of representations."[60] Meštrović explains Durkheim's view as follows: "For him, society is a representation, not the outcome of human agency nor material determinants. It is neither entirely objective nor subjective. And because the representation is a reality sui generis, not a mere reflector, it expresses its will-in part-independent of the will of human agents."[61]

Without surveying the burgeoning literature on representations, I would like to simply note the following. In his "Individual and Collective Representations," Durkheim insists that "representational life extends beyond our present consciousness."[62] Earlier in the same essay he opines: "Our judgments are influenced at every moment by unconscious judgments; we see only what our prejudices permit us to see and yet we are unaware of them."[63] Observations of this nature cast misrecognition in a different light. For what is being misrecognized is *the representation itself.* As Pickering describes it, "representations exist in the mind [*sic!*] of individuals, though they may not be consciously realized as such."[64] Meštrović believes that collective representations "are unknown to the consciousness of witnesses, agents, even the collective conscience. Consciousness is not inherent to the idea of the representation."[65] In other words, misrecognition also encompasses the inability to comprehend the influences of collectively generated representations.

Compounding the difficulties are the curious triangulations in Durkheim's thought between consciousness, representations, and what may be labeled "objective reality." It was Meštrović who argued that Durkheim adopted Schopenhauer's view that "the world can never be known as a thing-in-itself; reality can never speak for itself."[66] Accordingly, between the reality that exists "out there" and the consciousness that tries, in vein, to apprehend it, lies the representation. "Durkheim regards representations," writes Meštrović, "as *prisms*, refractions of reality that are themselves realities, not reflectors."[67] This reality is so impervious to cognitive apprehension that even science—the master representation—will never "adequately express all of reality."[68] This leads us to an intriguing deduction about the human condition. If society is indeed a system of representations, as Durkheim was so fond of saying, and if these representations imperfectly approximate reality, then we discover new levels of cognitive pathos.[69] For human beings can be said to misrecognize two realities; objective reality *and* the mediating, albeit partially autonomous, reality that is the collective representation.[70]

Now if reality is inherently unknowable, if it really exists but can never be apprehended by human cognition, then all recognition is misrecognition. Reality can *never* be recognized accurately—it can only be misrecognized *less*, by better, albeit imperfect, representations such as science. What emerges from this is *double misrecognition*; the agent misrecognizes empirical "reality," and the collective representation that only partly represents it.

Brief Critical Remarks: Conform *and* Transform?

This cursory exposition has collated and then sketched only the most rudimentary aspects of a Durkheimian theory of misrecognition. Prior to turning to the pedagogical implications of this initiative, it might be useful to call attention to some of its drawbacks.

In terms of consequential misrecognition, we must wonder if Durkheim really believed that outcomes were so difficult to assess, that sober calculation and reflection could not generate desired social ends. No reader of *Moral Education*, for example, could possibly doubt Durkheim's conviction that preselected pedagogical goals could be achieved by reading and carrying through the agenda promulgated in *Moral Education*. As far as that text is concerned, social outcomes *are* susceptible to human control. Durkheim's plan is intended to lead the child to cherish ideas of justice and solidarity.[71] "Morality," far from being something that organically happens, can "be built into, or developed in, the child."[72] Proper schooling will generate attitudes in the student that "will have the most fortunate influence on the general welfare."[73] A similar belief in the powers of (his) conscious social engineering is evident in Durkheim's reform-minded pleas on behalf of professional groups in works like *Professional Ethics and Civic Morals* or the preface to the second edition of *The Division of Labor*. I will discuss the inherent—but unavoidable—conceit of exempting his own thought from "the law of the heterogeneity of ends" later.

As for misrecognition of antecedents, we must wonder if humans could possibly be as oblivious to it all as Durkheim suggests. If consciousness is so feeble, if the world is so complex, if humans are so cognitively limited, if reality can never be perfectly recognized, then how does social life cohere? Insofar as social life generally *does* cohere, insofar as most societies are of the normal and not the pathological type, we are led to an intriguing possibility: accurate recognition is not essential for the healthy functioning of society. It emerges from this that the vast overwhelming majority of a society's members *need not* pursue recognition of the real. And this is a state of affairs that meshes splendidly with Durkheim's belief that the masses *cannot* recognize the real anyway. Of course, a small subset of scientists labors in pursuit of recognition, and among them an even smaller subset of Durkheimian scientists seems to make headway in this direction.

Whereas it was suggested earlier that this reality was never entirely recognizable, other aspects of Durkheim's writing imply that recognition is a possibility. This is most apparent in his various meditations on the law-like nature of societies. Society's laws "can be the object of a methodical study."[74] Sociology itself discovers "the general relationships and verifiable laws of different societies."[75] Our discipline, "by discovering the laws of social reality[,] will permit us to direct historical evolution with greater reflection than in the past; for we can change nature, whether moral or physical, only by conforming to its laws."[76]

The last, rather elliptical remark is especially interesting in that it points to a central tension in Durkheim's thought. The purpose of recognizing the laws—and note that here Durkheim does not doubt that they actually can be recognized—is described in terms of transforming and conforming. Somewhat puzzlingly, it is suggested that only by conforming to laws can we then transform historical evolution. (How can we transform that to which we must conform?) In other instances, however, a different view is proposed. Witness the following remark from *The Moral Education*.

> if it is not we who made the plan of nature, we rediscover it through science, we rethink it, and we understand why it is as it is. Hence, to the extent that we see that it is everything it ought to be—that it is as the nature of things implies—we can conform, not simply because we are physically restrained and unable to do otherwise without danger, but because we deem it good and have no better alternative. What prompts the faithful to see that the world is good in principle because it is the work of a good being, we can establish a posteriori to the extent that science permits us to establish rationally what faith postulates a priori. Such conformity does not amount to passive resignation but to enlightened allegiance. Conforming to the order of things because one is sure that it is everything it ought to be is not submitting to a constraint. It is freely desiring this order, assenting through an understanding of the cause.[77]

Durkheim now appears to stress that recognition only permits us to conform to the laws; transformation is simply not an option. This view is consonant with Durkheim's insistence that sociology does not endeavor to describe or explain "what societies *should be,* [and] *how they should be organized* in order to be as perfect as possible." Rather, its simple goal is *"to know them* and *to understand them."*[78] Earlier, of course, I noted that transformation of the social order was a possibility that Durkheim believed his own powers of recognition could bring into play.

Conclusion: Their Common Humanity

Transposing the theory of misrecognition into the key of pedagogy is the task that remains for us now. Enfolded within the ideas examined here, I wish to claim, are intellectual orientations and theoretical approaches that social theorists may use in the classroom.

Misrecognition theory is predicated on an undeniably and inescapably arrogant assumption. Implicit in the claim that human beings cannot accurately recognize social reality is the belief that the theorist in question *can* accurately recognize social reality. "One of the weaknesses of Durkheim's reasoning," writes Pickering, "is that he assumes the existence of a reality which the scientist knows but the nonscientist does not know."[79] As Lehmann puts it, "the subject of true social knowledge is a collective subject, but it is an élite collective subject, composed of modern, rational men, imbued with the scientific spirit. The subject of true social knowledge is a homogenous collectivity of men like Durkheim himself."[80]

But if we agree to divest Durkheimian theory of its patriarchal dimensions, the aforementioned arrogance and elitism strike me as not only inevitable but as part and parcel of the theoretical enterprise. Good theorists recognize what nontheorists (and bad theorists) misrecognize. In so doing, they must invariably attribute to themselves powers of recognition that almost all others lack. We still read Marx, an often pretentious and aggressive writer, albeit one who, more than any other, has helped us identify previously undetected material determinants of social life. "The reform of consciousness," he wrote in his youth, "consists *only* in enabling the world to clarify its consciousness, in waking it from its dream about itself, in *explaining* to it the meaning of its own actions."[81] Not a shred of humility is evident in this remark, and this underscores the truism that modesty is not necessarily a virtue when practicing social theory. Ostensibly, an immodest orientation, in and of itself, does not assure that the theorist in question will have anything of interest to say. It is simply the obligatory starting point for theoretical investigation.

When teaching Durkheim on religion, our basic goal is to get students to understand—not believe—the claim: "Religion is . . . the system of symbols by means of which society becomes conscious of itself; it is the characteristic way of thinking of collective existence."[82] This is not, I would submit, a popular insight among K-12 religious educators, and this means that this conception of religion is typically incommensurable with anything the undergraduate has been previously taught. That Durkheim (as with Marx) truly believes that he is in possession of a rare and superior insight pertaining to the workings of the social is something that should be relayed to students from the outset. Problematically, the sobriety of Durkheim's prose (contra Marx) tends to obscure the audacity of these claims. Accordingly, we need to highlight the assumption of scientific supercessionism on which his confidence rests. Students should be ushered to those sections of Durkheim's work where he celebrates the scientist's privileged status qua knower of reality. The remarks on the first page of *Suicide* about "the confused impressions of the crowd" and his discussion of "the layman's confused notions of society" in *Moral Education* are useful in this regard.[83]

Presenting his thought as, among other things, an assault on the common sense and preconceptions of the students is wont to create a tension in the classroom that can be effectively exploited for pedagogical purposes. By underscoring these dimensions of his theory, we can conceivably make Durkheim more intriguing (as opposed to more accessible) to his readers. As noted earlier, free-thinking dissent is, paradoxically, a value in American popular culture. Having been warned from the outset that counterintuitive ideas are headed their way, students are now primed for engagement with his theory of religion. My own recommendation is that professors accentuate the negative, as it were, in order to create precisely the sort of disorienting intellectual environment that may motivate students to grapple with a deceptively dry corpus of texts.

There is much to recommend in W. E. H. Stanner's observation that "Durkheim did not see that his thesis was very depreciatory of man."[84] I have observed that his thought involves a problematization of the integrity of the conscious knowing self, as well as a deep skepticism about the efficacy of human agency. Contentions of this nature, if stated with a modicum of teacherly dramatic flair, are likely to create the types of healthy tensions advocated earlier. As opposed to continually assuring those who sit in our classrooms that they are special creatures, empowered agents, and the sovereign authors of their lives, Durkheimian pedagogy demands that we apprise them of their limitations qua individuals. We do so, of course, solely in order to give them the requisite tools for the contemplation of an occluded and complex reality. For by disabusing them of the anthropocentric postulate, we enable them to begin seriously contemplating the world in which they live and the religions to which they adhere.

As regards misrecognition theory and religion, I would stress that much time must be spent teaching students a particular *form* of reasoning, one that challenges their ontological literalism. This type of thinking involves searching for causes that are real but not apparent. I would advise a specific sequence of questions, amounting to something of a Durkheimian ambush. First, our students should be asked if it is at all possible that there exist influences on their thought and action that they do not recognize. Experience suggests that most will incline, initially, to either resist, misunderstand, or garble the question. This is a telling sign of how little epistemological common ground misrecognition theory shares with common sense.

If students can make this concession, the next step involves asking them what these influences might be. As the process moves forward, some will come to speak of a new-found recognition of music, God, their parents or siblings, and so on. The more insightful participants might point to the economy, or speak of the way architectural spaces affect their mood and behavior. In all probability, students will, never, *ever*, conclude of their own "free will" that social forces or collective representations are also determinative. But even so, the mere phrasing of the question completes half of the task for the teacher. The query itself is subversive. For once they have been forced to confront the possibility that factors outside of their comprehension may indeed affect their thought and action, the path has been paved for an appreciation of Durkheim's specific sociological insights. It is only when they have grasped this conceptual form that they are prepared to learn about the Durkheimian contents: the notion of the collective representation and its generally indiscernible "working over" of human consciousness.[85]

The same conceptual form, incidentally, is present in non-Durkheimian variants of misrecognition theory. A text such as Frederick Engels's book *The Peasant War in Germany* assumes that "very positive material class-interests were at play," even though the interests of the belligerents "hid themselves behind a religious screen."[86] Similar logic is also present in Mary Douglas's essay "The Abominations of Leviticus." For what the Levitical legislator (and the Levitical reader) misrecognized as a meditation on clean and unclean animals was in reality a sign "which at every turn inspired meditation on the oneness, purity and completeness of God."[87] Paul Boyer and Stephen Nissenbaum's excellent *Salem Possessed: The Social Origins of Witchcraft* relays this form of thinking in a highly readable manner. What Salemites perceived as the devil was but the encroaching ethic of mercantile capitalism associated with the social network of the accused.[88] In bringing things up to date, students might be alerted to Pierre Bourdieu's ingenious discussion of how both the prophet and his audience misrecognize that the source of prophecy is to be found in that very audience. Bourdieu writes: "The prophet embodies in exemplary conduct, or gives discursive expression to, representations, feelings and aspirations that existed before his arrival—albeit in an implicit, semiconscious, or unconscious state."[89]

In closing, it should be noted that as presumptuous as Durkheimian misrecognition theory can be, it nevertheless retains an oddly democratizing classroom dynamic. Unlike other theoretical traditions, it tends not to split students along the lines of class, race, gender, sexual preference, and so on. On learning the theory, one does not have to wonder if one should cast one's lot with the powers that be or the oppressed of the earth. One does not have to rethink one's position in a field of gendered relations. Durkheim's ideas configure classroom passions in a most unusual way: they maintain that everyone present is equally oblivious to that truth promulgated by the arrogant master himself (and the instructor who functions as his local university emissary). His theory stresses their common humanity, so to speak. This is by no means to say that other, more divisive (and currently more fashionable) theoretical models in social theory are invalid. It merely signals, yet again, the singularity and vulnerability of the Durkheimian project.

NOTES

1. Robert Bellah, preface to *Emile Durkheim on Morality and Society*, edited by R. Bellah (Chicago: University of Chicago Press, 1973), vii.

2. Jennifer Lehmann, *Deconstructing Durkheim: A Post-Post-Structuralist Critique* (London: Routledge, 1993), 3.

3. On the cooperative nature of the research conducted by the Durkheimians, see the articles in *The Sociological Domain: The Durkheimians and the Founding of French Sociology*, edited by Phillipe Besnard (Cambridge: Cambridge University Press, 1983).

4. On collective representations in general, see W. S. F. Pickering, ed., *Durkheim and Representations* (New York: Routledge, 2000).

5. Durkheim, *Montesquieu and Rousseau: Forerunners of Sociology* (Ann Arbor: University of Michigan Press, 1960), 11.

6. Durkheim, *Moral Education: A Study in the Theory and Application of the Sociology of Education*, ed. E. K. Wilson and trans. E. K. Wilson and H. Schnurer (New York: Free Press, 1973), 107.

7. See in this regard Durkheim's rather unique definition of "autonomy," in *Professional Ethics and Civic Morals*, trans. C. Brookfield (London: Routledge, 1992), 91.

8. Durkheim, "Course in Sociology: Opening Lecture," in *Emile Durkheim on Institutional Analysis*, ed. and trans. M. Traugott (Chicago: University of Chicago Press, 1994), 69.

9. Stjepan Meštrović, *Emile Durkheim and the Reformation of Sociology*. (Boston: Rowman and Littlefield, 1993). Susan Stedman Jones, *Durkheim Reconsidered* (Cambridge: Polity Press, 2001), 2.

10. On Durkheim's foundation in academic philosophy, see John Brooks, III, "Analogy and Argumentation in an Interdisciplinary Context: Durkheim's 'Individual and Collective representations,' " *History of Human Sciences* 4 (1991): 223–259.

11. On the radical dimensions of his thought, see Frank Pearce, *The Radical Durkheim* (London: Unwin Hyman, 1989). On the wide range of political labels that can be applied to him, see Lehmann, *Deconstructing Durkheim*, 8.

12. He would certainly reject the notion, so common among scholars of my generation and the one that preceded it, that the work of the scholar is inextricably bound to his or her political activism. "The lecturer of today," Durkheim declares, "must not be suspected to be the candidate of tomorrow" ("The Intellectual Elite and Democ-

racy," in Bellah, *Emile Durkheim on Morality and Society*, 59). As for stimulating social change, it is a well-known premise of his thought that humans are beguiled by the illusion of being able to change the world through an act of the will (see "Intellectual Elite and Democracy," 74; also see *The Division of Labor in Society*, trans. W. D. Halls [New York: Free Press, 1984], 1, 32, and see the discussion hereafter). But note his participation in the Dreyfus Affair, and see my remarks on the moral/intellectual implications of this activity in Jacques Berlinerblau, *Heresy in the University: The Black Athena Controversy and the Responsibilities of American Intellectuals* (New Brunswick, N.J.: Rutgers University Press, 1999), 188–195.

13. Durkheim, *The Rules of Sociological Method and Selected Texts on Sociology and Its Method* ed. S. Lukes and trans. W. D. Halls (New York: Free Press, 1982), 107 n. 13.

14. Durkheim, *Division*, 76; *Rules*, 85.

15. Durkheim, *Ethics*, 60.

16. On the lack of popularity of such approaches in religious studies, see my "Towards a Sociology of Heresy, Orthodoxy and *Doxa*," *History of Religions* 40 (2001): 327–351.

17. We should note that in Durkheim's writings these terms are imbricated but not identical.

18. Lehmann, *Deconstructing Durkheim*, 63

19. Durkheim, *The Elementary Forms of Religious Life*, trans. K. Fields (New York: Free Press, 1995), 420.

20. Durkheim, *Professional Ethics*, 161.

21. Durkheim, *Elementary Forms*, 211.

22. Durkheim, " 'Marxism and Sociology: The Materialist Conception of History (1897)'; Review of Antonio Labriola, 'Essais sur la conception materialiste de l'histoire,' " in *Rules*, 167. In the same review he writes: "For a long while historians have perceived that social evolution has causes of which the actors in historical events are unaware," 171. Lest we conclude that there exist some direct debt to materialist analysis, Durkheim immediately assures us that "we arrived at this postulate before we had learnt of Marx, whose influence we have in no way undergone," 171. For an interesting and widely neglected discussion of the relation between sociology and history, see Durkheim, "Prefaces to *L'année sociologique*," in Durkheim et.al., *Essays in Sociology and Philosophy*, edited by K. H. Wolff (New York: Harper, 1960), 341–353.

23. Durkheim, *Rules*, 171.

24. Durkheim, *Suicide: A Study in Sociology*, trans. J. A. Spaulding and G. Simpson (New York: Free Press, 1951), 43. The remarks on "intent" suggest the possibility of something like "interpersonal misrecognition," though I shall not explore this theme here.

25. Ibid., 299–300.

26. Durkheim, *Montesquieu and Rousseau*, 11.

27. Ibid., 42–43.

28. Steven Lukes, *Emile Durkheim: His Life and Work, A Historical and Critical Study* (Stanford: Stanford University Press, 1985), 30–36.

29. Jorge Larrain, *The Concept of Ideology* (Athens: University of Georgia Press, 1979), 92.

30. Discussed in Durkheim, *Ethics and the Sociology of Morals*, trans. R. T. Hall (Buffalo, N.Y.: Prometheus Books, 1993), 103.

31. Ibid., 81.

32. Ibid., 103.

33. On the influence of Wundt, see Theo Verheggen, "Durkheim's 'Représentations' Considered as 'Vorstellungen,' " *Current Perspectives in Social Theory* 16 (1996): 189–219.

34. Durkheim, "Course in Sociology," 65.

35. Durkheim, *Division of Labor*, 1; also see *Ethics*, 97.

36. Durkheim, *Ethics*, 72.

37. Durkheim, *The Division of Labor*, 62–63.

38. Ibid., 63.

39. Jones, *Durkheim Reconsidered*, 11.

40. Durkheim, "Sociology and the Social Sciences," 79–83.

41. Ibid., 83.

42. Durkheim, *Division of Labor*, 201.

43. Ibid., 278.

44. Ibid., 285; also see Durkheim, *Moral Education*, 61, 62; Durkheim, "Individual and Collective Representations," in *Sociology and Philosophy*, trans. D. F. Pocock (New York: Free Press, 1974), 24–25.

45. Durkheim, *Rules*, 45.

46. Durkheim, *Division of Labor*, 278; "Marxism and Sociology," 171.

47. Durkheim, *Division of Labor*, 201.

48. Durkheim, "Sociology and the Social Sciences," 79; also see *Professional Ethics*, 60; Susan Stedman Jones, "Representation in Durkheim's Masters: Kant and Renouvier. II: Representation and Logic," in *Durkheim and Representations*, edited by W. S. F. Pickering (New York: Routledge, 2000), 69, 74–76.

49. Durkheim, *Ethics*, 117.

50. Emphasis added; Durkheim, *Rules*, 46.

51. Ibid., 52. This is an idea certainly related to Auguste Comte's surmise that "man" believes "that he is, in all respects, the center of the natural system, and consequently endowed with an indefinite control over phenomena . . . men . . . form exaggerated ideas of their importance and power. Such an illusion constitutes the most prominent characteristic of the infancy of human reason." "Plan of the Scientific Operations Necessary for Reorganizing Society," in *Auguste Comte and Positivism*, edited by G. Lerner (New Brunswick, N.J.: Transaction, 1998), 34.

52. Durkheim, *Rules*, 46. C. Bouglé opines that what Durkheim meant when he proclaimed that we treat social facts as things "is to help us free ourselves of prejudice and to warn us that we must not rely on ourselves and consult our own feelings when we seek to establish the essence, origins and functions of the different human institutions" (preface to the original edition, in Durkheim, *Sociology and Philosophy*, xxxvii). It is difficult to tell in Durkheim's writing whether misrecognition is the cause or effect of misattribution.

53. Durkheim, *Ethics*, 105.

54. Durkheim, *Division*, 331.

55. Durkheim, *Elementary Forms*, 213–214.

56. Lukes, *Durkheim*, 6.

57. W. S. F. Pickering, preface to *Durkheim and Representations*, xiii.

58. Durkheim, "The Dualism of Human Nature and Its Social Conditions," in Bellah, *Emile Durkheim on Morality and Society*, 153.

59. Durkheim, *Moral Education*, 114.

60. Durkheim, *Elementary Forms*, 273. On the collective genesis of representations, see Durkheim, *Pragmatism and Sociology*, trans. J. C. Whitehouse, ed. J. B. Allcock (Cambridge: Cambridge University Press, 1983), 84.

61. Meštrović, *Emile Durkheim*, 13. Also see Durkheim, *Pragmatism*, 85–87, 92.

62. Durkheim, "Individual and Collective Representations," in *Sociology and Philosophy*, 23.

63. Ibid., 21; also see Durkheim, *Montesquieu*, 11.

64. Pickering, "Representations as Understood by Durkheim: An Introductory Sketch," in *Durkheim and Representations*, 11. Representations are sometimes conscious, sometimes unconscious; see Verheggen, "Durkheim's Représentations," 199, 214.

65. Meštrović, "Durkheim's Concept of the Unconscious," *Current Perspectives in Social Theory* 5 (1984): 267, also see 268, 278, 282.

66. Meštrović, *Emile Durkheim*, 2. Also see Jones, *Durkheim Reconsidered*, 31.

67. Meštrović, *Emile Durkheim*, 11.

68. Durkheim, "Dualism," 153.

69. See, for example, Durkheim, "Sociology in France in the Nineteenth Century," in *Emile Durkheim on Morality and Society*, 13.

70. Of the relation between representation and reality, Durkheim writes: "There is a sense, of course, in which our representation of the external world is itself nothing but a fabric of hallucinations. The odors, tastes, and colors that we place in bodies are not there, or at least are not there in the way we perceive them. Nevertheless, our sensations of smell, taste and sight do correspond to certain objective states of things represented," *Elementary Forms*, 229.

71. Durkheim, *Moral Education*, 102–103.

72. Ibid., 129.

73. Ibid., 50.

74. Durkheim, "Course in Sociology," 46. Also see "Sociology and the Social Sciences," 72, and *Rules*, 37, 63.

75. Durkheim, *The Rules*, 85. Also see 71, 72, 74. We would hope for greater clarity from Durkheim, but we must assume that these laws can be correlated with reality.

76. Durkheim, "Sociology and the Social Sciences," 75.

77. Durkheim, *Moral Education*, 115.

78. Durkheim, "Sociology and the Social Sciences," 71.

79. Pickering, "What Do Representations Represent: The Issue of Reality," in *Durkheim and Representations*, 103, 113.

80. Lehmann, *Deconstructing Durkheim*, 167–168.

81. Karl Marx, "For a Ruthless Criticism of Everything Existing" [1859], in *The Marx-Engels Reader*, ed. R. C. Tucker, 2nd ed. (New York: Norton, 1978), 15.

82. Durkheim, *Suicide*, 312.

83. Ibid., 41; *Moral Education*, 116.

84. W. E. H. Stanner, "Reflections on Durkheim and Aboriginal Religion," in *Durkheim on Religion*, ed. W. S. F. Pickering (Atlanta, Ga.: Scholars Press, 1994), 298.

85. It goes without saying that it is important to focus students' attention not only on their own personal misrecognition but collective acts of misrecognition as well.

86. Frederick Engels, *The Peasant War in Germany*, trans. M. Olgin (New York: International, 1984), 51.

87. Mary Douglas, "The Abominations of Leviticus," in *Purity and Danger: An Analysis of the Concepts of Purity and Taboo* (London: Ark, 1966), 57.

88. Paul Boyer and Stephen Nissenbaum, *Salem Possessed: The Social Origins of Witchcraft* (Cambridge: Harvard University Press, 1974).

89. Pierre Bourdieu, "Legitimation and Structured Interests in Weber's Sociology of Religion," in *Max Weber, Rationality and Modernity*, edited by S. Lash and S. Whimster (London: Allen and Unwin, 1987), 130.

REFERENCES

Bellah, Robert, ed. 1973. *Emile Durkheim on Morality and Society*. Chicago: University of Chicago Press.

Berlinerblau, Jacques. 1999. *Heresy in the University: The Black Athena Controversy and the Responsibilities of American Intellectuals*. New Brunswick, N.J.: Rutgers University Press.

———. 2001. "Towards a Sociology of Heresy, Orthodoxy and *Doxa*." *History of Religions* 40: 327–351.

Besnard, Phillipe, ed. 1983. *The Sociological Domain: The Durkheimians and the Founding of French Sociology*. Cambridge: Cambridge University Press.

Bourdieu, Pierre. 1987. "Legitimation and Structured Interests in Weber's Sociology of Religion." In *Max Weber, Rationality and Modernity*, edited by S. Lash and S. Whimster. London: Allen and Unwin.

Boyer, Paul, and Stephen Nissenbaum. 1974. *Salem Possessed: The Social Origins of Witchcraft*. Cambridge: Harvard University Press.

Brooks, John, III. 1991. "Analogy and Argumentation in an Interdisciplinary Context: Durkheim's 'Individual and Collective Representations.' " *History of Human Sciences* 4: 12–15.

Comte, Auguste. 1998. "Plan of the Scientific Operations Necessary for Reorganizing Society." In *Auguste Comte and Positivism*, edited by G. Lerner. New Brunswick, N.J.: Transaction.

Douglas, Mary. 1966. *Purity and Danger: An Analysis of the Concepts of Purity and Taboo*. London: Ark.

Durkheim, Emile. 1984. *The Division of Labor in Society*. Translated by W. D. Halls. New York: Free Press.

———. 1995. *The Elementary Forms of Religious Life*. Translated by K. Fields. New York: Free Press.

———. 1994. *Emile Durkheim on Institutional Analysis*. Edited and translated by M. Traugott. Chicago: University of Chicago Press.

————. 1993. *Ethics and the Sociology of Morals*. Translated by R. T. Hall. Buffalo, N.Y.: Prometheus Books.

Durkheim, Emile. 1960. *Montesquieu and Rousseau: Forerunners of Sociology*. Ann Arbor: University of Michigan Press.

————. 1973. *Moral Education: A Study in the Theory and Application of the Sociology of Education*. Edited by E. K. Wilson and translated by E. K. Wilson and H. Schnurer. New York: Free Press.

————. 1983. *Pragmatism and Sociology*. Translated by J. C. Whitehouse, and edited by J. B. Allcock. Cambridge: Cambridge University Press.

————. 1992. *Professional Ethics and Civic Morals*. Translated by C. Brookfield. London: Routledge.

————. 1982. *The Rules of Sociological Method and Selected Texts on Sociology and Its Method*. Edited by S. Lukes and translated by W. D. Halls. New York: Free Press.

————. 1974. *Sociology and Philosophy*. Translated by D. F. Pocock. New York: Free Press.

————. 1951. *Suicide: A Study in Sociology*. Translated by J. A. Spaulding and G. Simpson. New York: Free Press.

Durkheim, Emile, et al. 1960. *Essays on Sociology and Philosophy*. Edited by Kurt Wolff. New York: Harper Torchbooks.

Engels, Frederick. 1984. *The Peasant War in Germany*. Translated by M. Olgin. New York: International.

Larrain, Jorge. 1979. *The Concept of Ideology*. Athens: University of Georgia Press.

Lehmann, Jennifer. 1993. *Deconstructing Durkheim: A Post-Post-Structuralist Critique*. London: Routledge.

Lukes, Steven. 1985. *Emile Durkheim: His Life and Work, A Historical and Critical Study*. Stanford: Stanford University Press.

Marx, Karl. 1978. "For a Ruthless Criticism of Everything Existing" [1859]. In *The Marx-Engels Reader*, edited by R. C. Tucker. 2nd ed. New York: Norton.

Meštrović, Stjepan. 1984. "Durkheim's Concept of the Unconscious." *Current Perspectives in Social Theory* 5: 267–288.

————. 1993. *Emile Durkheim and the Reformation of Sociology*. Boston: Rowman and Littlefield.

Pearce, Frank. 1989. *The Radical Durkheim*. London: Unwin Hyman.

Pickering, William., ed. 2000. *Durkheim and Representations*. New York: Routledge.

Stanner, W. E. H. 1994. "Reflections on Durkheim and Aboriginal Religion." In *Durkheim on Religion*, edited by W. S. F. Pickering. Atlanta, Ga.: Scholars Press.

Stedman Jones, Susan. 2001. *Durkheim Reconsidered*. Cambridge: Polity Press.

Verheggen, Theo. 1996. "Durkheim's 'Représentations' Considered as 'Vorstellungen.'" *Current Perspectives in Social Theory* 16: 189–219.

Index